Praise for **PAND(**

MW00442333

"A gossipy and witty peek behind the real estate curtain. The author's voice is peppy and fun as she guides the reader through the relentlessly dramatic real estate scene. "So You Want To Be An Agent Quiz" at the end is a highlight of the book that's indicative of Griffith's extensive knowledge and chatty, relatable style."

— Kirkus Review

"*Pandora's Lockbox* is anything but predictable. Its hilarious stories will delight the general public as well as would-be and existing real estate pros. One thing is for certain: readers will never think of the real estate industry or agents in exactly the same way after absorbing the trials and tribulations that involve the agents inside Pandora's Lockbox."

— Midwest Book Review

"The stories I read here (in *Pandora's Lockbox*) completely blew me away. I'll suggest this to anybody involved in the real estate industry. If you're looking for a quick read that will make you giggle, this is it."

— Online Book Club 5/5 Star Review

"Fans of soap operas and daytime television will get a kick out of Griffith's jocular, episodic retellings of her most memorable encounters during her real estate career. At times funny and other times jaw-dropping, *Pandora's Lockbox* also attests to what it takes to make a career—and the value of creating connections as a woman in business."

— Booklife Review

"(*Pandora's Lockbox*) was a wild and compelling story! It fell into that category of the truth being stranger than fiction for me and I had no idea what to expect next. All the stories were an interesting way to explore memoir style writing. Anyone who has wondered about the insights and oddities of real estate would be interested and find this an enjoyable book."

— Judge, Writer's Digest Self-Published Book Awards

"*Pandora's Lockbox* by first-time author Nico Griffith immediately grabs you with its title. The escapades in the book are short, firsthand accounts written with a wicked sense of humor and in the same engaging manner as the types of tales told over a stiff drink…or two… or five. The author's descriptions of her agent cohorts, known as the Fab Five, are so vivid that one can't help but connect with a favorite in the same way they would with a television series character.

All in all, *Pandora's Lockbox* is a fun, eye-opening read!"

— Non-Fiction Writers Assn Review

Good book for a flight, should be a tv show . . .

"I've been reading a fun real estate blog and wanted to find something longer for a flight. This was recommended. Wow, insane times selling houses. Luxury real estate meets a wild memoir. A visually descriptive book, it made me want to watch a tv show about it. There is actually an alligator, but I don't want to spoil it."

— Hally F. United Kingdom

"I have to say your book is quite entertaining. I could not quit giggling. Your stories are full of humor, quirkiness, and adventure. When I finished the book, I was craving more. I am hoping you will write a sequel."

— Kara Schumann, author

"Nico, you've been living in my head ever since I started your book on the day I received it. If time had permitted, I would have finished in one sitting. It was gripping, shocking at times and kept me thoroughly enthralled."

— Stephenie Caughlin

"From soap opera lives and open house experiences to crime scenes that involve real estate agents, *Pandora's Lockbox* memoir offers a wealth of unexpected events that keeps readers laughing and learning about an industry that is sometimes privy to some closely-held (and potentially dangerous) secrets."

— Bookwatch

"*Pandora's Lockbox* is a MUST read for all real estate agents! I found it hard to put the book down — it was that good!"

— Emily Proctor

"Nico's hilarious peek-behind-the-scenes of the real estate world is riveting. As a former real estate agent myself, once I started Pandora's Lockbox, I couldn't put it down."

— Lael J.

"I am having the time of my life reading *Pandora's Lockbox*! I stayed up till 1:30 a.m. last night reading it. I had to force myself to go to bed. I'm a Realtor and I get it! You are funny!!! And oh so wildly entertaining. OK, I have to go back to finish reading your book."

— Kathleen Bailey

"A fun and interesting read . . . . lots of laughs!"

— Jenny C.

"I would just like you to know your book is interfering with my job . . . . I can't put it down and my work is suffering! I'm halfway through and it's GREAT!"

— Kathy Angello, agent

The stories were memorable and fun to read. I would recommend this book to real estate agents. I can only imagine how relatable Nico's stories would be to people in the same profession! I would also recommend this book to anyone who is looking to buy a home with the help of a real estate agent; the stories in the book will help bring levity to what can be a very stressful process. "

— Emily M.

PANDORA'S LOCKBOX

To Gayle,

Warm regards,

Nico

PANDORA'S LOCKBOX

A Wild and Wacky
Real Estate Memoir

True Stories of Love, Murders
and an Alligator

Nico Griffith

Lolo Press
Florence, Montana

DISCLAIMER

Everything in this memoir is true. It is a collection of creative non-fiction stories from some of my own experiences and some that were told to me. As such, it may not be entirely factual as is common in this genre. Conversations, for instance, are meant to convey the circumstances, not the actual word by word sequence.

Whenever I thought it necessary, I have compressed events; in others, I have made several people into one person. Almost all names and descriptive characteristics of people and places have been changed to avoid hurting anyone. I have occasionally embroidered events in telling my story to make myself look smarter, and perhaps, more or less sympathetic than I am in person. I thought you might want to know this before you start reading.

Published by Lolo Press
Editors: Elisabeth Chretien, Chretien Wordsmithery
          Bonnie Solomon, Voyage Media
Cover Artist: Rafael Andres
Book Design: Christy Day, Constellation Book Design

ISBN (paperback): 978-1-7377199-2-2

Printed in the United States of America

CONTENTS

ACKNOWLEDGEMENTS

I want to acknowledge my fellow agents, especially at RE/MAX, Realogy, and Century 21. After the doors of my first independent real estate office were chained together unexpectedly by the sheriff one Monday morning, I have spent my remaining time enjoying working for them.

There are many methods of selling real estate. One of the reasons I have succeeded beyond my wildest dreams is because of *Brian Buffini Coaching*. His '***By Referral***' method taught me how to work smarter, not harder, by working with buyers and sellers I already know. After you have tried some of the rest, try the best and go to *www.BuffiniAndCompany.com* for some great coaching to be your best self. Caution: his way only works if you actually do it!

Thanks also to the over 1,000 people who have bought or sold a property with me. Without you, this book couldn't have been written. Some of you appear in a story or two, but have been disguised so I can write these stories as accurately as I remember.

There are a few special people who come into everyone's life that truly make a difference whether they intended to or not. Some stay, while others just pass through. I want to thank the ones who have come into and through mine; I dedicate this book to them. I have always been a prankster with a sarcastic sense of humor *before* I met any of them, so it is not their fault. Each person, in their own way, has contributed to my fun and my experiences, usually by telling me *not to do that*!

Thank you to my special friends **Jim, Chris**; childhood friends **Bernie, Sue**; college roommate **Pam**; the rest of the Fab Five group of real estate agents **Loraine, Christel, Mary & Jennifer**; my motherly **Aunt Ramona**; and **my twenty-six cousins**. All have aided, abetted, and some have even joined me in fun escapades along the way while inspiring me to become a better person from knowing them.

A sincere thanks to my husband, **Gordon**, and his son **Isaac**, who are new companions in my continuing adventure. To my favorite son **Jeremy**, who has taught me as much as I have taught him. He grew up loving the other ladies of the Fab Five—they are his Aunties to this day. His insights and remembrances of some of these stories have helped me write more accurately.

A final 'Love You' to **Fannie Mae**, my parti-Yorkie, who, unlike the government's FANNIE MAE, does NOT take people's homes

SHE MURDERED HER DAD AND MADE ME AN ACCESSORY

I became an accessory to murder for the first time on a Monday morning at 5 a.m. when my phone suddenly rang. As I lifted up the receiver, I could hear sobbing getting louder and louder. The sobbing was emanating from my newest relocation buyer, Missy Ann. Missy Ann was THE Yellow Rose from Texas—meaning that, with all the yellow she wore, drove, and decorated with, everyone assumed that she owned the color yellow. Missy Ann was a force to be reckoned with. She was wider than she was tall, larger than she first appeared, and her laugh was so hearty, it took people by surprise. She sported a pair of 44's in her bra and ten gallons of yellow hair above it. Clients tend to overshare as they get comfortable with us agents, and Missy Ann had already confided to me that not only was her hair naturally yellow, but "the rug matched the drapes." In other words, she was a natural yellow blonde down there also!

I had been working with Missy Ann for two months, and she was having a hard time deciding on a home. However, Missy Ann was entertaining to work with, and she always bought me lunch or dinner after our showing appointments, so I was being patient while her *wants* frequently switched to *needs*.

Slowly and sleepily, the phone found my ear. For the rest of my life, I wished I had resisted answering this call. No good news can possibly come from a phone call when it's still dark out. Missy Ann's thick husky Texas accent, sobbing and wailing, forced itself in rising crescendos into my still-sleepy ear. "Ahm sorry to wake you up. Ah had to let him go, but it was so hard. He was sooo sick! Ah just had to put him down. Euthanize him. Ah didn't know who else to call. Ah had to talk to someone."

The rest was unintelligible as my ear closed for business and my brain fought to submerge itself back to its dream state. The sobbing and wailing and hiccupping continued uninterrupted for several minutes.

When Missy Ann finally had to take a breath, I could only offer, *"I'm so sorry, I didn't even know you had a dog. Those darn pets—they steal your heart, make you love them, and then they die. What kind of dog was it?"*

The ensuing silence was deafening, and I thought Missy had maybe passed out from lack of oxygen. Then, having recovered from her speechlessness, came a frosty, indignant "It wasn't my dog, dammit, it was my *father*. He's been unconscious for over a week now, and ah just could not see him suffer from the cancer anymore, so ah increased the morphine drip when the nurse took her break. Do you think ahm going to Hell? Or could ah go to prison? Oh, Lordy, ah'll just die right this second if ah thought ah'd spend the rest of my life in jail. Oh, Lordy, Lordy, ah deserve to go to prison—then what's going to happen to me in there, without my makeup or special shampoo. Ah really didn't think about that." And now her welcome wailing took over again.

It was my turn to be speechless. I didn't . . . I couldn't . . . hear any more. She was making me an accessory to MURDER, and she hadn't even bought a house from me yet. I glanced at the clock. It was 5:11 a.m. on Monday morning—a time that still makes me cringe when I notice it. Jesus, what kind of week was this going to be?

What was it about my sales demeanor that made people tell me EVERYTHING? I didn't want to know EVERYTHING—I only want to know how much money they earned, how much they had in the bank, and what kind of alimony they paid or received.

Don't tell me about your affairs, your abortions, or your hatred of your spouse or ex-spouse or soon-to-be ex-spouse. And *definitely* don't tell me you euthanized your FATHER.

Eleven days after Missy Ann's 5 a.m. phone call, I was chalking up some tax-deductible mileage coming back from her father's funeral. I was smiling sympathetically to myself as I remembered how Missy Ann's thick accent had disappeared among the family, neighbors, and friends in attendance. Even though I had never met her dad, I wanted to support Missy Ann.

After her dad's funeral, at her desperate sounding pleading, I had taken Missy Ann to the doctor who had been primary care for her dad for many years. Dr. Earl sat across his desk from us with his thinning colorless hair combed sideways over one ear. He wore the stereotypical white medical coat, accessorized by a stethoscope draped professionally around his neck. He had pushed his black rimmed glasses low on this nose so he could look sternly over them at Missy Ann directly. There was no smile on Dr. Earl's face or in his eyes as he advised her that her dad had died of heart failure in the hospital. He wanted her to know that was to be the official cause of death on the certificate and held out the paper so she could read it for herself.

If he expected a confession, I was ready to give him mine, even though I was only an accomplice. I was saved when Missy Ann, thick Texas accent back in place, rose from her chair to accept the paper and took Dr. Earl's hand between both of her hands.

"Thank you, Dr. Earl, and Bless Y'all for taking such good care of my father, especially in his final days. We both appreciated it. Ah'm glad his suffering is over." And with that, we left.

The following Friday, two dozen yellow (of course) roses were delivered to me in the office with an unsigned "Thank You for Your Time, I Enjoyed Meeting You" notecard. I have enjoyed lots of flowers from satisfied clients after closing, but flowers from a client *before* they buy a house are an agent's worst nightmare. It meant that I had been spending (wasting) a lot of time with someone who never buys. It meant that Missy Ann had decided not to buy a home in San Marea and would be staying in Austin.

INTRODUCTION

The legend of Pandora's Box has become an idiom that today means "starting/opening up something that will cause many unforeseen problems." According to Greek mythology, Pandora received a box as a wedding present, but was cautioned not to open it. When her curiosity got the better of her, she tried to peek inside her box. Her action let all the world's problems escape before she quickly closed it, leaving only Hope inside. That visual is synonymous still in today's world, to describe what happens when a real estate agent opens a lockbox. Inside that lockbox is a key to open a house so hopeful buyers can peek inside. Neither the agent nor the buyers know the chain of events that might be unleashed by looking inside that house.

The backdrop for PANDORA'S LOCKBOX is the 1980s and early 1990s. It was a world where real estate regulation was in its infancy. Elaborate perks, like office parties, gifts, vacations, limo rides, free advertising, wining and dining, were given to top agents as thinly disguised bribes for business. Satellite businesses like mortgage, escrow, title, pest control, and property inspectors provided increasingly lavish gifts too, depending on the perceived success of specific agents. That bribery no longer exists as it did then. At least, not overtly. At least, not legally either.

During the time covered in this memoir, offers were presented in person by both the listing and the buyer's agent in a seller's home at night, after work. There were no answering machines, no cell phones, no computers—only Selectric (look it up) typewriters. We learned the other agent's foibles and those of their clients too by the time a sale transaction was closed. Unlike current times, where we almost never meet other agents or their clients, everything in these years was done face to face, phone to phone, and sometimes fang to fang. These interactions spawned the phrasing of my stories about "clients and agents I have loved and loathed."

This was a time where potential clients and other agents judged success by the car you drove. These were fun, crazy, and financially rewarding years—while being heart-breaking, costly, and depressing at the same time. I'm talking about the successful agents, but it was even more heartbreaking and depressing if you *weren't* successful.

Real estate is an equal-opportunity career where everyone got paid the same IF they could get a transaction closed. In other words, novice or veteran, man or woman—all were rewarded, or devastated, equally. My single mother raised me in the 1950s to the lament "women don't get paid what they're worth, even when they do the same job as a man." However, I had stumbled into a career that my pre-women's lib mother could approve of—although, throughout her life, she rarely approved of anything I did or accomplished. For seven straight years, I was the Top Producing Agent in a boutique, one-owner company with 700 plus agents and 17 offices. I succeeded without any such expectations of myself and in spite of my mother's caustic criticisms.

In advance, I'm offering an apology to those of you who may be affronted by my references to women using real estate to husband-hunt, or prostitution to support themselves or further their career. This is just the way it was in this time capsule snapshot of my early years selling real estate.

ONE

NICO'S STORY

It was 1982, and the upcoming Sunday was Mother's Day. I had suffered a miscarriage in February, so Mother's Day this year was going to be a touchy subject, and I wasn't sure how we (I) would handle it.

My husband of fourteen years, on his way to work, paused briefly to look at me from the doorway, but instead of asking me what I wanted to do for Mother's Day, he said, "I want a divorce. And by the way, since I've put money down on a new apartment, I won't be paying our mortgage anymore, so get serious about finding a job."

This was the end of the beginning for me, a full collapse of life as I had known it up until today. It was a turning point that I still call The Royal Flush. Not as in the card game of *Poker*, but as in *down the toilet-kind* of flush. The first fourteen years of my married life was officially going down the toilet. It had started with the recent miscarriage that ended my four-month pregnancy, continued with the loss of my business containing my support group of work-associated colleagues, and would be followed shortly by our mutual married couple friends. I expected them to disappear (as is normal) as soon as they heard about our divorce. All this happened in the stalled-out, half-finished remodel of our money pit house due to our lack of funds. This announcement was made even more monumental because my husband, whom I have always described as 'a passenger in the car of life', had actually gotten into the driver's seat without me noticing and made a life-altering decision. A decision that would change the road map of my life forever. All in all, The Royal Flush pretty much summed it up perfectly.

Up until now, my life had been a well-paid, consistent monthly paycheck-type of life. For all outward appearances, I lived a perfectly normal, upwardly mobile life of new cars and different houses every four to five years. Nice vacations every other year. Our friends envied our seemingly emotionally and financially stable existence. However, we only *looked* stable.

They hadn't recognized that two months ago, I had started going by myself to Tijuana on Thursday evenings to get food. We were broke, and grocery shopping at Cali-Max kept our pantry from being empty. Four grocery bags of meat and food cost $10 at Cali-Max, where at my local neighborhood supermarket, it would cost $30. *Rollos* (or hard rolls, in Spanish) were twenty-five cents a dozen instead of ten cents apiece in the U.S., and filet mignon was half the price of the cheapest supermarket hamburger. However, items like Campbell's Soup were four times the price of the exact same can in the U.S., so I was careful what I purchased.

On the first trip, I made the mistake of buying four rolls of Hecho-en-Mexico toilet paper. Truth-in-packaging laws should have required it to be labeled Made-In-Mexico toilet *sand*paper. I immediately understood why I saw lines of women and children at the border coming back into Tijuana, portaging two or three Costco-sized packages of Made-In-The-U.S. toilet paper on their heads.

But, as I said, looks were deceiving. The mortgage loan industry had just been deregulated. It had started offering variable rate mortgages after hitting 18% for a 30-year fixed rate conventional loan. Buyers were afraid that the variable rates might raise their payments so high every year that they might lose their home and go bankrupt as a result. They were having none of it, so real estate sales stalled out, as did the economy in the early eighties. I was part owner of a mortgage company with twenty-four and one-half employees (the half being my alcoholic business partner), and times were really tough. Even my normal stress level was stressed.

After the miscarriage, my doctor sat me down and said, "Your miscarriage was caused by stress. I don't know what kind of work you do, but the stress of it killed this baby, so I suggest you find another line of work before you get pregnant again."

I never went back to my office. I just signed over my share of the business to my partner. I was not compensated, and I never looked back.

Without taking any time to recover from the miscarriage, I had spent the last two months combing the mortgage industry looking for a steady job. One that paid me, instead of me paying myself from a line of credit. I was finding that all my experience of processing loans, underwriting, doing appraisal reviews, funding, and shipping loans off to secondary investors was very intimidating to the people interviewing me.

It was slow to dawn on me that I had more experience than my interviewers, so who was going to hire someone whose job skills could replace several people in this slow economy? I could have saved myself at least ten weeks of the confidence-eroding interview rejection, had I been thinking more clearly. I could have turned my sights on some other form of employment outside the mortgage arena after the first blank stare and "We'll let you know". It was a combo that I experienced many times before reality bit.

My Soon-To-Be-Ex-Husband, who had very few good ideas during our fourteen-year marriage, in reply to my incredulous *"What the Bleep am I supposed to do NOW?"*, said, "Why don't you go sell real estate? People are always asking for your advice, and real estate companies hire everyone."

This exchange took place at our front doorway to our house— the one with a heavy plastic sheet nailed over it because the new door was still in the lumber yard awaiting the funds to pay for it. The one with a very low 14% interest rate and monthly payments thru the stratosphere. The one that a single-income family (namely me) could never afford. Need I mention that I was about to become a no-income single person, and not even a family anymore? Plus, having exhausted our savings buying this money-pit fixer, I had $801.40 in the bank and the next $2031 monthly payment, not including taxes, was due in twenty-eight days. I knew

I was in trouble—deep trouble—even before my gaping mouth closed.

My brain struggled to grasp the sound of my husband slamming the imaginary front door shut behind him as he left. I shuffled over to the garbage to retrieve the morning paper and comb the employment ads yet again. My husband's parting comment about selling real estate made me look in a different column in the help wanted ads, for lack of any better ideas of my own. As a by-product of The Royal Flush, I knew I wasn't thinking clearly. Somehow, I reckoned that the biggest real estate advertisers most likely had the most business, and I should probably try to work for one of them.

There were really just two choices: Distinctive Houses & Gardens, and Fakke & Company (rhymes with khaki). The running joke in the mortgage industry, after dealing with clueless new agent after new agent, was that a broker would hire 'Anyone who could fog a mirror' (or, in short, anyone). I've always done well on tests, so I knew I would pass one as easy as this might be.

Of the two choices, Distinctive Houses & Gardens sounded more my style. I prided myself as being unique and knew that I was too much of a maverick to be associated with any national brokerages wearing matching jackets. So, despite my crumbling life, off I went the next day for my first interview at Distinctive Houses & Gardens. It was another beautiful sunny California day—one that in no way reflected my mood.

Their office was in a new square glass and white stucco ultra-modern building, and it was hopping. The phones were ringing, the agents were yelling back and forth, swearing liberally, and my immediate thought was 'this is perfect'—a thought I always had when something was about to go wrong.

The brokers were a husband-and-wife team who went perfunctorily through the extensive mortgage lending background on my resume. Mr. Broker stated the obvious: "You have no experience selling real estate. Your mortgage background is useless. Selling a home is a lot different."

I'm sure I must have looked close to tears as Mrs. Broker added,

"Why don't you go to another office to get trained and then come back here after you have some experience? My husband and I have a policy that we only hire experienced agents." (That they didn't want to bother to train me was left unsaid.)

All in all, it was almost a coup-de-grâce to my fragile ego, to be dismissed so blithely and without even any questions or mirror test or apology. "They hire everybody . . ." meant that my Soon-To-Be-Ex Husband was wrong again.

Would I have felt better had they said, "We just love that you have so much good background. You've owned your own company, and know what it's like to be self-employed. However, under the circumstances, you are an unknown quantity, and we are unwilling to risk that you might use our phone to call China. We can't incur expenses from someone who has never sold a home before."

Probably not, but at least I would have had a chance to practice fine-tuning my BullSh...t Detector; something I quickly realized was a tantamount skill necessary in successful real estate agents. Another rejection—this time because I didn't have *any* experience instead of *too much*. What a bummer. They didn't have to pay me anything. I would have had to buy my own cards, For Sale signs, lockboxes, advertising and forms printing. I would have to pre-pay one year of membership to the MLS, the California Association of Realtors and the National Association of Realtors. Interestingly enough, the cost of those three memberships totalled $800—virtually my entire bank account—and they STILL didn't want me.

After all the rejections I had faced these past two months in chasing a mortgage banking job with a monthly paycheck, and a Soon-To-Be-Ex-Husband who was divorcing me, this was the final straw that strangled the camel. Although I am normally a calm, collected individual (one of my clients laughingly once told me that "being around you is like smoking a joint"), I was distressed to the point of being deranged, and angry enough to bite my lower lip bloody in lieu of crying. I felt friendless, penniless, and was trending towards hopelessness. I concluded that I only had one more chance to land a job in a prominent real estate firm, and I couldn't waste it.

I could feel myself slump down behind the steering wheel as I drove back to my unfinished money pit. I needed to give myself some time to calm down and formulate a plan of attack for the next day. There was a do-or-die kind of day ahead of me.

TWO

THE FOG-A-MIRROR TEST FOR AGENTS

The next morning found me outside Fakke & Co., gathering courage to face this do-or-die job interview. As I focused my observations of the real estate office more closely, I saw that it was a way cool office. It was San Marea contemporary box architecture, tall and square with a flat roof, a shingle wood exterior, and windows of narrow, slatted glass. The windowsills were full of live plants and the interior walls were covered with rough-sided, vertical wood paneling. The street level of the two-story office was filled with authentic old roll-top desks which, I found out later, were for the top-producing agents. Regular inexpensive flat-top wood desks were all on the lower level for everyone else. Wood, glass, and green. Yes, this could work—it had to! Now, how to get a job.

I sat scrutinizing everyone who came and went, hoping to find a familiar face to fortify my ebbing courage. Unexpectedly, out walked Dan, a loan officer from my old mortgage company. I leapt from the car to greet him and get some advice on how to land a job at Fakke. Dan laughed heartily, saying that virtually any real estate firm would hire me—all I had to do was walk in the door. He joked with the familiar refrain "All you have to do is pass the 'fog and mirror' test". In other words, if they held a mirror under my nose and could see that I was breathing, I would be hired. Well, I was breathing this morning—barely—but was positive I could fog any kind of mirror when the test came.

Dan marched me right into the Fakke & Co. office, knocked on the broker's open office door, and said, "This is Nico. I used to work for her mortgage company. She's great, hire her," after which he saluted me and left, saying, "You'll be fine."

So, alone and with stress-wet armpits, I turned to face my first broker, Granville Fakke.

Granville Fakke looked me over with his little beady widespread eyes recessed into his bulldog-wrinkly, jowly, well-fed face. He granted me a wide smile which framed his also-widespread pick-et-fence teeth. (He referred to himself as Grant, but I soon found out that his agents all called him 'Granny'.) I didn't realize until many months later that, lurking below his unconventional out-wardly ugly bulldog features, hid the heart and aggressiveness of a pit bull, with all its negative connotations. His oily hair, oily complexion, and oily personality masked his age, which could have been late forties to maybe even sixty.

Grant/Granny looked me over yet again, not seeming to get any higher than my ample chest, and said, "So, you want to sell real estate? Okay, you can start tomorrow."

I was stunned. I had a job, just like that. I was hoping that my overwhelming sense of relief wasn't too obvious on my face.

As I started to go over my resume of no-experience-selling-re-al-estate, Granny cut me off.

"Never mind, you'll do fine, I can always tell. Is there anything important that I need to know about you?"

I was so close to tears (tears of relief, of ridiculousness, of how easy this was), who knows what prompted me to say, *"Yes. If you ever make me cry, I'll quit!"*

He snorted and said, "Come back tomorrow at 9 a.m. for the office meeting and meet the gang. By the way, I'm buying lunch for everyone on Thursday, so be here by noon on Thursday, too."

I had a job (elation, celebration, exultation!)—I had a job at Fakke & Co., and I started tomorrow! I was so excited, I had to tell someone, but old habits die hard. I acted on my instincts to call the one person I told everything to: my husband. I needed to tell him the good news, forgetting for the moment that he was now my Soon-To-Be-Ex-Husband. He had news of his own.

"I got a new job as assistant manager of my company. I got a raise and everything. But unfortunately, I have to turn in my company car in two weeks when I'm no longer an outside salesman. So, you have two weeks to get yourself a new car or drive the Chevy van you won on that TV show. It's probably not a good real estate car, though. I'm sorry."

I had been on the TV game show Concentration about eight years earlier. I had won everything in sight, including a car, for solving two Bonus Puzzles in less than sixty seconds. Our neighbor at the time was the district manager in Southern California for Chevrolet, so he had arranged for me to take the base price of the car and apply it to anything else Chevy had. Although I toyed with getting a Corvette, my practical side kicked in, and I opted for a one-and-a-half-ton van instead.

We had equipped it for camping and had not only traveled to Guadalajara, Mexico for three weeks, but we then drove to Alaska for five months, all the time camping and sleeping in the van. It had two front seats (called 'captain's chairs'). The rest of the interior was a queen-sized mattress upholstered with carpet and built-in wooden boxes along the sides, filled with camping gear. In a nano-second, I realized that my van was not an option for showing houses to potential buyers. I started to cry.

"Don't cry, honey. We'll figure something out. Perhaps I can get an extra month for you to use my company car."

He wasn't able to negotiate that, so two weeks later, on a Friday afternoon, he drove away in his company car while I disparagingly contemplated selling real estate in my 180,000-mile, eight-year-old camping van. It caused me a lot more tears and consternation.

After a week of driving the van, I resorted to a phone call begging my Soon-to-be-Ex for some help, even if it was to be able to use his car on the weekends when he wasn't at work. After one more week of feeling like I would have to quit real estate for lack of proper transportation, he drove up in an older model yellow Mercedes 4-door sedan.

He said, "The people in my office said the only kind of car a real estate agent should have is a Mercedes, so I found one in the neighborhood Penny Saver newspaper for you. It's got an extra gas tank in the trunk, so you can drive over 900 miles on a full tank of gas—oops, diesel. It runs on diesel. If you keep grocery shopping in Tijuana, diesel down there is only twelve cents a gallon, so that will save you lots of money."

Although I realized he must be feeling guilty about the divorce and who knows what else, I said my proper thank-yous for the gift. I knew nothing about Mercedes, but I loved yellow, so I appreciated whatever had prompted him to buy it for me.

Two weeks after my Soon-To-Be-Ex dropped off the Mercedes, I got a fat envelope in the mail containing the title to the Mercedes, with me as the sole owner. Also enclosed were several loan papers needing my signature. The loan papers for $8,300 were also solely in my name, along with the repayment schedule of $315 a month.

Even if it were $25 per month, I wouldn't have been able to pay it. I literally had NO money. However, I had just received an unsolicited credit card in the mail a few days ago. Although I always had cut them up in the past, I knew that The Universe had tossed me a life-line to give me some breathing room in which to make a sale. Three thousand dollars wasn't much of a lifeline, but within ninety days, I had closed my second escrow.

If only I had known what a roller coaster ride I was in for by selling real estate, I would have forgiven my Ex a lot sooner. My real estate career began with that first of several yellow Mercedes cars that I owned and enjoyed through the years. At a time where my share of a normal commission check was to be under $2,400, I would earn my one millionth commission dollar less than five years later. Fate was my co-pilot, guiding me along a path without steady paychecks while jettisoning that passenger from my Car of Life.

THREE

GRANNY BLEEP, INCORPORATED

Today was the second day at my new real estate job at Fakke & Co. I had only learned the names of a few of the thirty-one agents, and some limited office procedures. I was cautioned that the two-hour free parking along the main street in front of Fakke & Co. was closely monitored by parking police, who walked by every hour to put chalk marks across rear tires. By the third mark, you got a parking ticket instead. It was important to have clients park underneath our building off the alley, if possible, because showing even five houses took more than two hours. I hadn't been asked to take the 'fog mirror test' or had a chance to find a customer who wanted to buy or sell property. I learned that buyers and sellers are 'never a customer, but always a client' in my rapidly expanding real estate vocabulary.

But selling real estate would always be a love-hate relationship. We agents all loved and helped each other, and we all hated and avoided Granny and his deceptive, misleading, and (at times) downright dishonest schemes. These practices were affectionately known as Granny Bleeps (I call them Bleeps because I don't say F—k out loud). His motto was, "I give heart attacks; I don't get them!" When he got tripped up in what he laughingly called a 'good plan gone bad' scheme, we agents all rolled our eyes on the latest 'Granny Bleep, Number __'.

What kept us all working at Fakke & Co. was that Granny had the best office location in San Marea, plus he was a master magician at advertising and inspiring us agents to get out there and make a sale. Granny made the phone ring by running newspaper ads with extremely low fake (Fakke) prices. "Steal This" as a headline made buyers walk thru the door with the newspaper in hand—and most of us took full advantage of what he generated.

He locked the office doors on Wednesdays so we would caravan the new broker listings. Caravans, also known as Broker Open Houses or Broker Caravans, were only for us agents to preview the new inventory. There were no computers yet, and The MLS Blue Book of real estate listings only came out every other Friday. It contained a bad newsprint 1/2" x 1/2" photo and a perverse three-digit coded description instead of words for each home (twelve to a page). If you wanted to know what was new to the market in between books, and what it looked like inside, agents had to go on Caravan every Wednesday afternoon.

Grant Fakke had once been a car dealer, but should have been an attorney to save money on all the lawsuits he was continually involved in. Instead, he contributed his not-so-small scheming efforts into giving real estate agents a bad name by association. Still, while no one ever made the mistake of trusting him more than once, Granny had the top-producing office and the best agents in San Marea, one of the toniest, priciest towns in Southern California.

Thursday's lunch was coming quickly, but today was my first day, and I was still elated. Today allowed me to meet fifteen of the other twenty-three women and eight men that comprised Fakke & Co. in those early years. For the most part, these agents were an industrious crew, with their minds on their work, except for two strikingly beautiful young women named Lolly and Krista. They looked like they were going to be trouble, and I was right. My mother used to tell people that I was born looking for trouble, so these two were just my types, and we bonded immediately.

Lolly and Krista were polar opposites that were a great pairing, like salt and pepper. The gorgeous petite brunette, Krista Heinrich, was a waitress with a college degree who waited tables at the local greasy spoon. She had a lean, athletic body that looked good in any outfit—even the cheap ones she bought regularly. She never said an unkind word about anyone, she never swore, and she always burst onto any scene with boundless energy. If there was ever a negative thing to say about Krista, it was that she dressed in clothes she bought at Safeway and the local drugstore. She was working part time selling real estate and had started a couple of weeks before me. When Granny hired her, he assigned Lolly Goldsmith, the other office beauty, to be her mentor.

Lolly was a life-sized Barbie doll, the same height as Krista. She was the daughter of a famous local doctor and an art patron mother. She was a class act, born of a rich upbringing in a rich town. Her dad provided her with carte blanche on his membership account at the La Jolla Country Club, where she and her friends could hang out after school and order whatever they wanted. Listening to those stories, I surmised she had father issues like me and had tried to get his attention by running up outrageous country club bills that he never seemed to notice. After he left her mom for his secretary and cut off financial support for her and their two kids, she had to find a job.

She was a honey blonde, slender, and with baby blue eyes that stopped men in their tracks. In contrast to Krista, Lolly was always impeccably clothed from Nordstrom and Saks Fifth Avenue and was fashionably accessorized. She drove a pale yellow Cadillac named Buttercup, while Krista drove a ten-year-old gunmetal grey Nissan. Like I said—this pair of agents were salt and pepper.

Lolly had been Granny's personal secretary for over a year, but had been forced to start selling real estate herself only three months previously when Granny fired her to cut some of his office expenses. He also gave her a Buyer to get her started.

"I just know what's best for you," he had said to her in answer to her tears of protest. I was to find out later how prescient I had been with my hiring condition to never make me cry. Rarely a week went by at Fakke & Co. that at least one person wasn't crying. Sometimes it was even a guy. But, to Granny's credit, there was truly very little about people or making a real estate deal that he wasn't dialed into, especially the sketchy ones.

I instantly became a mentor for both Lolly and Krista, after they learned I could help them with qualifying and finding the right financing for their buyers. Variable interest rate loans had come out about six months earlier as a solution to 16% interest rates, but everyone was afraid of them. If buyers weren't able to buy homes, the economy of the United States would suffer. A multitude of other industries from inspections to loans to home improvement to new furnishings depended on our sales.

Having just come from owning my own mortgage company, I was well versed in how to use variable rates to help our clients buy a home. As real estate 'newbies' in this unsteady economic mortgage and sales climate, both Lolly and Krista were sticking close to me. Since they were experienced agents (by at least a few weeks), I was sticking close to them, also. Lolly had sold two houses that had yet to close, but she was my hero, and was to become my role model in dressing and decorum as the three of us struggled to succeed. It was Granny who started the Fab Five count when he saw Lolly alone in the office one morning and asked her where the rest of her Fab Three gang was.

Back to my first day. In a torrent of information from the Fakke agents, all at the same time, I was told where the real estate forms were kept, where to get Open House signs, how to answer the phone. More importantly, I learned how to answer and then *transfer* the calls without disconnecting them. I was introduced to the Thomas Brothers Map Book so I could find addresses once I had some clients. About every two years, I had to get a new map book, as the worn-out pages of the old ones kept falling out and the San Marea area was booming with new construction and new streets.

This client stuff was so pretentious, to me. Psychiatrists and lawyers had clients, CPAs had clients, architects had clients—but I never thought of real estate as being high-classed or in the same league as all those well trained, well-educated professions. By the time I sold my first home three weeks later, I realized that a good, successful agent really did need to have a working knowledge in every category of the trained professions listed above.

At the minimum, I needed to have a list of a variety of experts that could be relied on for accurate information. Our clients, on average, only bought or sold a home every twelve years. They relied on us to educate them, as well as point them in the right direction to get proper legal and tax information.

But here I was on my first day as an agent, with no business cards or name badge officially marking the transformation. I had absolutely no idea of what I was doing, so I just pretended to look like what I thought a seasoned agent should look like. I sat perkily at my empty desk on high alert, scouting the horizon for a client and unwilling to admit that I wouldn't recognize one, or even know what to say or do if I accidentally found one. It felt kind of like having a pebble in your shoe inside your nylons. It was uncomfortable, but I couldn't take off my pantyhose in public, so I put on a stiff upper lip and tried not to limp, metaphorically speaking.

Every moment spent looking for a client was precious, since my mortgage payment was looming, and my new credit card would only cover one month. It was the biggest incentive I'd ever had (or ever HAVE had), to this day. My mortgage payment, my mother's criticisms, and my unwillingness to fail, were the foundation of my successful career selling real estate.

Darlene was the old timer at Fakke & Co., with ten years of selling experience, although Lolly whispered that Darlene hadn't had a sale in over a year now. She and eleven of the women huddled together around me that first day to apprise me of the situation. They were disgruntled employees, to say the least, and I was starting to have second thoughts about my assumption that Fakke & Co. was a solid, reputable company. According to them, the roof leaked on some of their desks, the downstairs toilets overflowed continuously, and the toilet paper was always missing. Furthermore, the copier rarely worked, light bulbs were out in the steep stairwell, several homeless people who occupied the lower-level garage were constantly confronting agents and clients for money, and one of the male agents smelled bad. They were putting together a formal list for Thursday's meeting to highlight these issues.

Lolly typed away furiously, trying to keep up with the fast flow of grievances. Eventually, on the second page, they all signed one below the other, like voter registration, leaving space for the others to sign when they came in. Under Darlene's leadership, they were Organized Labor pushed to the breaking point, and were determined to get Granny to agree to fix every item at lunch tomorrow—or else!

I surmise, in retrospect, that had the market been better and they were earning enough money to pay their own bills, they would not have had time to complain. (Just like the rest of life, when someone explodes over a minor issue, it was because the bigger issues were too heavy to bear any longer.) I didn't sign, of course. I hadn't needed to use the bathroom yet, so didn't have personal knowledge of the grievances, plus I was parked on the street and was distractedly keeping my eye on the clock so I didn't get a parking ticket.

On Thursday morning, the sun broke through the early coastal fogginess on this, my first business lunch in my new office. The fogginess in my brain took a little longer than usual to dissipate, but I felt ready. On that particular day, I didn't know enough to even know what I was ready for. But I was READY.

I walked with Lolly and Krista down the street to Murphys, a pleasant, pricey Old Boys Club-type restaurant smelling of stale booze and cigar smoke. The décor was real red leather banquette seating, faded carpet that always looked dirty, low lights, and lots of good food that wasn't on the printed menu. You had to Belong in order to order off the Other Menu. By the way the bartender and maître d' greeted Granny respectfully, he Belonged. However, Belonging, as I found out in later years, was not synonymous with them actually liking him.

Lunch was truly memorable. I ordered the open-face lobster club, which was an Other Menu Thursday Special. The ladies, though stressed, were chatty and outwardly cheerful. The men were focused only on their food and their drinks. Everyone ordered like they hadn't had a good meal in months (which might have been true for some of the agents). Lunch hour faded towards 2 p.m. and everyone had had a glass of wine, a Margarita, or two Wild Turkey bourbons (in Granny's case), so our nerves had subsided.

Darlene called the meeting to order by tapping her wine glass with a knife. All eyes shifted (some expectantly, some sinisterly) towards Granny. With one last sip of wine, Darlene started with "Grant, first, we all want to thank you for buying us lunch. You've never done that before, but we've all been working really hard, and as you know, times are tough." Then she launched directly into the list of grievances with no further preamble.

Granny sat passively. His little eyes sparkled with flashes of what I mistakenly thought was Wild Turkey, but which was, ultimately, of murderous intent, as became clear a few moments after the twenty-two grievances had been aired. I realized that everyone was holding their breath as they waited for Granny to respond. And, respond he did. He stood, slowly looked the group over one by one, then announced loudly and effectively simple, "You're all FIRED!"

After which, he stalked out and left the almost $450 bill unpaid. (I was to find out, in the fourteen years that I worked for him, that Granny virtually never paid. If, on occasion, he did pay in front of everyone, a title company, a mortgage loan officer, or some other supplier was standing behind him to reimburse him in order to garner his favor to access his office and solicit business.)

I sat in stunned silence. Granny had just fired me. I hadn't done anything. I hadn't complained, I hadn't signed the letter, and I'd only had one drink. Why did I deserve to be fired? Three of the female agents openly sobbed. As the sobbing subsided, individuals looked in their wallets for some money, but no one said a word. I had $3, not even enough to cover the glass of wine I'd had. Krista had her tips from the morning restaurant shift, so she covered for several of us. Finally, Darlene cleared her throat and said, "Okay, let's go back to work."

Like small children with their heads hanging low, knowing they had done something wrong, we all quietly went back to our desks at Fakke & Co. No one, including Granny, ever talked about that day again.

FOUR

THE MISTRESS OF ACCESSORIES

I was enjoying getting to know my new set of co-workers. I had never had any interest in the clothes I wore—I concentrated on cheap and comfortable. Lolly had a knack for dressing that made her look fashionable even in sweatpants. So, I started paying close attention to her appearance, as she epitomized how I thought a successful salesman should dress and act. Regarding fashion, Lolly was a walking Cosmopolitan Magazine. Her wisdom on appearance was sought out by many of us on a daily basis. She once told me that when she was growing up in her wealthy, society-conscious family, she unlocked the secret of looking well dressed—*accessories* were that secret.

Over the years, except for Krista, we all took note and evolved into wearing basic plain colored clothing emphasized with belts, large costume-jewelry pins, scarves, and oversized necklaces. Lolly could have written a book on all the ways she tied and draped scarves on her body.

Lolly never criticized me for a fashion faux-pas or pointed out my dated outfits. I cared nothing about clothes. I had grown up poor and wore hand-me downs from the daughter of my mother's boss. That meant that I grew up not knowing what my own taste was, or how to shop for clothes. I remember the very first time I went to buy a brand new outfit during my first year in college. I was unable to answer the sales lady's question about what size I wore (it was size twelve). When I arrived at Fakke & Co., I owned four pairs of shoes, including one of tennis shoes and a pair of hiking boots. I had five sets of cotton slacks and blouses, one for each weekly workday. So, when Lolly's closet was in danger of exploding from too many clothes and accessories, in my early years at Fakke & Co.,

I looked forward to being invited over to shop in it. It was a win-win activity for us both: she made room for new items, and she could tactfully help me look better.

After I closed some escrows and had money to upgrade my wardrobe, I took advantage of the fact that Lolly was always up for the shopping adventures we called Retail Therapy. She accompanied me to Nordstrom and helped select clothing items that went together. She told me the Nordstrom buyers always went on buying trips together, so all the departments carried stock that complimented each other. It was important, she said, to start with the shoes on the first floor because it was easier to find outfits to go with the shoes than vice versa.

However, Lolly was a complex woman with some hidden attributes that led me to have to re-categorize her occasionally.

My first recategorization happened one Tuesday morning about six months after I started at Fakke & Co. Knowing that most agents would be there for the weekly office meeting, two armed police officers came in, asking for Ms. Lolly Goldsmith. They were as serious as a heart attack, and although Lolly came to greet them with a smile on her face, her smile quickly turned to tears as one read the Miranda rights to her as the other handcuffed her hands behind her back.

Off she went between the two policemen without even her purse or her morning cup of coffee as we all stood by with our mouths hanging open. Buttercup was parked on the street in front of the office, as usual, just waiting for the parking police to make their rounds. Everything happened so fast that no one thought to look for her keys and move the car for Lolly.

About eight hours later, right after the office closed for the day, here came Lolly, in a taxi. Her makeup was streaked by trails of tears and her hair was disheveled. It was so uncharacteristic of her to look awful that Krista and I instantly braced for the worst.

So, what was Lolly's crime that warranted her being callously shackled in front of us all? Unpaid parking tickets. Eighty-five unpaid parking tickets, to be exact. Plus, two court-ordered appearances that she missed or forgot or something. As standard procedure, the court had issued a warrant for her arrest. The parking tickets were $40 apiece, plus the fine for missing her court appearances was $2,500 plus attorney fees. Lolly was going to have to have some big escrows close, and soon! No one wanted to tell her that Buttercup had accumulated three more parking tickets today; one for each two-hour time period that she hadn't been moved while Lolly was gone.

Lolly morphed into the 'Angel-Convict' in my eyes that day. That was before she revealed yet another aspect of her personality some months later.

This new aspect of Lolly's complex personality came into focus in December of my first year, when she came into the office with a thick, 8" x 12" plain brown envelope. She'd had a professional boudoir photographer take photos of her for her boyfriend's Christmas present, and she wanted our help to pick out the best one. Although that type of photography began with a hair and makeup session, Lolly hadn't needed that. She was a perfectionist with her appearance, so the stylist had not been needed.

Krista and I protectively crowded around Lolly's desk to keep her photos private from the male agents close by. I involuntarily let out a yelp when she slid out the first one. I expected to see Lolly in typical boudoir poses. She would have bright red lipstick and nail polish, be wearing skimpy lingerie, and lying on her stomach on a bed with a seductive look on her face. The edges of the photo would be blurred to soften the mood.

Instead, out of that plain brown envelope popped a new version of Lolly that made our mouths drop open. A version that made Krista laugh nervously, and one that I always referred to from then on as the 'Angel-Slut'. Since Krista never said anything bad about anyone, it came out as endearing instead of critical. In the top photo, Lolly was lying fully naked on her back, on a red Harley Davidson. She had one stiletto-heeled foot cocked over the handlebars for dramatic effect and wore a full-length leopard fur coat draped just so on the motorcycle, but not covering any of her important parts. It took three or four more similar photos before I blinked and noticed that she also had on giant pearl-drop earrings and different colored velvet ribbon chokers.

Lolly was, and still is, a beautiful woman, and almost every one of the twelve pictures was fabulous. Krista and I both assured her that any one of them would please her boyfriend. She couldn't decide, so she chose two and put them in a silver-hinged picture frame that he could stand on his desk.

By the following Christmas, Lolly did not have that same boy-friend. She had become engaged to a highly successful businessman who had moved to San Marea in June. His first weekend in town found him at Murphys, where he spotted Lolly and Krista having a glass of wine. This successful businessman was used to getting what he wanted, so things moved fast between them.

Over the years, Lolly proved to be as creative in having fun as she was in accessorizing. Her other talent—one that rivaled her success as Mistress of Accessories and annual awards as one of Fakke & Co's top agents—was hosting mega-successful parties. Her parties were elaborately staged, with meticulous attention to detail and outstanding food choices.

One Halloween, she and her new husband hosted their first annual costume party of their married life. He was dressed as a clergyman and Lolly was a pregnant nun. A few years later, it was a Valentine's Day party with the theme of "Doomed Lovers". Miriam and her husband won First Place when they dressed as Bonnie and Clyde and drove up to the party in a red Aston-Martin convertible holding plastic tommy guns.

Another of her well-remembered soirees was a party they hosted on a yacht in San Diego Harbor. She gave her guests a highly inventive party favor. It was a Certificate of Authenticity, showing that each person had a star named after them. It was accompanied by a chart of the heavens, showing where their star was located. I missed that party, so sadly, nowhere in the heavens is there a Nico's Star.

Lolly was, and still is, a well-known, well-liked, and phe-nomenally successful real estate agent. I became a nicer, more thoughtful person by knowing her. She was a role model for many of us agents (except for the convict or the slut persona— at least in my case).

FIVE

THE MILLION DOLLAR CLUB

Missy Ann's act of euthanizing her dad made me reflect on what I would do if I found myself in that position with my mother. I had been raised by a bitterly unhappy single mother who, I'm sure, did the best she could. What I remembered in my later life is that photos of Appalachia always looked familiar, somehow. We lived in a dirt cellar (to call it a basement would be exaggerating) of a large home where, in the winter, I wasn't allowed to touch the dirt walls because they crumbled.

It was fascinating to watch the frost line come down the wall as the ground froze deeper and deeper beneath Mother Earth's icy breath. In the spring, my mother's dark blue living room carpet remnant got soggy around the edges when the dirt thawed, and moisture seeped into the carpet. There were a couple of 8" x 12' planks set end to end that she and I had to walk, tight-rope style, on the way to the bathroom over an especially low patch, so we didn't get mud on our bare feet or my one pair of shoes.

My father walked out on us when I was five, never to return, and never to pay a dime of child support. My mother made so little money and never, ever had any left over, so every bump in life was a financial disaster. So, I think the natural thought progression here was to deduce that I would be happy when I had some extra money and could live in a nice house with real walls and floors like all my childhood friends.

My mother was also an alcoholic, and all her judgments, pettiness, and downright meanness were amplified after 7 p.m. She told me I was fat when I weighed 127 pounds at almost six feet in height. She was against my getting married right out of college. She was against my divorce almost twenty years later. She told me

I should just suck it up and stay, ignoring the fact that I was not leaving, I was being left.

When I couldn't find a job and decided to try selling real estate, she then focused on my recklessness in leaving the safety of a regular paycheck for a commissioned job. She conveniently forgot that the financial and real estate industries were in one of their biggest slumps ever, and no regular jobs were to be had. She refused to agree that I had nothing to lose by attempting to sell real estate while I looked for a steady paycheck job. She knew what she knew and didn't want any facts.

My adult self has never grown past the ability of my mother to make me feel guilty or not worthy. About something. About everything. It seemed that no accomplishment was ever great enough to warrant a congratulation instead of a criticism. Somehow, she always found some tiny failing to deflate the satisfaction I might have enjoyed over my accomplishments—which were many by the time she died.

I had started at Fakke & Co. in mid-May, 1982. I had never sold a home, but failure was not an option in my mind. In four months, I jumped from a starting commission split of 65% to an 80% commission split with Granny. By the end of that first year, I was ranked the fifth top earning sales agent out of thirty-one agents. This fifth-place ranking was from selling and closing around $2.5 million worth of property (almost $8 million in today's value) when my average sale was less than $180,000.

That first year, I had earned gross commissions of almost $60,000 in spite of interest rates hovering around 16%. (Today's equivalent would be $168,000.) I was selling roughly two properties per month, and two years later, was averaging four per month. (My personal one month's sales record was in June of 1987, when I sold eleven properties totaling over $6 million—an equivalent of $14 million today.) I had no secretary, no buyer's agent, no computer, no cell phone—it was the result of grueling, old-fashioned, hard work.

But that day at January's first office meeting, I was pretty pleased with my accomplishment. I was expecting my fifth-place ranking to quell my mom's concerns about me not having a regular paycheck.

"So, are you in the Million Dollar Club, then?" she casually asked over the phone from 1,400 miles away. I could see another failure looming large in her eyes as I had to admit that, no, I had never heard of the Million Dollar Club, so likely was not in it.

Her chilly reply informed me that Tess Moretti, who lived across the street and was my mother's regular drinking buddy, had a daughter who was a real estate agent in Ohio. Tess's daughter had been inducted into the Million Dollar Club for her real estate sales. Mom didn't really like that neighbor, and together they played the one-upsmanship game constantly in a passive-aggressive dance, frequently pitting one unknowing daughter against the other. Needless to say, my mom was mortified that her daughter was eclipsed by an unknown agent in Ohio. An agent who was a member of the Million Dollar Club, not to mention that it now gave Mrs. Moretti bragging rights for the entire year.

Mom ended the conversation abruptly by saying, "Next year, I expect that you will also be a member of that Million Club, so get to work and don't let me down." She left the word 'again' off the end of the sentence, but it was understood.

If this story had ended here, the answer to the hypothetical question I posed in the beginning of this chapter would have been 'yes'. Yes, I would have euthanized her, too, just to get rid of her dispiriting and disparaging ways—not because I loved her too much to let her suffer, like in Missy Ann's circumstance. However, most things look different with perspective.

My second year in real estate was a whirlwind. I had a $12,000,000 goal on a sticky note on my bathroom mirror. It resembled a thermometer, with twelve marks above the bulb at the bottom, where I filled in the milestones of each month's closings. I worked nonstop, as only a motivated self-employed person will do, under the assumption that the Million Dollar Club was a *monthly* goal. It was a logical assumption since I had earned $2.5

million the prior year and heard nothing about the Million Dollar Club from Granny.

I was determined to please my mom and give her back her bragging rights with Mrs. Moretti. As a result, I have them both to thank for my incredible success that year, and for establishing my work ethic and my sales career for many years to come. I became such a high-producing agent that several of the newspapers took note, writing stories about me in ensuing years and calling me for my 'expert opinion' quotes for their real estate articles.

Title reps, escrow reps, termite companies, mortgage reps alike all left me notepads, pens, gift cards, discount cards, invitations to lunch, and bottles of wine in hopes of attracting some of my business. The inducements piled up on my desk during the week, as I was rarely in the office. At my insistence, Lolly and Krista regularly gleaned from the pile and distributed the rest, although they knew to leave my two guilty pleasures: anything chocolate or any bottles of red wine.

By the end of that second December, however, I had only sold $11,998,800. I was $1,200 shy of selling $12,000,000 and achieving my Million Dollar Club sales goal. I was beyond embarrassed to have to admit to my mom for the second year that I missed The Million Dollar Club award, but I had nothing that would close in time to push me over the top in this calendar year.

Desperate and humbled, I braced myself and slunk into my broker's office with a request. I was to be the top agent out of seventy-four agents now in his growing company, but I needed a favor. A big favor. *A really big favor.*

I sat across the desk from my slimy shadowy broker and took a deep breath, steeling myself to ask a favor of him. Granny was famous in the real estate industry for all his sales schemes, his deceptive advertising, and the gifts (bribes) he was always extracting from mortgage, title, insurance, and escrow company reps wanting to do business in his office. This knowledge made me feel like I was sitting across from the Godfather. Which also meant that if he granted me a favor, I would then owe him. Lord only knows what I would be signing up for as an IOU to Granville "Granny" Fakke. It makes me shudder even today to look back on the moment.

I started out awkwardly by explaining my mom's request and my need to be able to give it to her so she could be back on even footing with her neighbor Mrs. Moretti. I ended it awkwardly, also, by admitting I was $1,200 shy of my $12.0 million dollar closed sales goal, but could he at least give me the award anyway, just for my mom, just so I didn't lose face with her and she didn't lose face with Mrs. Moretti? I closed my pitch with, *"No one at the company has to know; it will just be between us."*

Granny's mouth dropped open as he sat across the desk, his eyes bulging in disbelief at the suggestion that he lie on my behalf. He seemed to be having trouble finding the right words. Then he did a surprising thing. He put his head down on his desk and his shoulders heaved soundlessly. Quickly, I realized he was laughing. And laughing and laughing and laughing, to the point that when he raised his head, tears were running down his reddened face.

I jumped to my feet, indignant and embarrassed and furious that I had stooped to ask a favor of a man whose duplicitous ways of running his business I detested.

"I'm sorry you think it's so funny. I don't; and furthermore, it's important. I've sold forty-four houses this year, and the least you can do is help me out this one tiny little bit." I turned to leave his office.

He continued to laugh and sputter and motioned me to sit back down while he regained the ability to speak. I didn't sit down. I stood there glowering with my arms crossed in the universal body language signaling rejection, while inwardly feeling devastated.

Finally, he was able to get out, "The Million . . . Dollar . . . Club . . . . is for Coldwell Banker agents with . . . total sales . . . of a Million Dollars . . . in one YEAR . . . not per MONTH."

I had heard stories of people who did unbelievably amazing things because no one told them they couldn't, but this story was about me. My arms dropped to my sides as I stared dumbfoundedly at Granny, slowly comprehending what he was saying.

He continued. "Screw the Million Dollar Club. Don't you realize you've set a new MLS record for total sales in *one year*? You sold more this year than the next four Fakke & Co. agents below you, combined!

"What's your mother's phone number? We both need to call and thank her."

SIX

TEEN FOR A DAY, PROSTITUTE FOR A WEEK

I was working harder than ever, and didn't notice the arrival of Granny's newest agent, Ginger. Lolly and Krista, however, took an immediate liking to her, and the comments they made about her caused me to take a look.

Ginger's arrival at Fakke & Co. and her desk placement next to Lolly, Krista, and me had caused a quick expansion of our Fab Three to the Fab Four. It was an Assumptive Close on Ginger's part—she assumed that, since she sat next to us, she was included in everything we did. And so she was. Our bonding glue was always the sharing of our most intimate stories. We were each other's confidants, confessors, and co-conspirators; and Ginger was a wealth of intimate stories. She was a self-described 'Wild Child' which, we came to realize, was likely a watered-down version of her escapades.

When I first took a closer look, I saw a woman who was perfection for how someone with carrot-colored hair, pearlescent skin, and faint freckles should be constructed. Ginger was a head-turner. She had a great figure. Her breasts were matched cantaloupes sitting high in her sweaters—large, but not too large for her 5'5" frame. According to Ginger, they were already in place when she was thirteen.

Ginger was very talkative. One night, after two bottles of wine between the three of us, I encouraged Ginger to tell us about herself. Not needing any prompting, she started to reminisce. After hearing her background, I knew she had had such a life that, at twenty-four, she should be writing a book about it instead of me.

In short order, we knew she had grown up in Brea, a poorer

section of Los Angeles known worldwide as THE source of re-assembled dinosaur bones in museums. We had all heard of the La Brea Tar Pits. Or, as Ginger paraphrased it, she came from the pits of L.A.

Her whole life goal was to turn thirteen, on which day she decided she would be an adult and start her life without all the years in between being wasted as a teenager. She took her mom's annual birthday present of a $20 bill down to Goodwill where she invested in a new wardrobe. This new wardrobe consisted of some good-quality, designer label, sparkling, form-fitting clothes to make herself look older.

Ginger was both determined and resourceful. She told us she had asked her mother for the deluxe "All Day Tour of Homes of the Hollywood Stars" for her thirteenth birthday, along with the accustomed $20 bill she always got. She sat on the upper deck of the red bus with binoculars to better see the exact addresses and took notes on her map.

Instead of scholarly reading of the *The Old Man of the Sea* or a book on world history, Ginger read all the Hollywood Reporter magazines for star sightings, castings, and dirt. She read Cosmopolitan Magazine for the latest in makeup, dress, and accessory trends, as well as a source for sex education. Ginger's knowledge of accessories turned out to be the one thing that bonded her to Lolly, who was all about 'accessories, not clothes' being the secret of the well-dressed-for-success woman, no matter how much money was spent.

Ginger's mother was another source of addresses and dirt. According to Ginger, her mother was a "Psychic to the Stars" with a major following of Hollywood glitterati and, after a flattering and reassuring prophetic reading, would get heartfelt thank-yous and invites such as: "I'm having a party on Saturday, please come."

By fourteen, she was sneaking into the Hollywood mansion parties of major stars. Not really sneaking, just jutting out her already generous chest and walking brazenly up to the front doors in her 'couture de thrift store' skimpy outfits. She wasn't old enough to drive, so she had to take three different buses up to Mulholland Drive, where she sometimes walked several miles to that evening's party. She was smoking and drinking with an adult attitude, but never wavered from her declaration that she never, ever took drugs of any kind. That is, AFTER the first time, when someone deliberately slipped her a Quaalude and she saw kaleidoscope-colored monsters trying to eat her for an entire weekend. Ginger had 'street smarts', so once was enough; especially since it had happened without her knowledge or consent.

I listened to Ginger's backstory with a grain of salt. I suspected it had been embellished to make it a wonderful-sounding story to tell at parties. If her mother was such a great psychic, why wasn't she 'seeing' what Ginger was doing? And why wasn't she rich from predicting the winners of the races at Hollywood Park racetrack, a place she and Ginger frequented daily during racing season? Nevertheless, Ginger was a source of inspirational and highly entertaining stories, and she was a great addition to our now Fab Four.

Ginger's path to becoming a real estate agent in San Marea began when, at eighteen, she widened her partying ways. She started going to Tijuana with another girl she hooked up with at a Hollywood party at the Playboy Mansion. They had met across the bed during a "three-some" with a director.

Marina claimed she was only a year older than Ginger, and felt that Ginger was a kindred soul immediately upon meeting her. She drove to LA on weekends from Pacific Beach/San Diego, and one weekend, suggested Ginger come down to San Diego with her to attend a party in Tijuana. Marina was somehow familiar with wealthy Mexican families and frequented their lavish parties at golf course or oceanfront mansions by Plaza de Toros, home of the Tijuana Bullfights. Marina had luminescent skin, too, framed by a wild mane of cascading black hair. Together, Marina and Ginger got extra attention (and offers) from their contrasting looks.

That first weekend in San Diego, one of Marina's Mexican businessman 'friends' did his final walkthrough in a two-bedroom oceanfront condo that he was buying in an exclusive Coronado high rise next to the Del Coronado hotel. He kept ogling Ginger, and repeatedly said that if she had a real estate license, he would be buying this from her and she would be earning 6%, too. (One of the Urban Legends of Real Estate is that every agent earned a full 6% commission and had no expenses eroding the bottom line. In reality, after splitting a commission 50/50 between listing and selling companies, then splitting it again with their individual broker, most beginning agents earn *60% of half* of the original commission. When you take out average business expenses of 25%, the net in their bank account is roughly 22% of a 6% commission—not 100%.

As an example, if a 6% commission was $16,000, Ginger's gross earnings for her company would be $8000 x 60% her share, or $4,800. Then, subtract 25% business expenses, leaving her $3600 to live on. Since new agents rarely sell more than two properties their first year, $7,200 is not enough to keep them working in real estate beyond the first six months. Keep in mind that many commissions start at 5-1/2%, not 6%, so the bank account is even smaller. Back to her story.)

Ginger was broke, weary of the LA party scene even at her young age, and she had loved last night's mansion party by the Tijuana Bull Ring. Marina had told her she could stay with her as long as she wanted, so on Monday, Ginger enrolled in Anthony's Real Estate School to get her real estate license. Thirty days later, after passing the real estate licensing test on her first try, she was hired at Fakke & Co.

Reality set in about sixty days later, when she was even worse than broke and had no clients or leads yet. She was still staying *temporarily* with Marina, although, from time to time, Ginger was asked to leave for the day (or sometimes two days) so Marina could get some work done. She was going to parties in Tijuana every weekend, which cut into her Open House time, but the parties were great, food was fabulous, booze was fantastic, and life was good. Until it wasn't.

Ginger Jones woke up in a total funk one Wednesday in 1985 and took stock of her life to date. She had been living in Marina's tiny guest room for four months, now. She was wearing Marina's party clothes on weekends, could barely afford gas to get to work six miles away in San Marea, and had no real estate $16,000 commission prospects. Now that she had two months of real estate expertise, however, she realized that Marina's condo likely cost $100,000, her Nordstrom outfits at least $250 per outfit, and her late model red BMW convertible another $25,000 (in 1985 prices). She also realized she had never seen Marina's 'work'. How was this all affordable, she asked herself? So, she asked Marina.

Marina proudly confessed to having been a paid escort who had morphed into a Kept Woman. She had arrived in San Diego broke, too, and after answering an enticing job ad that said "Get paid while dining out every night," had been employed with a high-priced escort service, earning $100 per evening (or $200 for 'value added'). Within a month, a wealthy Mexican businessman hired her for an evening business meeting and refused to let her work for anyone else.

It was very prestigious and accepted that a certain level of wealth in Tijuana entitled a man to have a business, a family with children, and a mistress—all of whom had his complete devotion.

Jose Luis was just such a man. He installed Marina in his elegantly furnished Pacific Beach condo, where she could see the ocean from her bed every morning when she woke up. She still pinched herself daily that this was her life.

After the first month, Jose Luis bought Marina the red BMW. After one year, he deeded her the condo as an anniversary gift. Her Nordstrom account seemed bottomless. As the occasion dictated, she called in to her personal dresser, Chloe, who selected several outfit choices, from earrings to shoes and everything in-between. Although the theory might have been that she would pick the one she liked best, Marina just signed and picked up all the bags, much to Chloe's delight.

For all of these perks, the contract Marina readily signed said she had to be available at a moment's notice and be his, and his alone. No more working lady, she was to keep herself in shape—no drugs, and no demands on him. She had started coming to LA out of boredom when Jose Luis was on a business trip or family vacation. She thought that was far enough away that she wouldn't run in to anyone who knew her or Jose Luis. She told Ginger she knew she was violating her contract with him, but she was young and fun-loving, and it didn't really feel like cheating when he was out of town.

Marina then threw out an attractive proposition. Jose Luis really liked Ginger, and he was coming tomorrow. Should she call him and ask him if he wanted to bring a friend? Just for dinner?

For one of the few times in her life, Ginger was speechless. But, her resourceful and determined mind was working at the speed of light, calculating and scheming simultaneously. Rent for a nice condo was $325 a month, gas was forty-five cents a gallon, and a car lease on a four-door Mercedes was $165 a month. Two hundred dollars would cover two weeks of her basic necessities. times four? times eight? times ? ? ?

As a wild child, Ginger was used to freely giving 'IT' away, but somehow had reservations about selling 'IT'. In her no-frills mind, that would mean she was a prostitute. But that also meant that she could support herself until her real estate work started to pay off. She could afford a nice car to work in, and perhaps her first client would eventually buy a nice ocean view condo from her, too. In ten milliseconds, she said yes. But, to dinner only.

After an unbelievable dinner at Mr. L's penthouse restaurant atop one of San Diego's premier buildings, Ginger had to then eat her words for dessert. Miguel Angel was just that—dessert. He looked like the Don Diego character in the Zorro movie or the groom on top of a wedding cake. He was kind, gentle, confident, and gorgeous; albeit married with three grown children. She was already five years down the road with him, in her mind. Cars, furs, convertibles, condos, jewelry, designer clothing, and maybe even travel to exotic places she had only seen in magazines. She had always been guilty of dreaming large, and this dream was very, very large.

Miguel Angel owned several businesses, mansions, racehorses, and even a private airplane. That first night, he also proved to be generous, leaving her $250 by the bathroom sink before he left. Miguel Angel came back several times, that first week, always leaving her $250. "Treat yourself," he said. And she did.

The second weekend was a big party in Ensenada at his ocean-front mansion. She was instructed to get a strapless dress from Nordstrom and just put it on his account. "Don't look at the price," he said. No problem, there. His driver would show up for her at three pm. No problem there, either.

After nervously drinking an entire bottle of Cristal champagne in the limo on her way to Ensenada, the ensuing night was a little blurry. All Ginger could remember about the mansion was that the floors and walls of the bathrooms were covered by slabs of red veined marble. The view was forever, and the champagne that was served was more of the expensive Cristal. The hotel-sized oceanfront patio was rimmed with buffet tables and platters of lobster, shrimp, cabrito (baby goat), exotic cheeses, caviar and more—way more.

She ate and drank so much in her nervousness that she went from an alcoholic haze to a food coma for the rest of the evening. While she devoured the food, Miguel Angel devoured her with his eyes, coming by occasionally to furtively caress her bare back and tuck folded $100 bills between her breasts in the front of her dress at the same time. He definitely approved of her strapless, backless, clingy black Christian Dior dress.

Miguel Angel's beautiful blonde American wife was the hostess, and Ginger knew not to talk to her. But he had gallantly provided her with one of his racing jockeys, Alejandro, as an escort to make sure she had someone to talk to.

And escort Ginger, he did. At the end of the evening, Alejandro escorted her back to San Diego. At the end of the drive, he escorted himself into her bed, and the next morning, Ginger found she was $1,000 richer from the party—and in love. For real.

Although she and Alejandro were married two months later, much to the delight of Ginger's mother who was counting on inside information from her new jockey son-in-law, Miguel Angel had no hard feelings. Over the next year, he and several of his friends bought condos in Coronado from Ginger, launching her real estate career.

The marriage to Alejandro lasted long enough to give her two children, but Ginger's career lasted long after he was gone. All in all, it was a life-changing event that evolved from just one week as a self-professed prostitute.

SEVEN

THE WICKED WITCH FROM NOWHERE

It was a misty day in San Marea, and an ill wind was blowing in from the East. Although it would normally be called a Santa Ana wind, on this particular day, it became the ill wind that blew Beatrice "Trixie" Titoslav into our office, and nothing good was to happen after that whenever she was around.

I took an immediate dislike to Trixie. As with any group, be they members of a class, a church, an office, or even a family, there are people you like and those you don't. I had discovered at both of my high school class reunions that I still liked the individuals I'd liked in high school; and the jerks, the jocks, the social misfits remained stuck in their respective categories even decades later.

I had no tangible reason to dislike her, but as her time at Fakke & Co. continued, I developed many. My observations and experiences with Trixie lent credibility to why real estate agents are mistrusted, along with attorneys and used-car salesmen.

It started out innocuously enough, but whenever someone politely asked where Trixie was from, she always replied, "Nowhere." If they corrected themselves and rephrased it to ask where she'd moved from, it was the same answer: "Nowhere." So, even in the beginning, she was Ms. Nowhere to us all. Even me, until one day my client came to the office with his uncle. The uncle took one look at Trixie and swore profanely, saying. "Well, if it isn't Miss Five Hundred. I wondered where she went." When I raised my eyebrows questioningly, he just snorted and said: "My nephew will fill you in later. Let's go look at houses."

Diminutive Trixie constantly wore four inch heels which made her strut instead of walk, she wore designer St. John knits from Neiman Marcus instead of Nordstrom, she *leased* a powder blue

Rolls Royce instead of *owning* a *Mercedes* or a *Jaguar*, and worst of all, she claimed Murphys as her personal 'farm'.

Trixie did not conform to our idea of a traditional real estate agent, and we local agents resented it. She knew nothing about real estate, yet, somehow, she was selling a significant number of properties.

Trixie was proportioned so that whenever she sat down, her breasts rested on the table, or the bar, or the counter. That maneuver earned her a rude nickname that you can well imagine, knowing that it rhymes with 'Pits'.

As time went on, we all came to have grudging respect for those breasts. Whenever there was a difficult negotiation going on with a buyer, a seller, or even Granny, Trixie would assume the role of a smooth-talking seducer, er, salesman. She took control of the situation by leaning back in her chair, wearing a 'closing outfit' which invariably contained a low-cut clingy top.

Then, at the perfect time, if things had stalled out and it looked like the deal wasn't to be made, Trixie would lean forward to slide her chest onto the table. That pushed 'the girls' to overflowing capacity in her top. The men were the easy ones, but truly, after a moment or two of resistance, the women were too. Their eyes dropped inevitably to the straining breasts while Trixie slid the papers across the table, put a pen in their hand, and in her polished closing voice, commanded, "Sign here. Press hard, three copies." I never once saw it fail. As much as we all tried and tried, we couldn't even come close to replicating the maneuver.

As the years wore on, her biennial breast implants became legendary. Ginger famously once said, "Look, Trixie has increased her brain size again."

In the years when she didn't increase her brain size, Trixie underwent other plastic surgeries. Just like the robins appear in the spring and the swallows come back to Capistrano, every January, we all waited to see what new Trixie would appear. One January, she walked by the office window, and no one recognized her. Although we'd met her with black hair, after a few years she was a deep redhead. A few more years, and she was a brassy blonde. While that was the first year of being Blonde Trixie, it was her face that confounded us. We all disagreed on the cause—her nose was different, her chin was bigger, and her eyes seemed to be higher in her face. In retrospect, it was probably all of those.

The nephew had indeed filled me in shortly after Trixie arrived at Fakke & Co. His uncle frequented street prostitutes in a seedy area of San Diego. Trixie was not her street name, but she was reputed to charge an unheard of $500 for a full night of companionship—hence the nickname Miss Five Hundred. I anticipated from the onset that Trixie was a nasty piece of work, but she was also a fountain of memorable stories.

Once Trixie got entrenched in her farm area, Murphys, the listings just kept coming. No one could figure out how she got them just by spending a lot of time in a bar. Murphys was an 'Old Boys Club', meaning that all the older men in this wealthy town had their favorite stools or booths. After the dinner crowd cleared, the drinking crowd regulars took over. Her continuing success illustrated another true-ism in real estate—if newly licensed agents have no sales history, they still get listings. Considering that gross commissions are primarily either 5% or 6% of a sales price, if a seller is paying the same cost for representation, you would think they would want the most experienced agent to handle the sale of their largest single asset.

And you would think wrong. Agents are often chosen because they were standing nearby when owners decided to become sellers. Or because they're cute, because they're related to the sellers, their parents are friends, or because they remind the sellers of their grandkids or themselves at that age. Or agents are chosen because they offer something all the other agents don't—like spending most every night in a local bar, maybe exchanging sex for business. Lots of unexpected variables determine who gets a listing, experience was just one of many.

In the beginning months, local agents were initially amused, then exasperated, and ultimately totally irritated by Trixie's undeserved business. Those feelings were amplified when she ran a full-page New Year's ad of addresses that had sold over the past year in the San Marea Review. The ad congratulated herself and the people of San Marea on their sales. She worded it to encourage readers to think the entire list was a list of HER sales, when in reality there were only a tiny percentage of the fifty-six that actually were hers.

Granny's phone was ringing off the hook from other agents and brokers reading him the riot act, not to mention the handful of people whose homes were never on the market, let alone sold, yet whose addresses still were in the ad. Granny's fiancé's house was on the list, too, which didn't amuse her one bit. As a result, our local MLS board enacted regulations making it illegal to advertise, in any manner, a property where you were not the listing agent or the buying agent. This rule spread nationally over the next five years, possibly originating in San Marea.

Later that same year, Trixie's newest listing was the straw that broke the proverbial camel's back. It was a huge shingled Coastal Contemporary house that perched over its elevated corner lot like Snoopy pretending to be a vulture while surveying his backyard from the top of his doghouse.

While its neighbor homes were 2,400 square feet to 3,400 square feet, this monster coastal contemporary box was 6,200 square feet. It loomed even larger because of the flat-sided architecture of the three stories, unsoftened by landscaping. The owner was a single professor at a local university. He had built it in preparation for his upcoming wedding, but he'd lost his fiancé from non-stop arguments during the building process. When he put his FSBO sign in front, he announced himself as a target to the real estate community.

At least a dozen highly trained agents came from miles around to give him a presentation. The less experienced agents only stayed fifteen minutes. Others were so experienced that they almost always were successful at the end of a listing presentation, but every agent came away from the professor empty-handed.

People like Tony (who espoused the Mike Ferry-scripted questions approach where he asked specific questions designed to get a 'yes' response to his listing presentation); Mario (who was a Floyd Wickman Sweat Hogs graduate: just put your head down and make phone calls or knock on doors until you got a 'yes'); or Lolly (who had mastered Tommy Hopkins' The Art of Selling Anything, with its psychological approach to gaining a listing 'yes'). They were highly trained agents at the top of their individual games, but collectively, they all came away saying the undeniable mantra of FSBO properties—*the owner was unreasonable on his price.* He wanted $950,000 and all of the rejected agents agreed it was only worth $800,000 at the most.

After two weeks of hungry agents circling the prey, Trixie's sign went up in the front yard. "NOOOO!" was the invisible scream that echoed through The Universe. Even worse, she priced it at an even $1,000,000. To add insult to injury, after three weeks on the market, she sold it herself at *full price.* This example illustrated another true-ism in real estate—if your agent doesn't believe in the price, Mr. and Mrs. Seller, you will never get it. By that, I mean that any other agent who believed it to be worth $800,000 could never have gotten that seller a million dollars.

With this particular sale, the gauntlet was flung to the floor, so to speak. Trixie had to be doing something to get all these trophy listings, so the agent network started asking around. The stories of sex and scorched earth tactics came gushing forth. Even Murphys' patrons were referring to her as '*Queen of the Knees*'.

The whispered stories were all similar. If Trixie went on a listing appointment and it appeared that she wasn't going to get the signature right then, she offered a sex bribe. If the wife was present, she asked the man to carry things out to her car, and she offered a sexual favor there (maybe even in the backseat of her baby blue Rolls 'closing car'), continuing to up the ante until she got a 'Yes'. If none of those worked, she went on a verbal abuse tirade that would ensure that these offending sellers would never in 1,000 years work with or trust a real estate agent again. EVER.

Granny was the primary source of this explanation. He fielded all the irate calls about his agent, but he was thrilled with her production, so seemingly did nothing to thwart it.

I had just had a major problem with Trixie over paperwork from a sale we had worked on together. I had a trophy listing of a designer's own home that Trixie had sold to her buyer, a local sports celebrity. As expected, Trixie was difficult and demanding over the tiniest of issues, but it had finally closed. The day of closing, Trixie went to escrow and brought both commission checks back to the office. Which was uncharacteristic of her, until I noticed that she handed me two envelopes. The second one was a mediation lawsuit, dated that morning. The time stamp at the bottom was during the time we'd both waited for confirmation of the closing. The mediation lawsuit said Trixie was unhappy with the commission she'd earned, and now that it was closed, she wanted more.

The mediation hearing was in front of a panel of five agent peers who had been trained in mediation resolution. Also present were Trixie, me, and Granny, as brokers have to attend any potential disciplinary hearings with their agent(s). Trixie claimed she had written an extra ½% commission into her buyer's first counteroffer, and it was agreed to by my seller. (The legalities involved are that the seller pays the listing agent/broker, and the listing agent splits that fee with the selling agent. That's why she had sued me instead of my seller.)

Now that the escrow was closed, she wanted to force me to pay her that extra ½% from my commission. She presented the mediators with a letter signed by my seller agreeing to the higher commission and the signed counter offer to prove it. (I had not seen either one of those papers before that moment.)

Unfortunately for Trixie, she didn't know that the seller's girlfriend was a personal friend of mine, plus she hated Trixie with a passion after her boyfriend laughingly told her that Trixie had offered him a 'sexual favor' if he would accept her buyer's low offer.

When she heard that I was being coerced to give up part of my commission, my friend called Granny to apprise him of the back story. She informed him that Trixie had come by with an unusual request the day before closing, when they were moving out. Trixie claimed she had forgotten to get the boyfriend's signature on one of the counter-offers, and also wanted a testimonial for her portfolio. She had hand-written herself a testimonial as though it had come from the seller and asked him to read it over for changes.

Then, as is a universal by-product of signing so many papers during a transaction, my seller signed the counter without reading it, and a blank piece of paper so Trixie could type the testimonial up over his signature. That way, Trixie assured him, it would be nice and neat and legible so she wouldn't have to come back. You can connect the dots as to what two papers she confidently presented at the private mediation hearing in Granny's presence, and what the outcome was. Although no details of mediation are ever made public, Trixie never spoke to me again.

About that same time, several other agents started noticing things disappearing around Fakke & Co. First, it was paperwork from a file. Lou Anna was the first to think she was losing her mind, along with missing paperwork. Then I noticed Ginger loudly complaining that she'd had a full file and now several important pages were missing. She couldn't get her commission until she got new originals. She hated her difficult clients in this case, and they hated her. She was mortified at having to tell them she'd lost some of their papers, and would they mind re-signing them. I realized that I had been missing papers, too, but had just assumed I had misplaced them in a different file, and that they would eventually show up.

Lolly overheard the discussion between Ginger and me. Both she and the agent next to her were missing items—loose change, expensive closing pens, single earrings which had been removed to talk on the phone. Krista hadn't had any problems, surprisingly. Miriam joined us and whispered her story. Her Day-Timer had been missing for over a week, with every name and phone number of every client and friend she knew lost along with it. She had come into the office this morning at 6 a.m. when no one was around to make a thorough search for it one last time. She looked behind every desk and went through every single drawer and shelf in the entire office. Her Day-Timer was nowhere to be found.

However, Trixie had first shift floor duty this morning, and when she saw Miriam with her head down on her desk crying, some iota of pity made her open up a drawer in the up desk sometime later and, with a flourish, announce, "Miriam, here's your Day-Timer. It was in this drawer; you must have left it there the last time you had floor duty".

That made sense of all the other mysterious disappearances, so Lolly, Miriam, Ginger and I marched straight back to Granny's office with our stories.

Granny had a lot of faults, like making the phone ring with his misleading ads, but knowing how devious minds worked caused him to look into our accusations. He personally had not seen anything, but knew there was one person who sees all, knows all, but says nothing unless asked: The night cleaning lady.

For all her top sales production, Trixie was gone two days later.

EIGHT

HOMELESS MAN BUYS A MILLION DOLLAR HOUSE

Trophy Clients were one of the perks of being a real estate agent in an area with expensive houses in the 1980s. If you're a good agent, within ten minutes of meeting someone, you know the new client's name, marital status, job status, income, bank account numbers and other assets. (If they are married, nerdy, or barely have a down payment, you just do your best to sell them a house as quickly as possible.) After knowing all the basics, if they get high marks in all the categories, they become your Trophy Client, and you exert extra effort to sell them an expensive property, and perhaps, even become friends. That meant you closed the office and took them to Murphys, the local real estate hangout, for a drink, like Miriam did one Saturday night. I learned about Trophy Clients from Miriam.

Miriam was the fifth and final member of the Fab Five sisterhood. She was hired at Fakke & Co. before Ginger, but Ginger's out-going personality and wacky stories got her the Number Four membership easily. Miriam was so private that it took almost a year longer for her to become Number Five. Like Ginger, Miriam was assigned to a desk right across from Lolly and me. She was such a hard worker and was kind to everyone, even after losing the lawsuit on her first transaction. (More on that later.)

Initially looking more like the stereotypical sixties hippie flower child, albeit living in the 1980s, Miriam proved to be the ultimate caregiver. She was a flowing, free spirit with a skipping type of walk that made it appear like her feet never touched the ground. We never saw her dressed in slacks—only in slim dark skirts at work and hippy-style, summery, flowing cotton dresses otherwise. She could have been a fairy queen or a gypsy queen, but overall, she was one unique individual for sure. She said offhandedly one day said that her idea of dressing up was to wear a bra and panties. But, from the day she walked into Fakke & Co., she looked ever the part of a successful real estate agent.

Miriam had arrived in San Marea straight from Detroit with her new husband, their new baby, and two little girls from her first marriage. Granny proudly told Lolly and me that Miriam had passed her real estate licensing test on her first attempt, and predicted she would do well, with our help. Since we were independent contractors and not employees, he was not giving us an order— he was *strongly* suggesting that we mentor her. (And by the way, Granny, all of us Fab Four had passed the test on our first try, too.)

Miriam was six feet tall and thin, with classic Greek goddess looks, a straight nose, high cheekbones, and a flirty yet regal demeanor. She exuded poetry and read books so deeply philosophical that, in spite of my college classes in philosophy, I had never even heard of them. Her habit of twisting a lock of hair over her ear when she liked something, or someone, was charming. She looked like she had just stepped out of a Nordstrom catalog, projecting confidence in a power outfit of slim black skirt, white silk blouse, black ribbon cravat, and black blazer. In the summer, she replaced the blazer with a black cardigan.

Like many new agents, Miriam had a second job until she could close an escrow. As she learned the basics of showing, listing, and selling, she could only work at night. We agents loved that she took the 5 p.m. to 7 p.m. floor slot many days of the month, so the agents with children didn't have to work late. The average time for a first closing was four to six months, so most second jobs lasted a minimum of a year, until that agent could accumulate some commissions.

At this time in real estate, a usual commission was $2,800 after the broker took his share off the top. In San Marea, however, a usual commission was easily $5,000, so there were brokerages full of agents about every fourth address along the three-block downtown zone. Competition for both listings, and the buyers who could afford them, was fierce. Listing fringe-benefit offers of sex and commission-ectomies ran rampant. (Commission-ectomies are how part of an agent's earnings are surgically removed by a seller while the agent is trying to get the listing signed, or during the final negotiating of the sales price of a property between a stubborn buyer and seller, in order to make the deal work.)

But powerful, confident Miriam never lost her cool look or her determination to succeed. Within two months, she proudly got her first listing. Our office liked Miriam, and it was a huge celebratory moment witnessed by Lolly, Krista, Ginger, and I– until we learned she had listed a cemetery plot down by the Tijuana border for $750. It was a full 10% land commission. However, because she had to split with the selling agent AND Granny, she would clear about $14.50. I almost choked, trying to swallow my laughter while still looking thrilled by her accomplishment.

No one, including Granny, was sure that a cemetery plot was even something that fell under 'real estate', but it was land, so he let her keep it. And, to his credit, he even advertised it for her, figuring buyers *buy up from an ad and down from a sign,* so this price was bound to make the phone ring off the hook. She eventually sold it herself, and her first commission was $29.

Her second listing effort closed just a month later. It was an odd custom home that was designed to fit a triangular lot in Cardin. At this time, unless an agent could find an old floor plan or public record permit about the house, the listing agent had to measure the property and report the square footage in the MLS. We all had a 100-foot cloth tape measure so it was easier to get a long wall in one try.

I started college by majoring in math, so I helped Miriam calculate the area of the triangular-shaped living room and master bedroom above it. She and I both measured the weird-shaped home several times before we were satisfied. But Miriam never told any of us that she had gotten sued because of it.

Apparently, after the sale closed, Mrs. Buyer sat down and

actually read the appraisal. The appraiser's measurement of the house had come up with a different number—a number that was almost 1,000 square feet *less* than Miriam's listing in the MLS. By using the appraiser's cost replacement figure of $100 per square foot, Mrs. Buyer sued Miriam for $100,000, even though she had only paid $250,000 for the entire home.

To sum up this fiasco, by the time the court made a ruling, there had been four more appraisals at $450 each. Furthermore, none of them came up with the exact same square footage measurements as Miriam and I, or the original appraiser. The judge finally ruled that the initial MLS square footage was off by *fifteen square feet*; and awarded Mrs. Buyer $1,500. Miriam had been negotiated down to a 2% commission by a shrewd seller and was on a 60% commission split at the time. After having to pay the $1,500, her share of attorney fees, and two of the appraisal fees, she didn't break even. (Errors and Omissions Insurance goes into effect when a judgment is more than the commission, so, in this case, only Miriam had to pay.)

Miriam was too embarrassed over the low commission, the incorrect square footage, and the lawsuit to let any of us know what she had gone through. It came to light when Lolly and I observed Granny calling Miriam into his office. When she came out sobbing a few minutes later, we rose to her defense and hustled into his office, only to be told what had caused her tears. It wasn't him—at least this time.

In the meantime, even though she was a very private person and we had never seen where she lived or met her husband or her kids, we were impressed by how hard she worked. We knew Miriam was going to be a lasting agent, so we tried to help her.

What we didn't know about Miriam soon came out when Lolly, Krista, Ginger and I celebrated with her after her closing of a $1.5 million dollar home in The Ranch about eight months after she started at Fakke & Co. After several bottles of pricey celebratory wine at Murphys, Miriam relaxed and became chatty. As with any commission-rich sale, other agents want to know where the client came from in hopes of discovering a magic bullet shortcut they could utilize from the details, so we do whatever we can to encourage a successful agent to talk.

No agent worth their salt would talk about their clients if they were sober. Mostly because we take confidentiality seriously, but it's also bad luck. There are, and continue to be, many instances where the details or names were overheard by other unscrupulous agents, who then figured out a way to find said clients and lure them away.

(Our office was still unhappy about a recent incident where Louise, a popular but struggling agent, scored big time when the newly drafted professional athlete for a local team walked in on her floor time. She showed him houses for several weeks, ending up at one of Ms. Most Mistrusted Trixie's new listings. Inexplicably, he quit returning Louise's calls a few days later. The next time she saw him was forty-five days later, when he came into the office to pick up the key to his newly purchased home. Trixie had represented both sides as a dual agent, and it was apparent to us all that she'd deliberately arranged the key pickup on Louise's floor time.)

At our favorite hang-out, Murphys, along with Miriam, we all agreed that reality is stranger than fiction and you can't make stories like these up because they don't sound real. That encouraged Miriam to confide the story of her $1.5 million sale. She embarrassedly told us that her other job had been cleaning houses (or, as she succinctly put it, cleaning toilets), so she had only been able to work evenings and Sundays.

Late one Friday evening a couple of months earlier, a tall, dark, handsome man dressed exquisitely in linen shirt and pants, with a groomed mustache (I visualized Rhett Butler in *Gone with The Wind*) and a proper British accent, stuck his head in the door looking for directions to Murphys. Tall, dark, and beautiful Miriam took one look at him and closed up Fakke's for the evening to personally show him where Murphys was located instead of just telling him it was four doors further down the block.

Over the Friday night din at Murphys, Miriam and Willems (yes, Willems with an 's') got to know each other. Willems was moving here from his vanilla plantation in South Africa with his family because of the weather. Willems' wife had a respiratory disease and the climate and proximity to several top-rated Southern California hospitals helped them make the decision to immigrate.

He had started looking in the LA area but was turned off by the smog. He'd kept moving further and further south over the past month to find just the right place for his wife and three small children. He was horribly lonesome for his family; he just needed to buy a house so they could join him. At this point, Williams pulled out a dog-eared photo of a thirty-ish willowy blonde woman with matching willowy blonde little girls all under the age of ten. Today he had come from the San Diego Zoo, where he spent most of the time enjoying its botanical gardens, which reminded him of home. Willems felt that The Universe had given him a sign that he was in the right place.

Miriam's hippy Earth Mother/Caregiver persona kicked in, since they had now shared two bottles of good red wine and had forgotten to order dinner. He couldn't remember where he'd parked his rental car, so of course she took him home with her. To her couch. Where he resided for three months while she found a great house for him and his family in The Ranch, the most expensive zip code in the county. Miriam said her husband seemed glad for the extra male energy to balance out all the females he lived with.

In hindsight, it was a risky proposition to bring a total stranger into her home, but that probably never occurred to Miriam. She never got bank statements or a bank letter to prequalify him, and she spent hours upon hours showing him expensive properties by vouching to listing agents that he was a qualified buyer. She had faith, and faith takes care of fools and trusting real estate agents, it seems.

Miriam persevered until she found him a house. Because Willems was not a U.S. citizen, he wasn't eligible for financing, so he paid $1.5 million cash for the house. He finally closed escrow after a rocky experience with the sellers over a faulty home inspection and items that they refused to fix. After closing, however, he stayed one more month on the couch, awaiting the arrival of his family while Miriam helped direct the renovation and furnishing of the new home. Good real estate agents have no job description, so she just did what needed to be done. The weeks Miriam spent on home decorating came at no additional cost—a random act of kindness on her part.

No additional cost, unless you count the successive commissions she earned a month later when Willems' wife didn't like the house he had purchased. Miriam listed and resold the house and represented them in the purchase of a $2.5 million home a mile away. Miriam was so pure of heart that she was generously rewarded for her kindness with commissions on $6 million in sales for those three transactions.

After celebrating Miriam's good fortune, we were all bonded confidants over the shared stories and the bottles of wine. The Fab Five evolved into lifelong co-conspirators as Miriam filled in more blanks between how she looked and her reality.

Her husband Claude, whom we had still never met, was described by Miriam as her polar opposite, physically. He was a roly-poly man with long hair and a beard who wore wrinkled, disheveled clothing and looked homeless to people who didn't know him. He was evidently about three inches shorter, but with a tall, warm smile. Miriam rolled her eyes while admitting she was a sucker for musicians and artists.

She had fallen head over heels for Claude between sets in a Detroit bar in 1980, where she was waiting tables and he was playing guitar. He was a weed-smoking, mellow hippie-type spirit, five years younger than Miriam. Impulsively, she left her husband (whom she had married at age fifteen to get away from her ultra-strict father) and her two girls to move in with Claude. He ignited her own hippie-ness, free love spirit, and dreams of living in California.

During her divorce, Miriam found out she was pregnant with Claude's child and hid it from everyone because she knew the judge would never grant her a divorce if he knew. After spending a few weeks alone with his two young girls without Miriam to do all the work, when the husband came to drop the girls off for their first weekend visit with Miriam, he never came back to pick them up. She heard from an old neighbor that he had moved out of Detroit.

Miriam and her two girls stuffed themselves into every available cranny to live with Claude in his tiny apartment until the baby came five months later. She quickly learned that he only got guitar playing gigs when he felt like contributing something to the table or replenish his drinking fund. She lowered her voice to share that there was a warrant out for his arrest in Detroit for non-payment of child support for his two older children, although he had never been married. In the middle of the night, they had piled the baby, her two girls, his German Shepherd-mix dog, and his guitar into an ancient VW van and drove as far as they could to get away from that warrant. When they hit the Route 66 highway, they turned west and drove until it ended at the ocean by San Marea.

Some things didn't change in this new environment, she said. Claude still only worked occasionally. When so moved, to avoid public parking fees, he would take the transit bus to downtown San Diego's Seaport Village and play his guitar for vacationers to throw money into his open guitar case. He got more money there than at Horton Plaza, but as all the security guards got familiar with him and surmised that he was a homeless man, he was chased away continuously, volleying back and forth between those two sites.

Miriam's most recent listing came about when her landlord apparently got tired of late rent payments coupled with discovering he was renting to three adults instead of the original two, three kids instead of two, and the neighbor's constant complaining about the midnight guitar playing. There was also the accidentally non-disclosed dog that was a shedding machine, who spent hours every day howling and trying to dig out of the patio.

The landlord wanted them to move before their lease expired, so he told Miriam he needed to sell the condo for financial reasons, and the listing was a bribe. (Although potentially discriminating against children was a federal crime even then, there were so many other issues that he needn't have worried about that one.) The third adult, of course, was Willems, who was still couch surfing while waiting for Miriam to finish decorating his new home. It was an unexpected bonus, as Miriam and crew had planned to move out anyway, now that she had a decent commission in the bank, so she gladly added the condo commission to her growing bank account.

As for the old grey 1972 Mercedes sedan she drove, it had belonged to her landlord, who'd loaned it to her whenever she had a buyer, hoping she would earn enough commission to pay her rent. She bought it from him with her newly found commission wealth when she moved out.

After this jarring revelation, we four were all drunk enough to start asking more questions—like, how was she able to expensively clothe herself from Nordstrom from the start?

This answer was a mindblower. Miriam had arrived in San Marea with only a few hundred dollars in hand, so she resourcefully opened an account at Nordstrom to charge her purchases, having faith that she could pay the small monthly payments until she closed an escrow. She was observant enough to know she had to look successful in order to be a salesman, let alone a salesman of high-priced homes along the coast. Miriam only owned six items of professional clothing. For the past ten months, she wore her 'uniform', as she called it, consisting of black blazer, black cardigan, black ribbon tie, slim black skirt, and black tights with a white blouse. Every night, she brought them to the office to change into before her floor duty and then changed back into her cleaning clothes before going home, so as not to wrinkle her uniform unduly. She hand-washed the tights and blouse every other night in the condo sink and ironed them every morning.

Fueled by the wine, the private Miriam had taken us into her confidences, and we took her into ours. The Fab Four became the Fab Five, that night.

The five of us remained a closely knit sisterhood from that night in 1984 until Miriam's death from a heart attack in 2019.

RIP my beautiful friend.

NINE

KRISTA AND FAT ALBERT

Four years after joining Fakke & Co., I was on my way, with Lolly, Miriam, and Ginger, to a funeral for Krista's mom.

Krista was my most favorite person from the first day we met in the office. (Sorry, Lolly, but you're a close second!) Krista had dark hair almost to her waist and large luminous dark eyes with insanely long eyelashes. Her exercise routine was legendary, as were her perfectly proportioned body and her 1,000-watt smile. As I said before, she never said anything bad about anyone, unless you count her saying "Be-ah-che' instead of 'bitch' like the rest of us. Her generous mouth with perfect teeth got lots of complements from both men and women.

However, when I first tried to compliment her smile, she just laughed, saying, "My teeth are nice, but personally, I'm prouder that my mouth is so wide, I can get both of a man's balls into it during oral sex. Guys love it, and they treat me like a queen, so it's really hard for me to break up with them."

After the funeral and the internment, we all drove over to see Krista's legendary and oft-described childhood home. It was a charming Spanish hacienda from an original Mexican land grant. Her reminiscences always sounded like a 'Leave It to Beaver' existence (except for the Spanish hacienda part). She was preparing to sell it right away and wanted our help in pricing and recommending what needed to be done prior to putting it on the market. She knew she couldn't be objective about that.

I'd been hearing many stories over the past few years, of Krista's loving family and her wonderful life growing up. I had great expectations about how grand and historical her Spanish hacienda would be. Today, she talked about her Dad and Fat Albert in the same sentence. When I asked what kind of pet Fat Albert was, she just smiled. "You'll see. I don't want to spoil your fun." (I was to learn she didn't tell me because she didn't want to spoil *her* fun.)

I loved animals, and they all loved me, so I was intrigued. Krista obviously was a Daddy's Girl, and Fat Albert had been her dad's favorite pet, so treasuring him after her dad passed away two years ago was homage to her dad's memory.

We arrived in a little, hard-to-find area of Tidelands about 2 p.m. Once, it had been sequestered in rural farmland, but sketchy zoning enforcement outside the city limits allowed commercial buildings, high-density apartment buildings, the Dew Drop Inn mobile home park, and Eddy Royal's Towing Yard to now crowd claustrophobically around a teeny-weeny adobe cottage, making it look like it was the prototype for a normal-sized hacienda which hadn't yet been built.

The mini-hacienda sat whitewashed, stained, and cowering in stark contrast to its large commercial neighbors, even though it was on almost two acres and was guarded by 100-plus year old oak trees dripping with Spanish moss. It sat low to the ground, likely because there was no foundation under it.

Krista will probably need to disclose that lack of foundation to potential buyers, was my initial thought as I unfolded my 5'9" height out of her compact car. We were greeted by a motley crew of assorted, colorful Banty and Rhode Island Red chickens. One of the red chickens was gigantic. It was the Godzilla of chickens everywhere.

"*Fat Albert?*" I asked with raised eyebrows.

"Nope," Krista and Lolly said, in unison with their secretive smiles.

I had to duck my head to go through the hewn wood doorway into Krista's childhood home. Stepping inside was like stepping through the rabbit hole and falling into a Freida Kahlo painting. The dim, almost windowless interior was a collage of large and small murals flowing together in bright blues, buttercup yellows, and sunset-intense reds and oranges adorning pretty much every inch of the whitewashed adobe walls. Even the kitchen ceiling had birds and butterflies in colors and swirls that only someone inspired by Freida could concoct.

There was no other art on the walls, but a multitude of frames filled with family photos were huddled together, competing for space on all of the horizontal surfaces. I almost laughed out loud at the photo of Krista's mom wearing an apron over her dress and a string of pearls, just like June Cleaver. Interestingly, Krista's dad greatly resembled Diego Rivera. Perhaps he was his own source of the Frieda inspiration?

Krista proudly gestured around the room with, "Isn't this place a Heaven on Earth? My Dad painted all this! Look around for a minute while I use the little girl's room. You all went at the mortuary, so I'll be right back."

I got a reality check of what humble beginnings Krista came from, and felt a warmer and deeper connection with her, from that knowledge when I compared it to my own. No matter what a house looked like, Home is HOME. I admired Krista's remembrances of her loving family, even though I couldn't muster up any of my own.

I checked out the two bedrooms and kitchen in twenty seconds flat without having to take a step, then headed out into the back yard while Ginger and Lolly looked around the kitchen for a bottle of wine and some glasses.

I could see an interesting pond with a handmade rock border, about 100 feet from the house. Since Fat Albert hadn't been that gigantic front yard chicken, I figured I was about to discover Fat Albert, the koi.

I had taken about ten steps and was still smiling when I caught some movement out of the corner of my eye. I casually glanced that way, only to freeze in mid-stride, hypnotized at the sight of an enormous live alligator a few feet away and only separated from me by a ten-inch decorative fence/border. He was sludging his way through his mud playpen towards me, mouth slightly ajar and crowded with a million gleaming white knives, ready to eat me. Maybe even two million.

I was so immobilized with fright, I couldn't scream; I couldn't breathe. I could smell the swampy-ness preceding the gator. I remember thinking: how is this going to look on my obituary—that I was eaten by an alligator in a backyard in California while helping to price a home? Agents everywhere would laugh at me, and most of them would suspect I deserved it.

I read somewhere that animals, when confronted with imminent danger, survived with a fight or flight reaction. Because I was still frozen in place, I couldn't do either and I guess I imagined that I'd wet my pants. It was like in a nightmare, but I knew for certain that I wasn't dreaming, because when you dream that you wet your pants, you wake up with a wet spot on the mattress, and I was still dry, having recently come from the 'little girls' room'.

"Hey, I see you just met Fat Albert. Were you surprised?"

Her voice startled me so much, I jumped at least six feet and was hopefully out of danger.

"Isn't he cool? He's looking for a meal. Step aside, and I'll throw him one of the chickens. I just wrung its neck, and it's still warm. This is his favorite meal; he's going to love it."

I couldn't say anything. I felt I was going to gag in front of my friends and fellow agents! Once I started breathing again, that is. (Over the years, I've noticed that the occasions that have taken my breath away always make the best stories!)

Krista was all animated now, remembering her childhood days. "My Dad loved Fat Albert; probably almost as much as he did my sister and me—probably more, some days. He always said that when his time was up, there was a provision in his will for Fat Albert.

"Oh, I forgot about that. I need to remember to ask my brother what it says. Anyway, Albert is about fifty years old now. Dad brought him back in a sock from Florida before we kids were born. Did you know that alligators can live to sixty-five to seventy years years old? Albert, here, is one bite shy of fifteen feet and likely weighs 400 pounds, but no one wants to try to pick him up and put him on a scale to find out.

"Think I should try to sell him with the house? Kinda a novelty, don't you think? Maybe get a little extra money. Just kidding.

"Fat Albert uses that pond over there for soaking and catching the fish we stock from time to time with the free koi we find in the classifieds. We got migratory birds through here in years past, but not so many now. Not sure if Fat Albert contributed to that decline, or all the new development around here scared them away. I'm just kidding—about selling him with the house, that is. My dad loved him; I'll find him a good home.

"See where that towing yard is, over there? Used to be the County Pound. Dad would go over there Thursday nights to shop for Albert after they put that weeks' worth of stray puppies and kittens to sleep and stacked the cans to overflowing outside for the garbage pickup on Friday. He'd only bring home the smaller ones, at first, and put the extras in the freezer so Fat Albert didn't cost much to feed. After the Pound burned down, we had to start raising his food—hence, the chickens. We just bought the injured or chick culls from the local Ranch and Feed Store at first, but then Fat Albert was eating so much, we had to go around and adopt kittens and dogs from the various area pounds. Pretty ingenious, huh?"

Yes, ingenious indeed, I thought. I couldn't say it out loud as I was still afraid I might gag. I couldn't believe that charismatic Krista, who would never even swear or say a bad word about anyone, was talking about dead puppies and kittens in a conversational way.

After much problem solving, a month later, Fat Albert went to Northern California. He was transported in an enclosed horse trailer driven by Krista's brother, who used part of Fat Albert's $22k inheritance to build a new pond and a dugout cave under his back yard for Albert's hibernations during winter. I suspected that Albert wouldn't live much longer, since alligators and cold weather are probably incompatible.

The teeny-weeny whitewashed adobe hacienda sold in the first week to developers who tore everything down, including those magnificent oak trees, to add a new section for triple-wides to the existing Dew Drop Inn Mobile Home Park.

Two winters later, Fat Albert died at age fifty-four—which, coincidently, was the same age that Krista's dad had died. It caused another funeral event for Krista; an event to which I was invited, since, like many of my Fakke & Co. associates, I was considered family.

However, since I'd heard that alligator tastes like chicken, when Krista served us all lunch after the funeral, I declined to eat any of the chicken fingers that were the main course.

TEN

SELLING REAL ESTATE BY BUS

One day, a monster motor home stopped in the street outside Fakke & Company and dropped off our newest agent. Lou Anna was a short, plump, frumpy, monochromatic beige woman who looked like she would be more comfortable in a faded, flowery, full-length apron with flour on her hands instead of a worn briefcase in them. Instead, she wore a black blazer over her cotton dress. Lou Anna had just moved down from L.A., where she had owned a catering business that had gone bankrupt after being sued for something (she never told us the details). She had no sphere of influence to help start her new career here, nor had she ever owned a home to have an inkling of the process involved; but Lou Anna was a mom, and that meant she did whatever she had to do for her two kids.

After joining Fakke & Co. in 1986, she picked Lolly and my brains about everything. I had been the top-selling agent at Fakke & Co. for four years running, so far. Miriam was usually second, and Lolly and Krista volleyed between third and fourth. Every time we sold a property, she grilled us for details about how we'd met the clients, how we determined what to show them, how did we price the listing, what kind of closing gift did we give, ad nauseum. She picked our brains for suggestions about how to find an area so she could get listings, and quickly selected an area that was about ten miles away, to be her official farm.

'Farming', in real estate terminology, means to find a sales territory and go there repeatedly, knocking on doors or sending mailings to 'dig up or cultivate' listings. There are also 'People Farms', where you maintain repeated contact with people you already know (think Brian Buffini), to 'harvest' repeat business. She had read in detail about several real estate trainers' formulas for success. They all advocated listings instead of buyers because listings guarantee you'll get paid when it sells. Buyers are time-consuming while they decide what, where, and when they want to buy. Thus educated, Lou Anna decided to knock on doors to get listings.

Within two weeks, Lou Anna had a small condo listing that she priced at $40,000. She grossly underpriced it, and it sold immediately, way above her listing price, with twenty offers to pick from. She still had to wait forty-five days for it to close escrow. Even though her commission would only be about $800, she now had something in her 'pipeline', and was encouraged to keep going. To keep her family afloat, one day Lou Anna came into the office with remnants of her L.A. catering business. She was selling stacks of chafing dishes, metal buffet trays, silverware, white cloth napkins, plates, etc., for almost nothing. But it was enough to feed her family until her escrow closed.

Every single day, for several months, Lou Anna had the same routine. Her small desk sat just outside the ring of desks for Lolly, Krista, Miriam, and me, so we saw a lot of her. Mornings, she was in the office by 7 a.m. to call expired listings. She left at 11 a.m. and came back around 6 p.m. Rinse. Repeat. Every day, the same regimented routine.

Except for the day she came back in the office about 6 p.m. looking dazed. Only Lolly and I were in at the time, and our raised eyebrows and worried looks finally prompted Lou Anna to say, "A man came to the door today, after I knocked several times. His door was open, and the TV was going, so I just figured if I knocked louder, he would hear me. I smiled and opened my mouth to say hello when I saw him coming to the door until I saw HE WAS WALKING TOWARD ME NAKED FROM THE WAIST DOWN, AND MASTURBATING. He very calmly said, 'I hate real estate agents', and then had his happy ending before I could even turn around. It was disgusting. I hate this business. Is this what you go through all the time? Please tell me it will get better. Please."

I told her my story about a wacky seller that I'd had, early in my career. He was the weirdest little guy, but his listing was almost

$400,000, so I figured I could put up with him for at least a little while. After he signed the listing paperwork, he casually mentioned, "Oh, by the way, I am obsessive-compulsive, and having people come through my house will make me crazy. So, just know that when you are here showing the house, there will be one bedroom with the door closed and a 'Don't Open' sign on it. Don't open it. I'll be in there, walking back and forth around the room, naked and masturbating as a way to calm myself while strangers look at my house. When you get to the bedrooms, please have them hurry so they are gone before I'm finished. Otherwise, I'll be moaning loudly. I have to do this to keep myself calm. OK?"

I explained to him that price determines how fast it sells, so we agreed to deliberately price it low, and it sold after the first showing. (I'd told the buyers' agent that one bedroom door would be closed because the seller was sick, but they could look in the closed room during the home inspection, if they bought the house.) So, yes, it gets better, I told her.

The next day, she got a second listing! Embarrassed from realizing how badly she'd underpriced the first one, she was overly aggressive on the new one. It didn't sell for three months, until she had lowered the price several times. We watched her face grow grey from fatigue and the bags under her eyes become sunken and blackish. We were worried, and Ginger finally asked her what her husband was doing for work.

Lou Anna said, "Tim hasn't found work yet because we don't have a car for him to go look."

Leave it to Ginger to be blunt and to the point. "No car? How is it that you are getting these listings?"

Turns out that Lou Anna used the bus in lieu of a car. She and her family were living in an RV park in that monster motorhome, and she was walking two miles into the office every day to learn about real estate. She read book after book about real estate, about selling, about marketing, and about paperwork. Thus armed and educated, every morning she made calls to expired listings between 8 a.m. and 11 a.m. Then she left the office to walk down the street to the bus stop to take two buses to the end of the line in Bay More and start knocking on doors. Her daily goal was to was knock on 100 doors. Sometimes she missed the 5 p.m. bus, and it was 7:30 p.m. before she got back to the office to start the two-mile walk back to the RV park.

We had already noticed, when Lou Anna had been at the Up desk one morning, that she needed new shoes, and now we knew why. (The Up desk sits right inside the front door of a real estate office, and agents who have been assigned a four-hour slot sit there to greet potential clients who come in. If they aren't working with an agent yet, the 'Up' agent gets the opportunity to work with them. Car dealerships work this same way.)

When Lou Anna sat at the Up desk, she had crossed her legs at the ankles so the holes on the bottom of each shoe were visible under the desk. The sizable holes appeared to be covered from inside with layers of cardboard. Ginger thought she wore the same size shoes, and casually announced the following day to a couple of us that she was getting rid of some of her size eight shoes she never wore, and did anyone want a couple of pairs? Lou Anna jumped at the offer without ever knowing that we knew.

Then came a Monday when Lou Anna came into the office with a childish flowered thin chiffon scarf wrapped around her neck a couple times and knotted on the side. After the second day of the same stupid scarf, Ginger bluntly said, 'Get rid of the scarf; it's cheap and doesn't look right." When Lou Anna undid the knot and opened it up for us to see, what we saw were huge, round, yellowing bruises on both sides of her neck. It looked like someone had tried to strangle her, and we collectively jumped to the conclusion that her husband had done it because she'd only had two sales so far. But that was not the case.

Lou Anna had found a man on the upper floor of a condo building in her farm area who seemed ready to sell his condo, but it had taken several visits to get him to invite her in to look at it. She said that on the first visit, he rudely just sat in his condo while she stood at the top of the stair landing and talked to him through the screen door, asking him some scripted questions about buying or selling. He finally said he was thinking about getting out of this "sh-t hole" of a condo because all the neighbors were spying on or plotting against him, and he was tired of it.

Totally encouraged, Lou Anna went back every single day, and every day the man ranted about moving away. Last weekend, after ten straight days of perseverance on her part, he had actually invited her into the condo to give him a valuation. She had seen a huge telescope pointed at a building across the parking lot and walked over to get a closer look. When she realized it was a rifle with an enormous spotting scope mounted on a tripod, she started backing away towards the front door. When the man realized she was afraid, he started screaming about being a sniper in Vietnam, that everyone was out to get him, and he guessed she was no different. He taunted that he was a trained killer—he could kill the people in the other building whenever he wanted to, and he could kill her, too.

As Lou Anna reached the safety of the front door without fainting or dying of a heart attack, he lunged for her and grabbed her by the throat. The attack knocked her backwards through the door, causing her to slide headfirst down the stairs on her back. That broke his hold on her neck, and although she was really banged up and bruised, she got away without breaking any bones. She had walked the fifteen miles from her farm back to the RV park without taking the bus, as she didn't want anyone to see her crying.

Lolly, Ginger and I looked at each other with raised eyebrows. Crying? CRYING? What was she thinking? He tried to kill her, and she was worried about people seeing her crying?

No, she hadn't called the police. He had her business card, and she didn't want him showing up at Fakke & Co. with that rifle. She had kids to think about.

When Lou Anna got to her desk the next morning, there were two lovely silk scarves waiting for her, courtesy of Ginger and Lolly, the Mistresses of Accessories. She never did call the police, and eventually stopped worrying about him as she got busier and busier with listings and sales.

ELEVEN

A LIFE-ALTERING KISS

My life unalterably changed late that last Friday in April when I *finally* got my first commission check forty-five days after I started at Fakke & Co. To this day, I'm not sure what made me do this, except that banks were ready to close for the weekend and The Universe had a plan for my new life. That plan was to begin with a chance encounter in that particular bank lobby. Inexplicably, this was to lead to the highest of the high points of my life (and the absolute depths of despair in it, also—but I wasn't to know that until years later).

A few minutes before the 5 p.m. closing time, I hurried into a different branch of my regular bank to deposit that much-needed escrow commission check—one that the escrow officer had rushed to pay to me so my mortgage payment wouldn't bounce. The other choice was to go on Monday to my own bank's drive-through window, as usual, but, in absolute faith, I had mailed my mortgage payment yesterday, and was nervous that it would clear on Monday before the bank posted my commission.

After completing my deposit, I turned to walk back towards the entrance door. A Robert Redford twin, complete with golden blonde, gently curly hair, brilliant blue eyes, and incredible Tony Lamas, came through it moments later. I couldn't say whether it was his height, his confident stride, or that I'm magnetized to men wearing VERY expensive cowboy boots, that caused me to stand, frozen, mid-lobby, with my mouth hanging open. A shock of electricity surged through me. I couldn't move or say anything. I just gaped. I'm not ashamed to admit that I could likely have been drooling, in another moment or two, over the ruggedly handsome cowboy walking towards me.

I had never laid eyes on him before, but somewhere on a cellular level, I recognized him as the love of my (soon to be single) life. I had read about love at first sight, but no one mentioned it felt like a sledgehammer ringing an internal gong. I guess The Universe was making sure that, at this moment, this chance meeting didn't go unnoticed by me. It needn't have worried.

Before I could even think, I viscerally responded to the overwhelming magnetism that drew me forward. I walked up to Cowboy Redford, threw my arms around his neck, and said, *"I love you— want to buy a house?"*

Ya, right. Never happened. Not even close.

What did happen is this: I watched the bank manager and both secretaries rise from their desks to effusively greet this stunning cowboy with movie star features, whom they obviously had been expecting. If anyone was looking, they would have seen a crazy woman talking to herself out loud, saying, *"I am coming back for you someday."* In a state of emotional shock, I left the building without even making eye contact with him.

Opportunities are so fleeting they are incredibly easy to miss in this life. That night, all night, and for many nights to come, I reran that scenario over and over in my head with various outcomes, all leading to me kicking myself for doing nothing. For not giving him my business card or asking for his. I despaired of ever finding him again, so I didn't concern myself with being careful about what it was I was asking from The Universe. I was asking It to bring this man into my life. I didn't ask It for 'the right man for me'—I asked for *this* particular man.

Ah, life. It's what happens to you when you are wishing and making plans and The Universe complies.

The following year, (excuse me, I'm trying too hard to sound casual. I know EXACTLY when it happened.) on July 4th, HE walked into my real estate office in San Marea. The agent at the up-desk had his feet on top of the desk and crossed at the ankles while reading a dime store sci-fi book. He quickly put down his paperback as the Cowboy walked in, but he didn't even have time to stand up because, when the Cowboy's eyes swept the office, they locked instantly with mine as I glanced up from some paperwork to see who had walked in. With a flip of his hand, he stayed the up-agent in his sitting position as he instead strode over to my desk.

The effect was the same as that April day in the bank. This time, I was able to stand and reach out to shake hands. But, in trying to introduce myself, my brain had short-circuited from the jolt of electricity generated by my contact with his hand, and my mouth quit working. This exchange didn't go unnoticed by the other agents, who were looking at each other with raised eyebrows as they bore witness to the tangible torrent of sparks flowing between us. Yes, it was Fourth of July, but the fireworks were early, and they were inside my office.

"Hi, I feel like I know you. Have we met before?"

And with those few words, Jamison Rivers walked into my life. Into my heart. Into my soul.

In the conference room, I learned that Jamison was from Texas and his friends called him J.R. Those were his initials, but he clarified he was not named for the infamous 'Dallas' TV character, J.R. Ewing. Those were his real initials. He was a venture capitalist in town for his monthly meeting with a business partner to work on their joint venture into residential solar systems. After inking a contract with his partner this past month, he could see that he would soon need to be here weekly. The solar business was taking off, and he was ready to purchase a west coast home.

As I listened, I had to keep reminding myself to breathe. His proximity affected me so profoundly that I was beginning to sound like a fish out of water, gasping for air every few minutes. Because I was afraid to ask, I skipped my normal vetting questions and didn't know he was married with a daughter until the second time we met. Mentally, I had decided on a pet name for our future intimacy and was already calling him Junior instead of J.R.

I did manage to write down a few things he said, like "up to $1 million, no pool, ocean view, within twenty minutes of the airport." At a time where the average sale in my office was just under \$300,000, the specter of a million-dollar sale was contributing to my breathlessness. Also, he was leaving in the morning, and would be back in a couple of weeks to give me time to find some houses to show him. He cautioned me that he would insist on a great deal, and not to waste his time by showing him homes that he couldn't 'steal'.

Whatever you say, Cowboy!

Two weeks later, I was nervously awaiting his arrival. When he had called to confirm his appointment, he mentioned in an 'oh-by-the-way' manner that his wife and daughter would not be moving with him, initially. Sh-t, my worst fears were confirmed. He was *married*. Still, I had waxed my legs and bikini line, shaved my armpits, and had my hair cut and styled. I was decked out in new underwear and a stunning new pale grey/green \$400 Nordstrom outfit with \$120 (a \$350 cost today) alligator leather shoes. I looked and felt like a million dollars—pun intended. (This was also the beginning of my life-long affinity to all things Nordstrom.) I was ready for anything, and everything, and wanted to be confident that I looked good.

He was *married*. I don't think I've ever to this day spent that much money on one outfit, but practicality was not part of this confidence equation. *Why did he have to be married?*

I could immediately tell that Jamison appreciated my efforts. His smile lit up the office as he took me all in. I had read in chick lit romance novels that "he devoured her with his eyes," but now I was living it.

And loving every minute of it. I knew he was married, but I couldn't help myself. I was a moth, circling his candle's flame.

Jamison was a man who was used to being in control, and he insisted on driving. He apologized for being late to meet me, and now he only had time to see two houses. I quickly shifted gears from the five I was going to show him. Both Lolly and Krista were there to see the new client I was so excited about, so I asked Lolly to call the other three to cancel my appointments.

All I remember is that neither of them could take their eyes off Jamison, so that I had to place the list of houses to cancel into Lolly's outstretched hand. I came to realize that he wasn't aware of his stunning good looks, nor their effect on women. He didn't use them, he didn't flaunt them, and he didn't flirt. He was what he was, and I was magnetized by him.

The first house was a sprawling six-bedroom Spanish home in The Ranch with a commanding view over the Diegueno River Valley that ran out to the ocean two miles away. It had Saltillo tile floors throughout, hand-troweled walls, and stained-glass clerestory windows under thick dark brown wood beams that spanned every room of the 6,000 square foot home. It had been on the market at $1.3 mil for almost a year, and I had heard that the owners were desperate to sell it.

Although I emphasized its best feature—the opportunity to perhaps buy it for $1.0 mil—Jamison said, quietly, "too much house, I need something smaller." Ever the gentleman, he was polite enough to take a quick walkthrough so as not to offend the listing agent, who likely had spent an hour opening it up, starting the fountains, drawing back the drapes, and turning on all the lights for this potential buyer.

My nerves and hormones were humming. I wanted to walk more slowly just to spend some extra time with him, but he was a man on a mission, and sped back towards the freeway and the ocean, where the next house was waiting.

The second and last house was, again, a typical San Marea coastal contemporary house (meaning a three-story, wood shingle-sided building with a flat roof) sitting on the bluff overlooking the Pacific Ocean. It was fairly priced at $950,000. This house's selling feature wasn't so much a steal of a price as its unparalleled ocean view. This was a location, location, location house. The shingles had greyed out, it was down a long private driveway, and the sunset was promising to be vivid tonight as they often are during Santa Ana winds. (Santa Anas are winds that blow in off the desert to the East. They shove the smog out to sea, where it refracts the sunlight spectacularly at the end of a clear day.) As a selling point, I explained that we might even see the elusive green flash that happens just a split second after the sun goes below the horizon.

As Jamison and I stood on the patio and absorbed the spectacular sunset colors, he turned to look at me. Didn't say anything, just looked. If there had been an orchestra present, the cymbals would have clashed at the moment our gazes met. His was longing; mine hungry.

The next moment, he wasn't there. I blinked, and he was back inside the house and halfway across the living room. I had to raise my voice to tell him to wait while I turned out the lights and locked up. The motor was running when I got to the car, and without a word, he drove me back to my office.

What did I do wrong—did I say something wrong? Was I wrong to meet his gaze with so much longing? Did I accidentally have something stuck in my front teeth? Did my breath offend him? These and other insecure thoughts raced through my mind in the few minutes it took to reach Fakke & Company.

In the darkness of the alley parking lot behind my office, I cleared my throat and inquired, *"Do you want to make an offer on the second house?"* It was answered with a quick "No." I turned to get out of the car, still confused as to what had gone wrong.

A hand touched my shoulder, and as I turned back to him, his other hand cradled the side of my face as he leaned over the console to kiss me.

Time ceased altogether. Even today, I can recall the smell of the leather interior of the car, the subtle fragrance of his musky cologne, and the trace of brandy and cigars on his breath.

As our lips met, the overpowering sensation of my heart plunging down an elevator shaft caught me by surprise. The kiss went on and on until inside my head I heard a soft wind rustling through ancient grasses. Jamison's kiss was the kiss my soul recognized, and it had waited many lifetimes for him to return. Waited for The Universe to finally realign Itself for us to meet again. It was a kiss that has lasted me this lifetime and probably future ones, too. *Why did he have to be married?*

He rested his chin on my forehead and quietly said, "I'll be back in two weeks, be thinking about what's next. And I'm not talking about houses."

TWELVE

SUNDOWNER I — WHY AGENTS DRINK

With experience, I found that working with real estate buyers and sellers is an uneven reveal, and it drives agents to drink. Most times, getting a transaction closed is akin to wizardry. While we see who our clients are, where they've been, and what the insides of their homes and their lives and their bank accounts look like, they almost never are able to pull back the curtain to see what the lives of us Agents of Oz look like.

Pandora's Lockbox is a chance to pull back that curtain.

After a few transactions, I saw that being a real estate agent and negotiating the minefield called a Sale is like leading a platoon of mismatched parts. Agents are expected to lead this ragtag group, consisting of buyers, sellers, a mortgage broker, an escrow officer, a termite company, and a physical inspector through a landscape dotted with bombs waiting to blow up a sale. It's one of those herding cats hilarious comedic scenarios that is only funny if it happens to another agent. It becomes NOT funny if the scenario is yours when one member of the platoon steps outside the path you've laid through the minefield to closing. BOOM—the mismatched parts fall all over each other, and the deal can blow up. Even up to the day of closing, unfortunately.

Being on commission isn't always what is appears to be, especially when it comes to the income valleys that even the highest producing agents have experienced. I heard of one unbelievable top-producing agent from Southern California who flew to New York to receive a national award for his pinnacle of production. It was a biggest of big deals!

The award ceremony, which was held in Javits Convention Center, never mentioned that he had twenty-seven agents on his team. His individual sales figures took credit for all their combined sales. Nor did it mention that, because he never kept track of his expenses, he would be declaring bankruptcy within the month, and all his team members would be left adrift to find another broker. Looks can be deceiving—especially in any sales job like real estate that requires you to 'fake it 'til you make it'.

Whoever invented the "Sundowner" for agents is my hero. Around San Marea, the business owner members of Rotary host "Sundowners" on a regular basis. Each new business, in turn, opens their doors after hours with poo-poos and booze (poo-poos being heavy hors d'oerves, and booze being booze). It was a great idea, and some of us agents took notice at the well-attended evening turnouts and adapted the idea into our business.

Keep in mind that since 49% of all licensed real estate agents nationally close less than one sale per year, they are always hungry. When the list of weekly Broker Caravans (where agents hold mid-week three hour Open Houses for other agents) is held on Wednesday, there may be sixty or seventy homes spread out over eight zip codes. Even on a good day, with homes clustered together, an agent can only see twenty at most.

The best way to make sure as many other agents as possible came to *your* Broker Caravan was to serve food and wine. Which was also a way to have agents linger and share industry gossip, or gossip about other agents. The serving of alcoholic beverages finally was banned after a couple of accidents resulting in DWI (aka Driving While Intoxicated or Duwie) convictions and one vehicular death. Not only was a Duwie conviction expensive, but if you got your driver's license suspended, that agent (as in Trixie) then had to employ a driver for six months or a year and sit in the back seat with their client. Luckily, none of us Fab Five ever came to know just how expensive that tally was, although we certainly drank our share of alcohol.

Agents started getting reputations for their food, so after too many of the seventy new ones on Caravan offered 'refreshments', it came down to who had the best food. Granny always locked the office door during Caravan hours on Wednesday, so we agents HAD to go on Caravan as we couldn't work at our desks.

Four other agents and I held the title for 'the best' refreshments. Sarah made baked BBQ chicken wings that were to die for. She was stingy with her recipe, so we had to see her houses to eat some.

Anora was of Middle Eastern heritage and made a jasmine rice and lima bean salad with mint leaves and chicken cubes that was otherworldly. She made so much, she always had lots of leftovers to bring to the following Sundowner potluck.

Carmen usually had a whole smorgasbord of Mexican items—two different entrees with a choice of toppings, a cabbage salad, and the inevitable salsa fresca, guacamole, and chips.

Lolly was famous for her Death by Chocolate fountain. She had baseline choices of chocolate mousse, chocolate ice cream, brownies, or angel food cake and a three-tier cascading fountain dripping liquid chocolate instead of water. After drowning your base in melted chocolate, you then added sprinkles, slivered almonds, shredded coconut, perhaps a mandarin orange, chocolate chips, and topped it off with canned Reddi-Whip real whipped cream. There was never anything left over from Lolly's caravans.

As for me, as the caravan competition got more and more fierce for agent attendance, I resorted to having a 'Sundowner Open House' that started at four pm, just as the others were closing up. Since I rarely had more than two new listings in any one month, and only a few were able to handle the amount of people and required parking, it was not an overly expensive endeavor. The gossip that was exchanged made it a highly anticipated Wednesday night entertainment.

I gained infamy and higher attendance by offering wine. It was outside the board-sponsored tour hours, so I got all the hungry agents who missed Caravan along with those who ate at other Caravan Open Houses but wanted/needed a drink. I also smartly snagged all the other agents who had their own listings open on Caravan and hadn't eaten yet.

The piece-de-resistance was my world-famous mashed potato martinis, served in stemmed margarita glasses. (Although I stole the idea from one of Lolly's parties, I was the one who served them regularly on Caravan.) It was laid out on a buffet table with white, yellow, and purple mashed potatoes (that turned lavender when the milk was added). The table was further laden with a variety of regular and unusual toppings. These choices included, but were not limited to, regular brown or white gravy; bacon pieces or sausage; grated cheese or melted cheese sauce; chives; black olives; sour cream; and chopped green or jalapeño peppers.

I always threw in one surprise—like blue cheese, capers, caviar, or even orange flying fish roe. One St Patrick's Day Caravan, I threw some blue food coloring in the yellow potatoes, and they turned a ghastly green. I tried that one time only—I strive to make the same mistake just once!

One of the side benefits of these Sundowner Open Houses (I sometimes varied that by calling them" Sunset Soirees") was that, after a long week of crazy buyers and sellers, it was an opportunity to let our hair down with each other and get some sympathy.

Friday afternoons at 5 p.m. were our own private Fakke & Co. Sundowners, consisting primarily of the Fab Five and a miscellaneous agent or two who had no pressing weekend plans. These were potlucks where we brought any leftover wine and food from Wednesday's Caravan into the office (just to make sure it didn't go to waste, or, for me, to make sure I didn't drink it all myself) and settled in for an hour or two of real estate stories after the front desk closed for the weekend.

One memorable Friday, as we snacked away on Caravan leftovers, the stories started with Krista saying, "I've been sworn to secrecy, BUT you're going to die hearing this one." Thus, she embarked on how the past Friday, Granny and his secretary Gretchen had been 'eaten' by a house he was spec building. (Spec was shorthand, meaning he built it on *spec*ulation that he could sell it to a buyer when it was finished.) 'Eaten' was her description, not mine. So, we poured ourselves another glass of wine and leaned in for the story, ready to enjoy the worst at our broker's expense.

Granny was so notoriously cheap that he never had enough food for office parties, so everyone went home hungry. He had such tiny supplies of copy paper that we all carried our own in our car, so at least WE would have enough to make copies. Don't even get me started about toilet paper. Office legend was that he even skimped on food for his cat so it would catch its own food, so the vision of him being 'eaten' by his own hungry spec house was karmically perfect.

All we knew was that one week ago, Granny went missing after having a problem closing the escrow on one of his spec houses, so we were eager to hear why.

The story had begun during Ginger's noon-6 p.m. floor time. Ginger had observed Granny leaving during lunchtime last Friday with his retired Army Colonel (nee secretary) Gretchen, and they had not come back for the rest of the day. Granny was about 5'8" with stringy, thinning hair that grew down the back of his neck to disappear under his collar, and a paunch. Gretchen was a 6'1" Amazon warrioress and an uptight, no-nonsense piece of work. She was a real retired military colonel who never married, had closely cropped hair, buff arm muscles, and wore sturdy, sensible shoes. We all assumed she was a lesbian, so the specter of an 'afternoon delight' wasn't part of the equation for their absence together.

Ginger said that Granny had Friday appointments waiting and waiting in the office, and he had even missed an appointment with his attorney. "I'm sure the attorney didn't care," she said. "He just left the fare meter running in its twelve-minute increments for the entire hour that Granny missed." Phone messages were piling up, the end of the month paychecks needed signatures, and he had just disappeared. Not that anyone cared, except the people needing their money.

According to what Ginger had pieced together, Granny's buyers had done their final walk-through on his spec house at 7 a.m. before they went to work. The escrow was supposed to record once they signed off on that final inspection, but the picky buyers had been totally unhappy to discover that the utilities had been turned off. There were some repairs that they couldn't test, and it appeared that a large amount of building materials was still in the garage. Everything had to be removed *prior to close,* according to their sales contract. Because there was no electricity for the garage door opener to work, and there were no windows in the garage or the hallway approach, it had been too dark to see anything. This was a final item they were unwilling to cross off the walk-through. These buyers weren't closing unless Granny got everything taken care of by 1 p.m., or the recording would be next week.

As always, Krista continued, Granny was cutting it close. He needed that closing to pay off the overdue construction loan at the bank and the end-of-the-month funding of office paychecks and sub-contractors' invoices. Under that pressure, Granny had stormed off with Gretchen in tow. He had a 1 p.m. meeting downtown with his attorney, and she would come back to the office to let the buyer's agent and escrow know it was okay to close.

But neither Gretchen nor Granny came back, and the list of unhappy people waiting for money grew by the hour. At 6 p.m., they still weren't back, so salaried staff and creditors had to leave without their checks when the office closed for the evening. A couple of people in the office wanted to call the police and report them missing, but ultimately, no one wanted to be involved in case Granny did show up. His volcanic temper was legendary, and the overall assumption was that Granny probably didn't have enough money to make payroll or pay his bills this month. True to expectations, and without any explanation, Granny was indeed back in his office on Monday morning.

Krista's source of details were her past clients, owners of the newly built house across the street from Granny's spec house. The other houses on the block hadn't been sold yet, and her clients were the only inhabitants of the cul-de-sac street. They came home from work about 7 p.m. and heard some faint yelling and some banging. Knowing that it couldn't be from another neighbor's TV, their curiosity got the best of them, and they walked across the street. The house was vacant, and they almost turned around, but something about the raspy, pitiful cries coming from the garage sounded frantic.

Granny and Gretchen were both hoarse from screaming since noon. Because the electricity was turned off, when they went into the garage from the house, the self-closing door closed behind them and instantly locked while they were groping for the light switch. They were in total darkness. Even moving a little, they were stumbling over trash, paint cans, boards, and were afraid to step on a nail or a screw, so they sat down in place.

All the exterior doors in the house were industrial strength Baldwins that automatically locked each time the door closed, so it was easy to lock yourself out. Krista's clients couldn't get in the front or back door because of those same locks. Granny had saved $170 by not installing either a window or a side exit door in the garage itself, so Krista's clients had to call Lee's Lock and Safe. Being that it was Friday, the locksmith took a couple hours wading through weekend traffic to arrive. Meanwhile her clients relaxed on their front porch in total amusement, with a bottle of wine and a snack of cheese and crackers, to enjoy the drama unfolding across the street. Her clients said when the door was finally opened, it was apparent from the smell that someone had peed in there recently.

Granny offered a bribe to Krista's clients to never, ever tell anyone what had transpired, but the husband was a fireman and subscribed to that old adage about spreading a good story: Telephone, Telegraph, Tellafireman. We were breathless from laughing and were finally starting to unwind.

In the true evolution of events of the week, the other agents still at the office volunteered their stories in an effort of 'one-upsmanship' over Krista's tale.

On Tuesday, Miriam had had to call the fire department out to her expensive mansion listing in The Ranch. Somehow, the toddler of the potential buyers became fascinated with a black toilet in the all-black powder bathroom. She wandered in and closed the door like her mommy had taught her. The door had an industrial-strength Schlage lock which promptly locked behind her, trapping her inside. The fire department had taken forty-five minutes to arrive, during which the toddler, who was not tall enough to reach either the light switch or the doorknob, wailed inside her jet-black prison while her mother wailed outside. No sale here either, and Miriam still had a headache from all the screaming.

Lolly had experienced a crazy week also, involving the fire department, so she paired her story with Miriam's. Her coastal contemporary, all-wood, three-story career listing by the beach was not selling because it had so much termite damage. Buyers just could not see past all the dollar signs they would need to correct the dry rot and piles of black, sand-like termite droppings. (A career listing means it's been on the market waaay too long. My record career listing is thirty-one years, but after six failed escrows, I finally got it closed—two months before the seller died of old age!)

Lou Anna had brought an extremely obese client to see it, and her buyer broke through the rotted wood deck when she walked out on it to look for an ocean view. Her leg was stuck through the hole over her knee, and she was too heavy for the both of them to lift. Lolly said she was privately afraid the rest of the deck might collapse from their combined weight if they tried to pull her out.

So, for an hour, the three of them just nonchalantly chatted away while waiting for help. "Inwardly," Lolly confided, "I was crossing my fingers that she wouldn't sue my seller and me, so I was trying to look sympathetic while trying not to laugh at the absurdity of the situation." (When people sue in a real estate environment, they sue everyone. Attorneys hope that the broker carries Error and Omissions Insurance [aka E&O] so there's money for a settlement.)

Ginger had drunk at least one of my bottles of wine by herself to drown out her recent real estate experience, and she went next. Her story made us all want another drink, as it was an all-too-common story for agents.

Ginger had been at her dentist all of Monday morning, getting a root canal complete with eight shots of Novocain. She had to go straight from the dentist's chair to the office, hoping to get a message from the Robinsons before they left town. She had been working with Don and Margie Robinson for almost four months, and they had enjoyed many dinners and lunches out while looking for a home. (Need I mention that many of them were at Ginger's expense?)

Don Robinson had gotten a promotion and they were relocating to San Marea as soon as they could find a home. Ginger knew the pressure was on to find them a house, so every weekend when they came, she put all her other clients on hold and spent three full days with them in her car. Additionally, most of the ensuing week, she spent hours searching far and wide for something to show them on the next trip.

Ginger had FINALLY found them a house the previous day, on Sunday, the last day of this most recent house-hunting trip. They signed a full price offer shortly after seeing it, but they wanted to sleep on it before authorizing her to present it. The house was a rare one-story right on the Diegueno Golf Course. It would have attracted multiple offers when it came out in the MLS Blue Book later that week, but Ginger's networking skills got them in early. The Robinsons seemed really pleased when they woke up that morning and left several messages for Ginger to go ahead and present their offer before they left for the airport.

Ginger arrived at Fakke & Co. still loaded with Novocain. She got their messages, then worked on it all afternoon, trying hard not to sound drunk. She pushed and pushed the listing agent and the sellers to sign it before her clients flew off. They finally signed it, much to Ginger's excitement. An hour before their scheduled departure, as her Novocain was finally wearing off, the Robinsons called her. Before she could give them the good news of the seller's acceptance, they excitedly said they wanted to give her THEIR good news first.

On the way to the airport, since they had an extra few hours, Don and Margie had driven over the bridge to Coronado to investigate that area. They found an Open House on a new listing and although it was on a busy street, they immediately signed a full-price offer with the agent/owner (who was there to give them a deal, they said, since she didn't have to pay another agent).

Ginger sarcastically parroted the conversation. "Ginger, please don't bother about the house in San Marea; we bought a better one on our way to the airport. Thanks for all your hard work, and we hope you're as excited for us as we are about our new house."

She ad-libbed: "Have a nice life, with no commissions to show for all your months of hard work for us!"

We were all collectively sad, but also breathed a sigh of relief that Ginger's sad story wasn't our story. This time. Even though the Robinsons legally had accepted offers on two different homes, since they hadn't left a deposit check to open escrow and the golf course house wasn't really on the market yet, those sellers didn't force the issue.

My weekly contribution almost bought the house down (I love real estate puns!). Dottie, an agent in our office, went on a ten-day cruise with her husband and asked me to cover for her in case her sole buyer clients wanted to make an offer on the house she had just shown them. She had them sign the offer but left it in her desk drawer while they slept on it before telling her to present it.

I hadn't seen the house or met the buyers, but it was no problem—it was just part of agents helping agents get a little time off. Of course, the day she left, Dottie's buyers called with instructions to go ahead and submit their offer. I was crazy busy with my own clients, but loved to negotiate, so I just made room in my schedule to assist them.

I called the seller's agent to schedule meeting at the seller's house with the offer at 7 p.m. that night. She was thrilled, but I gave her no details about the offer. It was customary to reveal it to them all at 7 p.m. tonight with my fabulous "Nico Special" presentation, designed to end with "three copies; press hard" as they signed it without a counter. I could be done by 8 p.m.

I arrived about ten minutes before 7 p.m. and walked up the driveway that was shared by two houses, built side by side on a steep incline. The porch light was shining on the left side home, so I knocked on the door, and after saying I was here for the appointment, I was invited in. Since their agent hadn't arrived yet, I sat in the living room making small talk about the neighborhood, kids, and grandkids with the older couple while we waited.

The wife offered me some coffee, so I accepted, thinking I was bonding with them, which would be helpful because Dottie's clients' offer was low. We moved into the kitchen, where we sat with our coffee cups and a piece of coffee cake fresh out of the oven. At 7:30 p.m. when I took my last bite of cake, I asked them if their agent had called to say she would be late.

They exchanged puzzled looks. "What agent?" was their response. I said I wanted to present an offer on their house, but their agent needed to be present. It was obvious there was a lack of communication in that household that led each of them to think the other spouse had made an appointment of some kind without telling the other. Their passivity didn't even allow them to ask me why I was there. It turned out that *their* house wasn't for sale; it was the one on the *right* side of the shared driveway.

I don't need to even finish the rest of the story, as you can guess the outcome of the thirty-minutes-late, wrong house, low offer scenario. Sorry, Dottie, I tried.

But, leave it to Lolly to be able to top all of our great stories that evening. Did we remember that really cute tiny 1940s bungalow in La Jolla? The darling one on the postage-sized lot with the peek of ocean view? Surely, we remembered it—it was white stucco with a red tile roof and black window shutters, surrounded in front by a white picket fence with that intertwined vine plant that attracts butterflies? The one with shiny hardwood floors, arched doorways, and a long hallway down to the bedrooms?

Well, confided Lolly, she had heard that the agent who sold it to a sexy young contractor buyer had taken him back through it to celebrate that the seller had picked his offer over the offers from five other buyers who had also been desperate for it. The hot contractor was wanting to take a second look to decide whether to just remodel it or tear it down, but instead, he tore off his agent's clothes and sealed the deal by having a *wham bam, thank you ma'am* up against the wall in the narrow hallway.

As we screamed with delight, and some envy, we begged Lolly to tell us who it was. Who in the world would have confided such a tale to Lolly, and how did she know that it was true?

"It's true, all right," said a blushing Lolly, with tears of laughter streaking her perfect makeup. "I believe I was there at the time."

THIRTEEN

MOMMY, LOOK — THERE'S A NAKED MAN

It's hard to imagine how difficult it is to be a real estate agent until you've tried it. Had I known this before I was hired by Granny, I likely would never have even tried.

Agents who are ultimately successful will do most ANYTHING to become (and to stay) successful, and that included me. I showed homes at 7 a.m. before the buyers went to work, or at 7 p.m. after they got off work. I walked from house to house with blisters on my toes while still smiling and making positive comments about the green shag carpet or purple and red flocked wallpaper (which is affectionately also known to us agents as the purple and red f..ked wallpaper. Buyers rarely make an offer on a house full of wallpaper. I wasted a lot of time showing houses with wallpaper before I understood that).

I've always smiled to myself when I hear new agents say that they got their real estate license because they love working with people. I know that means they don't have any clients and have not closed a sale yet. Buying or selling a home is one of the top three stressors in life, so unless you can sell and close a home quickly while the clients still like you (probably 20% are unhappy with their agents by the time the closing happens), no successful agent will ever say they stay in real estate because they love working with people.

A more real response is that they are workaholics, love looking at homes, they're good at problem-solving, and they love the income. If you've managed to stay in real estate at least three years, the income stream stabilizes and can actually support you.

During those first three years, and every year thereafter, in order to meet licensing renewal requirements, agents take classes ad-nauseum. While I took my eight or nine per year, there never was a class on "How to Deal with a Naked Man While Showing a House." I would love to take it, as it has happened to me several times, and I still never know the proper etiquette.

My first encounter with a naked man in a house was about to occur late on a Thursday. This house was someone's second home. That usually means that during the week it was vacant, but fully stocked and furnished for the weekends. My buyers were a young couple in their late thirties with their eight-year-old daughter, who was fussing through the last two houses as she wanted to go to McDonalds and get a Happy Meal. NOW!

Believe me, we ALL needed a Happy Meal at this point, but it was the last house, and the most promising. It was another coastal contemporary house, being square and flat-roofed, with a wood shingle exterior—very typical for the San Marea beach area. According to the MLS, this house was a weekend home for some wealthy L.A. owners. It was a compact 1,600 square feet plus a one car garage. The small living and dining room combination opened to the kitchen a few steps away and represented approximately 800 square feet of it, so the three bedrooms upstairs commanded the remaining 800 square feet. Very compact, indeed. It was well located, just a block from the ocean; and because it was summer, it was still light enough to show it at 7 p.m.

The listing agent had said the house was vacant, so, without knocking, I just opened the lockbox for a key without ringing the doorbell. As my buyers and I stepped through the front door unannounced directly into the living room, my first puzzling thought was, *"Why is the TV on?"*

A slight movement caught my eye over by the wrought iron and wood coffee table where a jockey-sized, very tan, wizened man with silver hair was sitting on the floor eating his dinner out of a can with one hand, holding an open can of beer in the other. The coffee table covered everything except for his bare tanned chest that sported some sparse wiry silver hair, and a red bandana stylishly tied surfer-style around his scrawny neck. He kinda giggled. Not very manly, I thought, but I apologized profusely for walking in on his dinner, said I didn't realize anyone was home, and did he mind if I showed the house since we were already in? He just kept bobbing his head and giggling some more.

The four of us walked through the living room into the kitchen, where I could hear the dryer running in the laundry closet between the kitchen and back door. As my ears took in the thumping sound of shoes being dried, my eyes took in the broken glass on the floor by the back door window where someone had broken a hole so they could reach in and unlock the deadbolt from inside.

Crap! Crap! Crap! (I couldn't say 'sh.t', even to myself, with an eight-year-old present.) My mind raced as I frantically processed whether this was a simple break-and-enter burglary or an armed robbery about to take place featuring me, my clients, and their eight-year-old hungry, whining kid. Should I go out the back door with them now, or turn back to the living room to confront the little man?

That decision was made for me when the daughter squealed, "Mommy, look, there's a naked man!" What followed was a scene from a Laurel and Hardy movie. Or, perhaps the Three Stooges minus two of them.

The wizened little jockey-man had jumped up when our backs were turned as we walked into the kitchen, and started his escape towards the still-open front door. After hearing the eight-year-old scream, he evidently realized that someone had seen that The Emperor Had No Clothes, so he pivoted to run upstairs, but then seemed to realize that if he went upstairs, he would be trapped. At this point, he turned yet again to dive back under the coffee table to give himself some modesty.

I recalled all of this later, because when I had turned around, all I could see was his skinny little wizened weenie, kind of a wrinkled mini-me representation of his overall body. It was bobbing and weaving out a fluff of wiry silver pubic hair in concert with his movements as he darted here and there, trying to decide in mid-stride which way to go. He could have been a ballet dancer or a wide receiver with all the turns and jumps he made every couple of steps.

Forever after, every time I read a news article about people who had been robbed at gunpoint saying they couldn't identify the robber, as all they could see was the end of the gun pointed at them, I would nod sympathetically.

How did we get out of that situation? I was still in shock at seeing a naked man in front of my clients, and I absolutely can't remember. I'm sure we didn't go back through the front door, as the jockey-man was jumping back and forth between us and it. I know we didn't go upstairs, as there was no exit. I don't remember any of us bleeding after walking across the broken glass at the back door point of entry, but perhaps we jumped so far backward from the crazy living room scene that we cleared it and exited via the back door without getting cut.

I do know that by the time I got us all back to my office and called the police and the listing agent, all they found was a beach house with two open doors, a warm but empty dryer, all the downstairs lights on, and a partially eaten can of chili on the coffee table. For all of his haste, the little wizened man still remembered to take the beer with him.

FOURTEEN

AN AFFAIR TO REMEMBER IN D.C.

After all my teachable moments in front of a class of new agents, I am often quoted as saying *"Sell a client a house BEFORE you sleep with them. That way, if it doesn't work out, you won't lose both a buyer AND a commission."* I don't know of anyone who has ever listened to me on this issue, including myself.

I didn't have to wait two weeks for Jamison's return. Ten days after I showed him the two houses, he called me at the office. The receptionist announced his call. "Hey, Nico, your client with the cool Texas accent is on the phone for you. He's called a couple of times today, but never wants to leave a message."

"Hey Nico, been thinking about you."

"Me too." I tried to sound casual, but only I knew how obsessively I had been thinking about *him*. Thinking about answering his parting question in the car; thinking about what I wanted to do when he came back. Obsessing about ripping away my pride as I ripped off my clothes. 'Me too' was quite the understatement.

"I thought I might get back to look at more houses again later this month, but my plans have changed."

My heart sank and, unexpectedly, tears of disappointment welled up. Lolly was sitting next to me at her desk and startled at my tears. She raised her eyebrow questioningly, and I shook my head in response.

"I have to go to Washington D.C. for a business meeting instead, so I probably can't come back for several months now."

"Of course, I understand. I'm disappointed, though. I had a couple of good houses to show you, but they'll be gone by that time." I continued through a solitary tear finding its way to my chin. *"I was looking forward to showing them to you."* (This is what

my mouth said while my heart screamed: I was looking forward to showing MYSELF to you.)

There was a pause in the conversation while volumes of dialogue were being wordlessly exchanged across the phone wires.

I tried again. *"Washington D.C., huh. I've never been there, but always wanted to see the cherry trees in bloom. Are they still blooming in August?"*

"Well, I think you should check that out for yourself sometime. How about on August 21st? If I send you a plane ticket, will you come to D.C.? I'll get you a separate room in my hotel, so don't worry about your reputation."

My mouth dropped open and I think I must have quit breathing by the look on Lolly's face as she stood up to come check on me.

I stuttered, *"I, ah . . . I'm ah . . . I would really love that, Jamison. My birthday is in September, so that could be an early birthday present. Thank you, that would be really cool. Actually, I'm really excited."*

Hearing me say Jamison's name brought a look of understanding to Lolly's face, and she sat back down.

"I need to go; my clients just walked in, but I'm so glad I was in the office when you called. I'm really, really looking forward to Aug 21st. See you then. Take care."

The following week, after packing, repacking, and repacking yet again all my new underwear, new nightie, and three new outfits, I arrived on the East Coast. Jamison said he enjoyed flying into Washington National airport on Fridays because it was less congested when people were flying out for the weekends, and easier to get a rental car if your flight was late. I was flying so high at the prospect of spending a weekend with Jamison, I wouldn't have even needed an airplane, except for my suitcase.

At the end of the concourse by Baggage Claim was a sea of liveried men holding name signs. One was holding a sign that said 'Griffin'. I had never had a driver sent to pick me up at an airport before, but after a while, when everyone was gone and Jamison had not appeared, I took a chance to see if that might be a misspelled me. It was.

I was politely, but without fanfare, dropped off at an unremarkably conservative-looking two-story motel right off the Beltway. I could see the reflection of water a few blocks away, and a lot of trees without blossoms. While the room was clean and had four pillows on the queen-sized bed, I was a little confused, and a lot disappointed, by Jamison's absence. About three hours later, with my disappointment and outrage at being alone in an anonymous room in Washington D.C. running at peak velocity, the nightstand phone rang.

Jamison's captivating baritone hurriedly said, "Hey, Nico, welcome to Washington D.C. Sorry I couldn't meet you at the airport, but I see you made it to the motel. Hate to do this to you, but my meetings have spilled over to dinner, so I'll be tied up all evening. I left some money in an envelope for you at the front desk. Get yourself some dinner and I'll see you in the morning. I'm really looking forward to seeing you, but the Senators know I'm married, and I just can't bring you along with me tonight. I hope you understand. I promise I'll make it up to you. I'll leave your wake-up call for 7 a.m. so we can have breakfast before I go to my morning meeting. Thanks for coming—sorry, gotta run."

And, with that, he hung up. He was in such a hurry, I had said nothing.

As darkness finished its descent into my room—and into my mind—old feelings of being abandoned (that began in my childhood with my father's abandonment of my mother and I) started up again. Once more, I felt like I was waiting for a man who wasn't coming. To top off all these abysmal realizations, it occurred to me that instead of becoming the mistress of a handsome stranger in a romantic movie, it felt more like I was becoming the prostitute. In denial, I left the envelope at the front desk and paid for my own dinner!

No one thought to tell me that 7 a.m. in Washington D.C. was 4 a.m. at home, so when the wake-up call came, I was barely civil.

I pulled myself together in one of my new outfits and, with disappointed outrage still intact, I went to the motel restaurant to tell Jamison I was leaving today.

But as he rose from the table and folded me into his arms while chastely kissing my forehead and apologizing again profusely, all thoughts of leaving evaporated. The sight of his smiling face, the smell of his cologne, and the touch of his arms around me initiated the electricity between us again. Not even in the movies would an outraged woman walk out on Robert Redford. It was crazy and unthinkable. I don't remember anyone ever calling me crazy.

Just being next to Jamison at the table caused me to vibrate under his direct gaze. I think he was sizing me up to decide if he was crazy for sending some woman/real estate agent he really didn't know a ticket to fly across the country for a weekend. Or, maybe he was sorting out his own intentions or reservations. No matter, my skin hurt from the vibrating, my eyes were shining, and I could feel myself blushing like a teenager. I watched his pupils dilate as he looked at me. I've heard that, when Chinese shopkeepers see dilated pupils, the price of the desired object goes up; and I was watching my value go up right there over the breakfast table.

He cleared his throat (and probably his head, too). "Unfortunately, I have to meet my Senator at 9 a.m., but will positively be done before noon, as he's catching an afternoon flight back to Texas. I thought I'd pick you up at the motel and we'll have lunch in Alexandria. Bring a list of what you'd like to see. I'm thinking if we do the things on your list for the next twenty-four hours, then tomorrow at lunch, I'll lay out the things I'd like to see before we leave on Sunday night. Okay?"

Yes, Jamison, it was okay. Everything is okay now that we're here together. We had a nice breakfast, and he did a good job pretending he wasn't in a rush to make his 9 a.m. meeting. Then Fate stepped in to speed things along.

When we went by the front desk after breakfast, the clerk called Jamison over. It seems they were overbooked, and only his room was available for tonight—mine was taken. The clerk had called all around, but virtually all the local rooms in the city were reserved for a busy D.C. end-of-the-summer concert weekend. The clerk hesitated nervously before suggesting that since Jamison's room had two queen-sized beds, perhaps it be okay to move me there?

On the outside, I hoped I appeared nonchalant, but my insides were quaking. I felt like I might throw up my breakfast. *"Sure,"* I said. *"These things happen; no problem for me."* I could have hugged that desk clerk.

Seemingly innocent twists of fate can change the trajectory of the rest of your life, and I was totally aware we might be making such a change at the very moment it occurred. It was like walking down a street and suddenly going around the corner in a different direction entirely. This new trajectory was preordained from the instant that I had seen Jamison in the bank months earlier, and had been nudged along when he walked into my real estate office. Fate was still at my side, looking like She wasn't done, yet.

To fill in the hours while I waited for Jamison's return, I went over and over potential erotic scenarios in my mind while I watched an old western movie on TV in my room before packing up to move to the new room. I had never been affected by someone's presence like I was when Jamison was around.

That afternoon, we rode a paddlewheel riverboat to George Washington's plantation, but I hardly remember anything else. I was so distracted by the prospect of sleeping in the same room with Jamison. All night, even. And with Saturday night and Sunday ahead of us . . . my mind burned out its clutch, shifting through all the imagined good, bad, and possibly ugly outcomes.

Jamison spared no expense to take me to one of the highest-reviewed steakhouses in the city. He had removed tie and unbuttoned the top three buttons of his shirt after his morning of meetings. His casual demeanor only added to his attraction. We had a nice, relaxing, three-hour dinner of prime rib, baked potato, and salad. After sharing a great bottle of red wine, followed by dessert (consisting of a snifter of his favorite Hennessey XO brandy for Jamison and a piece of chocolate lava cake for me), we went back to 'our' room. In the course of getting to know each other, Jamison and I had talked so much since noon about so many different things that I was hoarse. The 11 o'clock news came on, and I went to take a shower, brush my teeth, apply my Obsession cologne, and put on my new red one-piece stretchy lace teddy with a snap crotch in hopeful preparation of erotic things to come.

When I came out of the bathroom, all clean and sexy, the news was over and so were my aspirations of a romantic interlude. Fate had gone to sleep—and so had Jamison. He was snoring lightly, having put on his pajamas, and crawled under the covers in his bed. I turned off the TV, moved some chairs around, and dropped my suitcase on the floor, but to no avail. Jamison was out like a light, so I turned off the light on the nightstand between our beds, and that was that.

Saturday morning started with Jamison slipping out of bed at 6 a.m. (3 a.m. California time) to take a shower and shave while I pretended to be asleep. I wasn't sure what to do. I was too insecure to just open the door and jump in the shower with him. I had never made love to anyone but my now ex-husband and wasn't confident enough to take the first step. I was at the same time both shy yet determined to make this happen with Jamison.

While I was lying there making up my mind, Jamison tiptoed out of the bathroom. When he saw I was awake, he said, "I'm done with the bathroom. I'll meet you downstairs for breakfast. Take your time, I'll just have coffee and read the paper while I wait."

I joined Jamison in the dining room thirty minutes later and had only two more things on my list for this morning. I wanted to visit the Lincoln Memorial and the Jefferson Memorial. Then, after lunch, we'd start on his list until tomorrow night.

At the Lincoln Memorial, he pulled a penny out of his pocket to show me a speck in the middle of the back side. It was Lincoln, sitting inside his Memorial. Amazing.

At the Jefferson Memorial, I told him I was surprised to see that it looked like the Parthenon in Rome, a place I had visited on my one and only trip overseas. I hoped I sounded worldly to him. I will always associate Jamison with August, Washington D.C., and those two memorials. It helps anchor the memory of the time I spent with him.

But the best that Fate had in store for us was yet to come. Because Jamison had initially thought he would only be in D.C. one night for his meetings, he was only able to extend his room for the one extra night. The motel was full, and so was every other one because of a big outdoor concert that Saturday night. So, Jamison changed his list and we left D.C. to drive to historic Gettysburg, a place he had always wanted to see.

It was ninety-five degrees and ninety-five percent humidity in Washington D.C. and the air conditioning in our rental car was working intermittently, so getting out in the country promised a more pleasant afternoon and evening. Although the ninety-mile trip should have been an hour and a half journey, we didn't leave until 3 p.m., and the traffic would give Los Angeles freeways some competition as the worst ever. We arrived in Gettysburg after 9 p.m. Nothing was open, there was no place to eat or buy any food. By 10 p.m., we were still looking for a motel. Gettysburg was more hot and more humid than D.C., and our rental car air conditioning had totally stopped about 5 p.m. I was murderous. At a tiny run-down motel, the clerk took pity on Jamison and called all the other remaining hotels and motels in the surrounding area, without success.

Jamison came back to the car to tell me the bleak news—there were no remaining motel rooms within forty miles. However, this little motel had offered him a small room with one bed, or we could go back to D.C.—what did I want to do? I got out of the car with my suitcase, saying, *"No, you do what you want to do. Sleep in the lobby, sleep on the ground, or sleep in the car for all I care. I'm taking this room."*

It's funny now, in retrospect, but it was not funny then. My romantic movie was rapidly turning into First Date Hell. We opened the door into a stifling storage closet—not a room, and definitely not even a small room. There were odds and ends of damaged nightstands, rickety chests of drawers, stacked plastic outdoor chairs, several dusty TV sets, cleaning pails, mops, and brooms surrounding a tiny, twin bed sporting a torn chenille bedspread and one pillow. I had to step from the door onto the bed to get over to the bathroom.

I desperately had to pee, but noticed, too late, that the bathroom had no door. After closing my eyes to pretend to be invisible and trying to pee quietly into a toilet with hardly any water in it, I flushed it, only to smell a horrible smell. It wasn't me, thank God—it was coming from the shower. This tiny bathroom's shower had no shower curtain and no grate over the drain. It was quickly apparent that when I had flushed the toilet, the sewer backed up into the shower pan through the drain.

Jamison was still standing respectfully outside, looking in the open front door. He had put my suitcase on the bed. In my most exhausted, crabby voice, I again announced, *"I'm going to bed; do whatever you want."*

In a series of fluid movements, I stepped back onto the bed, and back into the bathroom. I changed into my nightgown and got under the stained bedspread on the narrow bed. Jamison had disappeared from the door and, moments after I heard the rental car door slam, he reappeared in his pajamas and stepped onto the bed.

I can hardly picture that long, long night without cringing—Jamison at 6'3", me at 5'10" lying back-to-back in a twin bed, trying not to touch in the sticky heat. There was only one small pillow, which I selfishly claimed. The smell from the bathroom was so horrible, we had to leave the door to the room wide open in order to breathe. I wasn't worried about anyone coming to murder or to rob us—there was no space for anyone else to get into that room.

When I would turn to sleep on my back, half of me was hanging over the side of the bed. The one time that both Jamison and I tried to sleep on our backs at the same time, I fell out of bed.

In the early dawn, Jamison stepped over me to use the bathroom. I loudly whispered, *"Don't flush,"* but he didn't hear me. The sewer smell charged out of the drain and across the bed, trying to escape out the still-open door. I opened my eyes and, incredulously, I could hardly see the door from three feet away. The door was open, but the dense fog from all the heat and humidity was coming into the room and onto the bed towards me—maybe being drawn inside by the suction of flushing the toilet? It could have been a great scene from a horror movie. I started to chuckle. Even though I had been fantasizing for weeks for an opportunity to get intimate with Jamison, the specter of imagining making love in such surroundings was the trigger that made me start laughing hysterically. After a moment, Jamison started laughing with me at our inconceivable surroundings.

I finally quit laughing and tentatively reached up for him as he stood in the bathroom doorway beside the bed, looking down at me. And, just like that, the magic happened. Fate had made sure two hot, sweaty, exhausted bodies finally found each other in the stinky, dim, fog-filled storage closet with its pencil-wide bed.

The cost of one night on a twin bed that was to change the trajectory of two lives forever was $7.40, including tax. But the memories we made are priceless.

FIFTEEN

MY BEST CLIENT IS A PERVERT

My real estate career had been launched into the stratosphere with the first Open House I ever held in May, 1982. It was beginner's luck, that Sunday, when Wren and his wife Robbie wandered into my Open House.

Wren was over 6-feet tall. With a walrus mustache and wavy, longish salt and pepper hair, he looked every inch the movie director, or someone equally distinguished. Distinguished like the Senior Vice President of a major East Coast contracting firm that he was. Robbie was an elfin-like aging cheerleader who held camps for little girls who wanted to grow up and work on professional cheer squads.

Wren said he had always wanted to live in San Diego, so he'd volunteered to be the advance party for his Connecticut-based company. He was here to research corporate office facilities and housing prices for the fifty-plus employees who would be coming, and he was lost. He had been going up and down my street for the past fifteen minutes and, like a typical male, refused to admit he needed directions. They were now late to meet another real estate agent who was showing them a house on this same street as mine, but with a higher numerical house number. It was an easy fix—the street stopped just past me but continued on the other side of the freeway in an adjoining town.

I was so new to real estate that, although I recognized a huge opportunity, I didn't know how to seize it. I couldn't think of one single thing to say to try to make them want to work with me, so I gave them my Thomas Bros map book so they could find their appointment. I didn't have my business cards yet, so I wrote my name and company phone number inside the map book cover and asked them to please return it when they could. I didn't get their last names, their phone number, or even the town in Connecticut where they lived. All afternoon, I beat myself up, running and rerunning through my mind how I could have missed out on such an opportunity. Maybe there was more to this real estate stuff than just cashing a commission check.

The Universe smiled on me that day. Wren and Robbie actually brought the book back as I was closing up the Open House and insisted on taking me to dinner for my kindness. They said they were tired of all the pushy agents that entire weekend who tried to latch on to them when they heard why Wren and Robbie were house hunting. They had talked it over that afternoon and were both so relieved to find an agent who wasn't fawning all over them that they decided they wanted to work with me.

Perfect, I thought. Perfect. This real estate stuff really IS as easy as it looks.

Everything has its price, and although working with Wren and the NYSE-ranked company employees over the next six years was extremely lucrative, it caused me to question my ability to evaluate people—namely Wren.

Wren was a highly detailed engineer who was so picky that I couldn't find a house that passed his detailed mental checklist after four months of intense looking. As a result, I came to dread working with engineers like him. He was frustratingly slow to make a decision unless he had every question, no matter how petty, answered in advance. I learned to always show houses to an engineer's wife while they were at work. Buying a house is an *emotional* decision, and emotions are a trait sorely lacking in an engineer's left-brained, logical DNA.

But, in the beginning, it was all love and hugs. Five days after I met them, my phone rang at 5 a.m. as Wren called me from his Connecticut office to tell me he was really looking forward to working with me. He apologized for having called me so early, but it was 8 a.m. in Connecticut, and he wouldn't be able to call during his busy daily schedule. I assured him that was fine.

On Tuesday morning, my phone rang at 5 a.m. as Wren called me from his Connecticut office to tell me he was looking forward to working with me, and he had talked to five other top personnel, and THEY were all looking forward to working with me.

On Wednesday morning, Wren called me at 5 a.m. to tell me that all the top personnel AND the company directors were looking forward to working with me. Over the course of a couple of days, his voice had gotten softer, lower, breathier, and more endearing. As the months came and went, sometimes he almost sounded out of breath by the time he hung up.

But, 5 a.m. is still 5 a.m., and his calls hardly ever varied, so I never gave that detail much thought until later. Several years later.

I was feverishly looking to find Wren's company 100,000 square feet of office space. This was an absolutely huge amount of space, and hard to find all in one building. But, I persevered and was paid $33,000 for my share of the lease commission. I also found seven of the top executives (including the President, his personal secretary, and four other Senior Vice Presidents) homes that ranged from $400,000 to $750,000 in the next six months. In my second year of selling real estate, my commissions totaled over $200,000 in 1983, mostly because of Wren.

On the other hand, Wren was impossible to find a home for. He was now on the West Coast and didn't call me every day with his husky, breathy voice, but he still called several times a week at 6 a.m. before he went to work. At times, I flattered myself that he had a small crush on me; and other times, I thought he had already bought from another agent and was too embarrassed to tell me.

After four months of showing him five to ten houses every weekend, I had shown him over 130 homes. Robbie gave up at about the fiftieth house and told us both that when Wren found a house, let her know the address so she could order the movers and get their furniture out of storage.

One Monday night, I finally said to Wren, "There are only about forty houses in your price range left in the entire San Diego County that you haven't seen, and you need to buy something. So, this Saturday, I'm going to bring food, snacks, drinks, and a flashlight, and we are going to see all forty of them so you can finally make a decision. I'll meet you at my office at 7 a.m. and we will start with vacant houses. After it's dark, we'll finish with any vacant ones we haven't yet seen. On Sunday, you WILL eliminate every house you didn't like and pick a house to buy from whatever remains on the list."

And he did. He bought one of the very first houses I had ever shown him three months earlier. It was a three-story contemporary coastal home in San Marea with an expansive ocean view and a fully shingled exterior. The entire top floor was the master suite, complete with wet bar, refrigerator, coffeemaker, and hot plate. All he and Robbie had to do on the weekends was lay in bed and watch the waves crash on the beach. Robbie's only dry comment was that he could have spared himself all that looking, as I had told them, even then, they should buy it.

I learned to cringe when clients, who were difficult to please, introduce me to their friends, as they always seem to refer people just like them: "This is the real estate agent we told you about that showed us 147 homes, and we bought the first one she ever showed us." Fortunately for me, none of their friends were like them.

Eight months later, DeeDee, the managing broker for our office (and also Granny's new wife), came into one Tuesday office meeting in Total Disgust Mode. It was the first day of Nordstrom's yearly Half-Off Sale. The store had opened at 7 a.m. for their preferred customers so they could shop before going to work. The store was jammed, and she had to wait several turns to even get into an elevator.

After scoring some great clothes, DeeDee recounted that, on the way down the elevator to come to the office meeting, some tall pervert standing behind her kept pressing his privates up against her. The elevator was so packed that every time she tried to move away from him, he moved right with her. When she turned her head to give him a dirty look, he shifted his eyes to avoid eye contact. She would have slapped him, but her arms were full of shopping bags, so she was helpless for the entire ride from the fourth floor to the ground level of the store. Frustration and disgust prior to 9 a.m. on a Tuesday morning had left her partially unhinged.

DeeDee was still ranting at the end of the meeting when we all left to do the required office preview tour of the three new San Marea listings, one of which was mine. Wren had decided to move; the first of his six personal moves as my client. This current home was three levels above the garage, and the master bedroom was the entire top floor. His knees were giving him problems with all the stairs, so he planned to build a one-story home on a vacant lot he and Robbie had purchased right down the street.

The tour was going well. About forty agents had positive comments about the view and how I had priced it. They were taking turns going up or coming down the spiral metal staircase between floors when a piercing scream broke out, emanating from the top floor. It was DeeDee, screaming, "That's him, that's him—that's the pervert from this morning!" I rushed up the stairs and found DeeDee staring in horror at a framed photo of Wren and Robbie on the nightstand next to their bed.

Dear Lord, what next? My favorite, most lucrative client had (allegedly) assaulted my broker's wife in an elevator, and now she's in his house. Plus, she's rushing towards the stairs yelling "Someone call the police; call the police! I know who he is."

The Curse of Monday was happening on a Tuesday. (All of the weirdest things in my real estate career seem to happen on a Monday. Someday when I get to be President, or perhaps God, I'm going to rename that damn day and break the curse.)

I was able to deflect DeeDee's desire to call the police by pointing out to her that this sale would generate a $15,000 commission and, as managing broker, she would get some of it. That seemed to mollify her, and I sold the house without further incident.

Three years later, between Wren's third and fourth house purchase, several things happened in quick succession. Wren was first demoted from his Senior VP position after twenty years at his company, Robbie filed for divorce and moved back to Connecticut, and Wren retired at age fifty-eight to become a full-time real estate advisor.

He used OPM (Other People's Money) to buy, remodel, and flip oceanfront real estate. Those were also my personal glory years, for as soon as I earned $200,000, I would hit 'pause' in my business and take the rest of the year off to take a trip or two. Sometimes three. In those years, I was able to hit 'pause' in June or July. It may not have worked for everyone, but it certainly worked for me.

One day, I was enjoying a routine client lunch, something I did weekly with many of my favorite clients. That day I was with Marlene, the wife of one of the Senior VPs in Wren's old company. Lunch with her was always a three-martini event. I had stayed close to the original group of Wren's fellow employees, as they tended to move around a lot. The husbands were workaholics, and the women had a lot of time on their hands to shop, have lunch, and look at houses.

After her first martini, Marlene put pleasantries aside and went right to the reason she'd asked to have lunch with me. She said, "So, how are you and Wren doing?"

To which I innocently replied, *"How are Wren and I doing what?"*

She said, "Oh come on—you must have been involved with him, to keep working with him after the scandal".

To which I then incredulously responded, *"WHAT scandal?"*

After my seemingly innocuous question, lunch deteriorated into a four-martini affair. For the price of a lunch and four martinis, I learned the truth behind Wren's demotion, sudden retirement, divorce, and career change.

Marlene's husband told her that Wren had been caught having some type of unusual sex with the company president's wife, one afternoon. Wren was supposed to be out of his office at a meeting and the president, who was feeling ill, arrived home mid-afternoon unexpectedly.

Leading up to that startling confrontation, the president had been fielding/covering up reports from HR personnel for years about Wren's alleged sexual harassment from not only the old Connecticut office, but the other five satellite offices of the company. Wren was always attending this meeting or that around the country because of the government contracts, and apparently had seven or eight secretaries convinced that their continued company employment was predicated on keeping him sexually happy. Once the reports started coming from personnel departments of the sub-contractors also, the president was having a hard time suppressing the complaints about Wren.

A couple of days after being caught 'in flagrante delicto', Wren had been demoted, and within ten days, had retired. His divorce had already been initiated. The president filed for divorce from his wife about the same time, and by the end of the year, he was married to his private secretary. After Wren's retirement was announced, another dozen secretaries, both from the local and other out-of-state satellite offices, came forward with similar stories. Wren had been a VERY busy man, it seemed.

According to Marlene, it was common knowledge that the reason I was getting all the company business and Wren's continued real estate loyalty was because I must have been *keeping him happy also*, being single with big boobs and all. I think my mouth dropped open so far, she could see my lunch being digested.

I had never had a problem with Wren in that manner. Nonetheless, I felt chilled when I thought of all the breathlessness on his end of the phone in those original early morning calls after I first met him, and the bone-cracking bear hugs every time we got together.

I could see that Marlene was inclined to believe me. She was a smart woman, and likely understood that if Wren had such a character flaw, he picked on smaller, weaker women; and in no universe was that a description of me.

One of the advantages of being almost six feet tall myself is that 89% of the world population of both men and women are shorter than me. It seems improbable to intimidate or sexually harass anyone when you have to look up to talk to them, and I certainly didn't need him to help me keep my job. But, after Wren's departure, I was no longer getting any new business from his company. My old clients were calling me, but no new ones were being referred.

After that lunch, I never saw Wren in the same light. I was watchful of everything I said and did when I was around him, to the point of always meeting him with my arms full of purses and files to avoid his hugs.

SIXTEEN

SPIDERS AND SNAKES
ARE NOT OUR FRIENDS

I had a border patrol agent for a buyer who regaled me with stories of hair-raising drug busts. In his circle of work, it was common knowledge that ruthless drug dealers have snakes and sometimes tarantulas or scorpions housed in gigantic aquariums in their living rooms or labs. We're talking the 50-to-100-gallon size, full of reptiles and arachnids, in the middle of the main floor of a drug house. Police and border patrol agents dreaded raiding such a house knowing that the first thing the bad guys did was smash several aquarium sides to release the snakes and spiders, maybe venomous, maybe not, to give themselves extra time to escape.

I imagined the druggies congratulated themselves for being so smart as they walked casually down the street to their low-profile getaway car parked a couple of blocks away. In their aftermath, law enforcement agents were totally engaged in dealing with a writhing, hissing, undulating floor covering.

I remembered showing property in a rundown neighborhood south of downtown San Diego. My buyer and I drove by a house completely surrounded by police cars and paddy-wagons, and had laughed at uniformed men jumping from first floor windows instead of coming out the doors. It looked like a Keystone Cops segment was being enacted. I had sometimes wondered what caused that, until this border patrol buyer explained it. He also told me that when a big drug bust was scheduled, the officers always took a herpetologist with them for just such occurrences.

Lou Anna's kids were worried sick. It was almost 7 p.m. and they were hungry. They were now calling the office every ten minutes to see if their mother had come back from showing property at 3 p.m.

Their dad was working nights at his new job, and their mom was supposed to be home by 5:30 p.m. to fix dinner and help them with their homework. Daylight savings time hadn't started yet, so by 5 p.m., it was dark.

Krista and Lolly had finished their floor duty at 6 p.m. but resolved to stay until Lou Anna showed up. While it was not uncommon for agents to run late while showing property, her oldest girl was only eleven, so they promised they'd keep answering the phone to keep them calm until their mother returned. After two more calls from the increasingly worried kids, Lolly called 911 to report Lou Anna missing, and tried to figure out where to start looking for her.

While Granny had repeatedly told every agent to leave a list of houses they planned to show in the office in case of something just like this, no one did. He also told us to make a photocopy of the driver's license of any new male clients at their initial showing. We never did that, either. It was just too embarrassing, and we all knew we were good judges of character and would never have a problem with OUR clients. The one safety concession primarily used was to ask new clients to meet us at the office for the first time, so we could drive.

Just like our mothers taught us, we never got into cars with strangers. They got into ours.

Lolly's desk sat close to Lou Anna's, and she thought she remembered Lou Anna saying that her single lady client was ready to buy, and they were going to look at four newly listed homes today. She racked her brain to remember the price range to narrow down the possibilities for the police. Lou Anna's desk was a total mess. It was laden with papers, file folders, pens, blank forms, old sandwich wrappers, napkins, and the faint yellow duplicates of NCR (No Carbon-paper Required) messages. This all combined to completely cover the desk's surface and spilled off onto the floor. As Lou Anna often said, it was physical disorganization only—she knew where everything was.

With a stroke of genius, Lolly pulled last week's MLS Blue Book out of Lou Anna's trash can and found that it opened easily to a section of Cardin, a little beach town a few miles north. There were twelve fuzzy newsprint photos with barely discernible facts and descriptions in size four font per page. On this page, there were seven houses circled, all priced between $200,000 and $260,000. She opened her newest Blue Book to compare, and sure enough, there were four new listings in that price range, in Cardin.

With a mixed sense of elation and dread, Lolly met Officers Malloy and Pederson with the torn-out page with those addresses and a description of Lou Anna.

In answer to their questions, she said that Lou Anna was driving an older, dark-colored Mercedes that she had recently bought. It might be grey, or brown, or maybe black. Lolly admitted she really didn't pay close attention to Lou Anna's car, so it could be any color but it was definitely a Mercedes.

At close to 9:30 p.m., Officer Malloy phoned Lolly. They had found Lou Anna's car in an alley in Cardin and P.S. the color was called Astal Silver Metallic. Both Lou Anna and her client were safe but would have an interesting story to share tomorrow. And, by the way, he and his partner wanted to know what Lolly and Krista were doing on Saturday night. They'd like to take the ladies to dinner.

The next morning, Lolly, Ginger, Miriam, Krista, and I were in the office by 7:30 a.m. so we wouldn't miss Lou Anna in case she kept her normal routine. We were rewarded for our early morning arrival and sat with our mouths open while Lou Anna recounted her harrowing experience.

The 3 p.m. showing had started with Lou Anna's client, Sue, being thirty minutes late. Being late is the bane of real estate agents on a schedule everywhere. By the time they got to the third house, it was already dark. Sue had not liked any so far, but painstakingly went through each one at least twice before giving it the thumbs down.

It was almost 5 p.m. and Lou Anna was feeling hurried. No one had answered the occupant's phone number for showing the last house, so she hadn't been able to schedule that appointment. She prayed the owners wouldn't have had time to get home from work and was determined to rush Sue through it if she didn't like it immediately. Her kids were waiting, and she was already going to be late to make them dinner.

Cardin was a funky little town with many lots split in the middle, making one home face the street and one face the alley. This was an alley house. In her headlights, Lou Anna could see the lockbox on the back door, so they would be entering into the kitchen, probably, instead of the front door.

When she opened the back door and reached to flip on the light, she heard a noise in another room. That caused her to shout, very loudly, "AGENT!", at which time she thought she heard sounds of hurried footsteps and the muffled sound of breaking glass. After yelling "Agent" again with no further response, she and Sue walked across the kitchen to examine the countertops.

After that, things happened fast. Lou Anna and Sue both saw the first few snakes coming onto the kitchen floor from the adjoining room just as the house suddenly went dark. The snakes were slithering fast and were between the ladies and the back door. The door that Lou Anna had closed immediately after entering so any unknown pets couldn't escape, per Real Estate 101 protocol.

Lou Anna had read her daughter's biology book while helping her with a homework report on snakes. The book said there were two types of black and yellow snakes with red bands separating the colors. If the red was between black bands, those snakes were harmless; but if the red was between the black and yellow, that snake was extremely poisonous. Or vice versa—she couldn't remember. But she did remember seeing black and yellow and red on some of the snakes before the lights went out.

Lou Anna and Sue had scared each other so badly by the pitch and volume of their screams that they instinctively jumped, at the same time, onto the counter, where they sat in the darkness with their feet up under them. They couldn't see anything but could hear the dry rustle of a multitude of snake bellies crisscrossing the floor below them. Lou Anna estimated there were at least a million of them.

Lou Anna and Sue sat for hours on the counter in the darkness with their feet in the sink and their imaginations to entertain them. If that wasn't enough insult to their psyches, Sue had needed to pee before she left work, but didn't take the time because she was running late. After being scared witless by the sight of the snakes, the urge to pee became an emergency of its own. Lou Anna had lifted her feet out of the sink so Sue could use it. Mercifully, it was dark.

When the two policemen finally arrived sometime after 9 p.m. and located the fuse box hidden behind some bushes, there were only a few snakes visible. While none of them looked poisonous, there was no way to take a chance. It took another thirty minutes until a herpetologist arrived to identify the remaining snakes as the police crew carefully moved furniture and rugs and plugged cracks where some might have slipped into the walls.

There was also a second terrarium full of spiders, many of which WERE poisonous. The glass side had only cracked when hit, but it stayed intact. Although the spiders inside were now swarming all over each other again with the sudden appearance of light, apparently none had escaped.

Neither Lou Anna nor Sue could be convinced to come off the counter, so the larger buff policeman, Officer Pederson, had carried them one by one outside to the Mercedes, earning him the nickname of Prince Charming in the retelling of this story. Prince Charming had carried both ladies all the way to her car, a comforting vision that Lou Anna said she would replay again and again in her head for years to come.

Lou Anna was a perfect example of the One and Done. She closed one deal and wore herself out looking around for the next one. Without keeping in touch with her clients for repeat business, or asking for referrals, it was impossible for her to build a cliental or a continuing stream of business.

Things always seem to happen in threes. After the episode of the PTSD veteran choking her and the man in her farm exposing himself, we pretty much expected Lou Anna to give up selling real estate after the snake episode. But she was made of sterner stuff.

Her kids needed her to provide for them, so she lasted another year before finally burning out and moving with her family to someplace in Maine. Probably she picked a cold state as far away from California as she could get to lessen the chances of snakes.

SEVENTEEN

ACCOMPLICE TO MURDER
NUMBER TWO

U pon reflection, I realized these new clients were likely my karmic punishment for how much I'd enjoyed my weekend away
with Jamison. I looked forward to his calls that started with, "Hey,
Nico, I have to go to _____ for a business meeting, are you
able to join me?"

It never occurred to me to say 'No'. He always spoiled me with
massages, fine wine, excellent dinners, and lots and lots of sex.
Because these trips were rarely more than two days, no one missed
me. I could pick up my phone calls remotely from my answering
machine and tell my clients, *I'm booked today and tomorrow,
but let's schedule for Monday."*

On my way back (from Las Vegas, this time), being on Cloud
Nine and all, I was reliving some of our more special moments as
I languidly idled at Baggage Claim. Our lovemaking and joint bub-
ble bath this morning was so thoroughly relaxing, it had pushed
thoughts of the work week ahead out of my mind, for once. Jamison had been ever so clear from the very beginning, warning me
that he would never leave his wife. That had released me from
having expectations or worrying about that, so I could focus on
memorizing every moment we spent together. I reminded myself
over and over of his warning, but, like every woman in the world
in love with a married man, I still had hopes that on the next trip,
he would tell me he was getting divorced. Even now, I marvel that
an accomplished woman like myself, earning $200,000 a year in
the mid-1980s and credited with being a leader in the coastal real
estate market, could kid herself for so long.

To this day, I have no idea of how I attracted this particular couple, but it started innocently enough at baggage claim.

A nicely dressed couple in their late fifties, with matching Tumi leather carry-ons, were standing next to me holding hands and verbalizing a list of all the things they would want in their new home. When they got towards the end of a seemingly long list of awfully expensive 'must have' items, she speculated, "Honey, how much do you think this is going to cost us?" To which he replied, "It doesn't matter, Sweets, I'm buying."

Some people use coffee to jolt them awake. Dollar amounts of houses had the same effect on me. I inserted myself casually into their conversation by saying, "Prices here in California can really escalate depending on what area you select. I'm a real estate agent working along the coast—did you have an area or a price range in mind?"

Turns out they were looking for a large home in The Ranch (our highest of the high-priced areas in San Marea County. Prices were SOOO high that if The Ranch were a baseball stadium, their ticket prices would be located in the 'Sky Box' while the other homes in the county would be considered General Admission.) Homes in The Ranch were a minimum of 5,000 square feet, on mostly two-acre lots, with a starting price above $1 million even then. This couple was in town for a week to find something, and they didn't know any real estate agents. I was pretty excited.

My first clue that something might be unusual about them was, oddly, they wouldn't tell me their last name, but I smelled new business and I ignored the warning sign. "Just call us Eddie and Sophie and that will be fine," they said. (Oh my God, I can't believe I'm really risking telling this story, but it's far too good to be left out.)

At a time when a healthy sale for me in San Marea was $330,000, Eddie and Sophie wanted to buy up to $2.0 million. I was more than pretty ecstatic! Perhaps, they said, for the right home, they could go higher. Cash. I was over the moon. I strained to seem casual and confident when inside I was shaking and my Doubting Thomas/I Don't Deserve This mind chatter was screaming, "They won't ever buy" and "They'll find a better agent" and "They'll go to an Open House, and that agent will sell it to them." I resolved to stick to them like glue, solve their every need, and find them a perfect house before their week was over.

Sophie, especially, had some extremely specific requirements. The easiest of which was that the area for her shoes could not be inside the closet with her clothes. You would think this was the easiest to take care of—I thought easiest; we all thought easiest.

"No problem," I naively said, of course. As it turned out, it was a mountain of an obstacle. I never imagined there were so many expensive homes that ALL had the shoes storage *inside* their voluminous walk-in closet. Or closets. Who knew?

I put all my current eight buyers and eleven sellers on hold while I laid out a course of action for Eddie and Sophie. I didn't want them to be overwhelmed, I said, with looking at too many houses at one time, so I would pick them up at the hotel every morning about 10 a.m., show them houses while they were fresh, then have lunch before I would bring them back to the hotel at about 3:30 pm.

That was my first line of defense—Open Houses are usually held between 1-4 p.m., so being with them and stretching out the showings during this dangerous time slot solved one item of the Doubting Thomas chatter. What they liked and didn't like would help me refine the search for the next day, so at the end of the week, they would have eliminated everything that didn't work for them and only the perfect house would be left for them to buy.

(Most people think that buying a home is a process of selection, but it is just the opposite—it's a process of elimination. That can be daunting if the field to eliminate in one week is 113 homes priced between 1 million and $3.25 million that were available in The Ranch. It was a two-and-a-half-year absorption rate, or 1,000 Days on the Market, given the low number of sales in that price range. In that kind of Buyer's Market, I always looked for the homes that had been for sale the longest—equating time with seller motivation/desperation and the opportunity of negotiating a below-market sales price for my buyers.)

A client showing would probably take thirty minutes to an hour if they liked it, five to ten minutes if they didn't, and each listing agent had to go early to open up, wait and wait for the agent with the prospective buyer, then close up. After showing three houses, we could be early to the next one, or way late by number five—stressful, in any case, in this pre-cellphone era. Listing agents just waited and hoped the other agent hadn't changed their mind and had no way to contact them. This visual should help bust Urban Legend Number Four that agents do nothing but collect a big commission.

Before each showing, the listing agent started at least an hour before the appointment to open the drapes, turn on the lights, check the kitchen for dirty dishes, the master bedroom for underwear or sex toys (you'd be surprised), turn on water features, and generally air the home out from any lingering odors. To head off any potential bonding between Eddie, Sophie, and another agent, when I set up the appointments, I told the listing agents that my clients were very private people (true) and had requested that they be allowed to look at the home instead of being shown the home (sort of true). If they had any questions, they would ask.

Poof: another item off the Doubting Thomas list, as that actually worked.

As always, I was out my door at 7 a.m. in the morning to drive the proposed route for the day, then rush through paperwork at my office for my current escrows before picking Eddie and Sophie up. This daily routine ended when I dragged in about 7 p.m. every night to start returning the fifty-plus phone call messages my office had accumulated during the day from clients and other agents checking on my eleven listings.

Many of my fifty-plus calls were duplicated, had no message as to what was needed or had phone numbers written down wrong, so this greatly added to everyone's total frustration. By the end of that week, I was getting ninety-plus messages from people who'd originally called. They were returning my call and asked me to PLEASE return their call—it was URGENT (or as the week wore on—it was an EMERGENCY!). The bags deepened under my eyes literally every morning as I looked at myself in the mirror.

On the second day, I had to slam on the brakes to avoid a dog on the road in The Ranch. That caused Sophie's purse to fall over and an exquisite derringer with an inlaid pearl grip slid out, up under the footwell on the passenger side, and back down. She glanced over at me as she picked it up and said, "I hope guns don't frighten you, dear."

With a lump of fear in my throat, I casually said back to her, *"No, they don't. I grew up hunting with my dad. That looks like a really beautiful gun."*

The derringer episode prompted another event. As the agent for the potential buyer, I was supposed to check them out and verify with their banker (or see by their bank statement) that they could afford what I was showing them. It was a Scout's Honor type of thing. On our first day out, while switching between my real estate agent hat, my tour guide hat, and my bonding-with-them hat, I discovered that they owned a ranch outside Laramie, Wyoming. Not only did they own a ranch, but it also had a private air strip so that when they came in from Chicago, they could do so in privacy. (Chicago—this was a new piece of information.)

Given that Wyoming is a lightly populated state, and my old college boyfriend was a bank manager in Laramie, it was an opportune time to reconnect. Surely, someone with a private air strip was rich enough that he knew about them—last name or not.

After my drop off at 3:30 pm that day, I rushed back to the office and made that call. Exchanging pleasantries with Lorne about our wild and wooly drinking days from college (and there were more than a few) took twenty minutes! Finally, I got around to the reason for my call and asked him if he knew who had a local ranch with a private air strip.

I thought for a few moments that the line had gone dead, but it was only that he had stopped breathing and was struggling to regain his composure.

"How (*sputter*) in the world (*sputter*) did you find those people?

They are really dangerous. Don't call them or meet with them again—it isn't safe. They're Mafia.

"And don't mention my name, or that you spoke to me. It isn't safe for me, either."

Struggling to keep him on the phone, I pressed on. He admitted they probably had enough money to buy anything they wanted—they were part of an old-world, big-time, Chicago gangster family and he thought they might be in witness protection, given the money they had in his bank and the remoteness of their ranch. (He did tell me their last name, which I won't divulge—but if you had ever heard of Al Capone, you would recognize this well-known last name, too.)

F—K is the first word that leapt into my mind, and it kept repeating itself for days as though it was an echo in a large, deep canyon.

"Lorne, one more question—they have four kids, and they keep talking about the one who is away at camp. That sounds so strange for adult children. Is he mentally retarded or something?"

"Oh God, oh God, Nico, you've got to get away from those people. You're asking about Tony. He is not at camp, he's in prison. Our police chief is my brother-in-law. He says Tony's a mob hit man, but the police and FBI have not yet been able to prove it. He's serving five years in State Prison for tax evasion."

My mind was having a hard time processing this new information. They had told me nothing, I had been picking up scraps I'd gleaned from watching and listening, and Lorne had just laid it all out for me in one phone call. Eddie and Sophie were an unlikely-looking Mob couple. Eddie was a tall, slender man with a receding hairline and a slight paunch. He was slightly effeminate and more than a little coarse, saying 'F--k' at least once per sentence. He inventively said he was a retired doctor from New York, although I have to admit I couldn't visualize who his patients would be, to endure his vocabulary.

Sophie was a diminutive, classy, retired dancer. She was elegant in her mannerisms and wore Nancy Regan-type clothes and Nancy's bouffant hair style. She had retained the lithe body and erect carriage of a dancer, even though she was probably closing in on age sixty. They had four grown children, although she always described them as "three of my own and one that I adopted when his mother was killed. She had been my maid, so I felt somewhat responsible."

(Every time she said that I would mentally inquire the obvious of Sophie—you felt responsible for the killing? or responsible for the little boy?)

On the third day, to cover my nervousness of knowing so much about them after my call with Lorne, I asked Sophie how she and her husband had met.

"My husband saw me on stage in a lavish Las Vegas stage show, and when he was introduced to me backstage, he told me that he intended to 'whisk me away to have his babies' and be his trophy wife. I never performed again, although I still dance daily, to keep in shape."

Her eyes sparkled and she laughed a tinkly laugh. It was easy to see how much she still loved Eddie after all these years—as though it was still new. So, I relaxed and concentrated on finding them a house. Finally, on houses numbered seventeen and eighteen, I showed them two new-construction houses side by side, and they decided to buy both! One for themselves and one for their eldest son and his wife. Eddie bought a ticket for the eldest son to fly in the following day to see the houses, but the son didn't think the 5,000 square foot one was big enough for him. Darn, drats, and disappointment—so we moved on.

On day five, I deduced that Eddie was not Sophie's husband, but her boyfriend. Lorne had told me their names, so I had wrongly assumed that Eddie was using a Mob alias because of being in witness protection, but that was not so. The light went on in the closet of my mind, so to speak. It explained some of the more bizarre conversations between them.

For instance, that day we looked at THE most expensive home in The Ranch, a whopping $3.4 million. The owner had imported the rare blue-grey granite from a mine in Italy for the entire floor of this 10,500 square foot home. This included the entry, the entire kitchen and the main bathroom floors and counters. He then had the entire mine blown up so no one else would ever have the same granite. In the lavish main bathroom was a double piece of plate glass freestanding around the step-down shower-pond in the middle of the room. (Nothing screams 'I have sooo much money' than a 2,200 square foot master bedroom and bath with a free-standing, mid-room shower. Except maybe an exploded mountain.)

On this doorless shower enclosure were elaborate etchings on both sides of each piece of glass before they were sandwiched together. There were intricately etched palm trees, hibiscus flowers, flying parrots, ocean waves, and the profile of Diamond Head in Hawaii in the background. The end result was a 3-D scene on a plate glass sandwich an inch thick. Which, the listing agent casually assured us, was bulletproof.

Eddie said, "I really f--king LOVE this shower. I'll always know, when I'm taking a shower, that I can't f--king be shot. Maybe I could also sleep in here and be safe. Maybe we can also f--k in here—feeling protected makes me f--king horny. Whatdaya think, honey? Let's buy THIS house."

On the other side of this sprawling one-level home, we encountered a weird bedroom in an otherwise-classy, professionally decorated, and richly (emphasis RICH-ly) understated home. The bedroom was decorated in a western theme, complete with a wagon wheel headboard and a four-tier gun rack bolted to the wall at eye level. Its sliding glass door overlooked the lush, manicured lawn which gently sloped down to the Olympic-sized swimming pool. The pool was accessorized with three plastic pink floating flamingos and a cabana.

There were at least forty chaise lounges around the pool, much like the exotic resort spa setting you'd see in a magazine ad. This vista inspired Eddie to say "F-ck, honey, this is perfect for f--king Tony's room. The patio door slides open, and the pool is so private, no one can see who's here. Tony will only have to work one f--king day a year. He can invite all his clients over to relax around the pool, get them drunk, and look—he f--king won't even have to go outside. Whatdaya think, honey? I want to BUY this house."

The listing agent shook his head and looked perplexed as they chuckled at their own private joke. In an unguarded moment, I accidentally chuckled with them, and they both turned to look at me.

Eddie said, "I f--king know why I'm laughing, and I also f--king-know why Sophie's laughing, but why the f--k are YOU laughing?"

It was as though my strict mother was suddenly there in the room and had just said 'wipe that smile off your face, sister'. I stopped mid-chuckle, mumbling something like I was just being polite and was glad that they liked the room. Or something.

I skipped the next bathroom when Eddie and Sophie went in to look. I was afraid to see my face in the mirror in case what I was thinking was reflected there. Actually, for the first time, I was just plain afraid.

They were ready to make an offer, so I wrote up a full-price offer for $3.4 million for them to sign and presented it to the listing agent, who was a legendary top agent in The Ranch.

I had not been allowed to present it to the sellers, as was Mr. Legendary's way of client control. However, even with my good and accomplished professional reputation, in my excitement and haste in writing such a high-priced offer, I had forgotten to verify their funds to purchase, and was rudely chastised by Mr. Legendary agent.

"You're supposed to be an experienced agent. Get me the proof of their ability to pay cash before I present this to the seller. He's a busy man, and you can't waste his time." (He left unsaid: "or waste MY time either".)

Eddie had insisted on buying it for Sophie and I was mad at myself for not asking for proof of his funds *before* I presented the offer. I went through the options with them of what I could use to confirm his ability to pay over $3.0 million for this one-of-a-kind treasure, and that he had to do it immediately. A bank statement would work, a statement of the value of his stock portfolio, a letter from his private banker on letterhead—any one of them would work—just something that looked official and showed more than $3.4 million in liquid assets.

The next morning slightly before 6 a.m., my phone rang. I was still in bed and was not prepared for the deep voice that said, without introduction, "He got dah money". The voice was so stereo-typical threatening movie mobster that I was immediately awake.

"Who is this?"

"It doesn't matter," was the reply. "Eddie, he got dah money to buy dah house."

Click. The menacing voice was gone.

And suddenly, Eddie and Sophie were gone too. Physically gone and not returning my phone calls, gone. I called and called and called. After two weeks, I was having nightmares where I saw my commission check at the bottom of a resort swimming pool with the dollar figures soaked off. After an eternity of unanswered calls, late one night a month later, an obviously drunk Sophie answered the phone. I was so startled to hear her, I forgot all the scripted sentences I had composed for a lead-in when someone finally answered.

"Sophie, I have been so worried about you and Eddie. Is everything okay?"

"Dear," she slurred, "no, everything is not okay. Eddie is gone and my husband is dead.

"Two weeks ago, my husband was killed in a one-car automobile accident in Wyoming. That was the official report in the local newspaper, but I know in my heart that it was a mob hit. You know he was in witness protection for being an informant for the Feds. They were keeping him safe for an important trial, which was coming up at the end of this month. Safe, ya, right.

"As for Eddie, he was supposed to be a doctor here in Palm Desert. My pharmacist introduced us when I went to pick up a prescription about four months before we met you in the San Diego airport. I couldn't get ahold of Eddie to tell him about my husband's death, so I finally went over to the hospital, and no one had ever heard of him. He took me to the hospital's Christmas party, for Christ's sake, and introduced me to many of the other doctors there. I feel like I'm living a Twilight Zone episode.

"So, my dear, no; everything is *not* okay. I'm a widow with no boyfriend and I have no idea how they found my husband."

But, all of a sudden, the weird little string of odd events tied themselves together in my brain, along with Lorne's warning—the coarse un-doctor-like language, the bulletproof glass comment, the sinister-sounding voice saying Eddie "had dah money," the gifted airplane ticket for the son that would identify the departing city where the FBI witness protection was likely hiding the husband, and Eddie vanishing as soon as the husband was killed.

I sickeningly realized that I was again a witness and accomplice, albeit unwittingly, to a second murder. I really needed to find a job description for being a real estate agent so I wouldn't go through this type of event ever again. Was this perhaps a karmic retribution for loving Jamison and spending the weekend with him when I met them? Working with Eddie and Sophie had been a total waste of my time. I had nothing to show for all those weeks but a couple of Nordstrom lunches, a great story and a sick feeling from knowing about another murder.

EIGHTEEN

MORE OF THE WICKED WITCH

After being fired from Fakke & Co., Trixie moved on to a brokerage with blue and white signs. I was relieved to see her leave. She had tried to sue me using paperwork she had falsified. I didn't trust her, and I didn't want to be around her. Within a couple of months, strange things began to happen in her new company. Almost weekly, during Caravan, I heard about agents in her new company being accused of stealing stamps, rolls of toilet paper, reams of copy paper, and client gifts that were awaiting delivery. The more successful agents were having their For Sale signs taken down or defaced with spray paint in the middle of the night—something that was happening to several of us Fakke agents, too.

At the same time, the legend of Trixie grew. She listed an oceanfront estate that had been promised to Andy, a well-liked top oceanfront specialist in her new company. Andy single-handedly listed 30% of all oceanfront properties up and down the coast with the aid of a young buyer's agent/assistant, Raelene, whose side job was to be his eye candy (or, as Ginger referred to her, "Andy's Candy"). Not only did Trixie list the oceanfront estate, but she also started sporting a dime-sized diamond in an engagement ring from that seller.

It was always an extremely competitive market for San Marea's oceanfront listings and Andy had sold the seller this home. When Andy asked him why he broke his promise to give Andy his listing, the seller just smiled and mumbled something about liking whips and leather. Andy wasn't sure he'd heard that correctly. He knew his hearing was going, and perhaps that seller had said "Chutes and Ladders". He didn't ask for clarification.

Then there was the time of the Champagne Caravan Tours. The

title company and mortgage company reps were still able to bribe us agents for business, and the regulations preventing this were still years away. Some of the more adept agents got thousands of dollars of free advertising, free brochure printing, free limo use, and even occasional trips to Hawaii. We're talking heavy-hitter agents like Andy, Trixie, Lolly, and me.

Or heavy-hitter offices, like Fakke & Co.

Granny was a big abuser of this bribery mechanism. No title or mortgage reps were allowed to solicit business in his office until their company coughed up a minimum of weekly office meeting breakfasts, holiday party food and booze, office machine leases, or even prizes for the winners of his semi-annual Granny-Needs-More-Business contests. There never seemed to be any shortage of companies waiting in the wings to be taken advantage of by Granny.

Every Wednesday, Granny kicked all his agents out of the office to go on Broker Caravan to see the new listings inventory. One of the more resourceful bribes that evolved for Wednesdays was The Champagne Caravan Tour. Micah and Jan were industrious (but not 'preferred') title company and mortgage company reps who were not allowed in the Fakke office. Once a month, they chipped in to hire a stretch limo loaded with snacks and champagne and a driver, as a reward for the top five agents who had written their company's services into a sale that month.

The first Wednesday of the following month, the limo pulled up outside our office. Micah and Jan were good-looking and well dressed in suits and ties, as good sales reps should be. We agents looked forward to being chauffeured to the homes on Caravan.

The first Wednesday of this particular May, Trixie was a first-time guest of their tour. She was a prodigious drinker, and we shortly ran out of our usual allotment of Brut, causing her to suggest stopping at a Mini-Mart for more bottles. Micah got two more, and those quickly disappeared also.

It was 4 p.m. and closing time for the Open Houses on Caravan. Thank heavens, as Lolly, Krista, Ginger, and I were pretty much drunk, but still needed to go back to work. However, Trixie was having so much fun, she proposed dropping back by the Mini-Mart for a couple more bottles of champagne, and then going over to her house to watch some porn movies. She stated that she had a great collection of porn, and we would have some REAL fun, as the day was still young.

Although Ginger looked briefly like she might say yes, the rest of us were insisting to be dropped off at the office. The last we saw of Trixie and the two reps was through a cloud of dust kicked up when the limo squealed away from the curb in a hurry.

This habit of Trixie for farming Murphys and driving home drunk night after night apparently gave her a legal problem a couple after that Champagne Tour. She had just upgraded herself from the leased Rolls to ownership of a $60,000 top-of-the-line black Mercedes and had gotten a Duwie the first week she had it. Two months later, we read in the local newspaper that she had gotten her third Dewie, and her driver's license was suspended for a year.

Being the small town that San Marea was, Trixie knew she couldn't get away with driving home after drinking, even if home was only a couple of blocks away. Ever the resourceful agent, she hired a handsome young man from a temporary employment agency to drive her to work and to appointments. Just like in the movies *Driving Miss Daisy* and *The Lincoln Lawyer*, Trixie sat in the back seat of her Mercedes with her clients and a 'business as usual' attitude. She still closed lots of escrows, so it didn't seem to be a problem.

Then Trixie married a Mercedes salesman, Monte Grayson. We all snidely gossiped that Monte had seen how much she was earning when he sold her the black sedan, and now she would get really good employee discounts in the years to come. It was a win-win situation we agreed.

Three years after that, Monte called me to list his house—the one he had owned before he married Trixie. He wanted to buy one of my lower-priced listings and figured that if I were the listing agent AND the selling agent, I could convince the seller to take his contingent sale offer.

I was confused. First—I didn't want anything to do with Trixie, given my past experience. Second—I didn't want anything EVER to do with Trixie, given my past experience. And third—same reason.

Even though Monte told me they were getting divorced and she wouldn't be involved as a principal or his agent, I could sense a giant red flag. But he was insistent, so I told him he had to get her permission in writing before I would write his offer and take his listing. Trixie had a reputation for suing all sorts of people including her clients, her assistants, even other agents. I had no wish to get in her cross-hairs.

Two days later, I was at his house, east of San Marea, with listing paperwork in hand. I asked where his permission slip was, and he handed it over, saying, "She laughed when I told her what I needed, but she signed it, so let's get started."

NINETEEN

MARCI'S LAST DAY IN REAL ESTATE

Marci was a brand-new agent in the first few months of her real estate career in 1987. This Sunday was to be the last day of Marci's career, but she didn't know that when she picked up the phone at 7 a.m. Her husband worked a normal work week and was off on the weekends. Marci, however, had been holding Saturday and Sunday Open Houses non-stop all month trying to make a sale, and he was starting to grumble about being a real estate widower.

She had decided not to work today and was feeling guilty about taking an important weekend day off. To make this worse, last night, her husband had been offered one free ticket to the local professional baseball game, so she was destined not only to be alone and idle at home, but non-productive on a Sunday, as well.

So, when the phone rang suddenly and the voice of her favorite Fakke & Co. agent, Tom Little, came on to ask her to take his scheduled Open House (please, please, please) at his new listing on Valley Place, she was both relieved to not be wasting a Sunday and irritated at herself for thinking she could take a day off on a weekend.

It seems his sellers were expecting the open house, he had a large ad running in two papers announcing it, but a family emergency had come up. He would put out his own Open House signs around the neighborhood to draw in traffic before he left for the day, so all Marci had to do was show up for three hours between 1 p.m. and 4 p.m. He would come after 4 p.m. to take all his signs down. Please, please?

When Marci pulled up outside the rambling brick ranch-style home sitting on an oversized lot at about 12:30 p.m., she did as she always did—she took a good look around the neighborhood before getting out of the car. She had been well schooled on realtor safety, so she slowly checked out the street and, once inside the home, checked all the rooms and unlocked all back exits in case she had to leave quickly. She would reverse this procedure at the end of the day when she left, making sure all rooms were empty and all exits were locked.

Then she hid her purse in a bottom cabinet behind the boxes of Rice Krispies, Lucky Charms, and Smart Start (which signified that at least one adult, one teen and one small child lived here). There had been no man's clothing in the master bedroom closet, so this might be another divorce-motivated reason for selling.

Tom's listing was a corner house on a two-block-long cul-de-sac street with about ten houses further along on it. With the minimum two-acre lot zoning, the houses were gracefully spaced for maximum privacy. Marci was a little concerned that since this house was so close to being considered rural, she may not have many, if any, potential buyers through today. But, she had agreed to help Tom, so she settled in with a good book while waiting for potential buyers or neighbors to come through the door.

True to his word, Tom's personal Open House signs were out. There was another agent's sign from a competing brokerage out too, directing buyers to her listing at the far end of the cul-de-sac. You couldn't see it from Marci's house, but pretty much any buyers would stop at hers first, then continue down the street to check out the other one to compare prices, furnishings, and upgrades. She would have first chance at bonding with them to secure their commitment in working with her. She had passed her test almost six months ago and had yet to make a sale, but she could feel her luck changing today. Yes, today would be her lucky day.

The other agent had a photo of herself on her sign, a new RE/MAX-inspired industry wide change in real estate marketing. The photo showed her to be a cute young blonde with a winning smile. Marci's self-doubt surfaced again—a concern that her signs, with only Tom Little's name and photo on them, were less inviting. Oh well, things always worked out the way they were supposed to in Marci's world.

The day dragged along, a few cars came and went down the street, but only one couple had stopped to come inside when she first opened up. They had only made a cursory inspection after learning the price. Buyers "Buy up from an ad and down from a sign." That old adage about asking prices is still as true as ever.

Marci read almost 100 pages in her new true crime novel, uninterrupted for the next two hours. She smiled as she remembered when she had fallen asleep at her first Open House one Sunday. Granny had made a spot check and, finding her asleep on the couch, took her purse and her car keys and went back to the office. When she woke up and got ready to close up the house, she searched and searched for her purse. When it dawned on her that it truly was missing, along with her credit cards, wallet, money, keys to her car, her office AND her house, along with several things identifying her home address, she panicked.

That day, her husband was in his favorite brown leather lounger, drinking a beer and watching a crucial baseball game on TV. He was too engrossed in the close game to notice her frantic phone calls. In desperation, she finally called 911 and reported the theft.

The policeman who came to take the report was kind, and sincerely concerned for her safety. However, he sternly chided her at the same time for being alone in the house with the door wide open. She was lucky she was only frightened, he said. He would drop her back at her office, but since it was the end of his shift and it was his anniversary, he couldn't drive her all the way to her home, some twenty miles north. She would have to wait for her husband to answer the phone.

Marci had cried so much in the back seat of the police cruiser that she probably left a wet spot on his seat where the next person might think someone had wet his/her pants.

The light inside the office was on and Granny was working late, praise the Lord. Embarrassed and relieved at the same time, she sobbed through the retelling of her terrifying ordeal.

Granny didn't say a word, and when she was done, he pointed back over her shoulder towards her desk where her purse perched, perky as all get-out, unaware that it had been kidnapped. Granny kept the entire contents of her wallet as the cost of the lesson, he said—all twelve dollars of it. She wasn't able to laugh about it for months, but eventually her sense of humor kicked in and she never fell asleep again at an Open House. Nor did any other agent, after hearing her Granny Bleep story.

The wail of an emergency vehicle seeped into her reverie, growing louder as it came her way. Another siren started up, coming from a different direction and traveling fast, judging how quickly it got louder. The screech of tires from a cruiser taking the corner of Valley Place too fast happened right in front of the two Open House signs. Its siren was turned off after rounding the corner, although the phantom wailing continued in her ears for a few more moments.

Marci hesitantly put down the fascinating crime novel to go outside on the front porch to see what was happening, but she couldn't see where the cruiser had gone. Then the second vehicle, an ambulance, this time, barely made the corner and disappeared (without a siren) down the street and around the bend into the cul de sac. More sirens started up in the distance, coming from both directions now.

The hairs on Marci's neck, arms, legs, and head were standing on end as two more police cruisers and another emergency fire department ambulance whizzed by, with enough lights flashing to inaugurate a Presidential cavalcade.

She was still standing there, looking dumbfoundedly down the totally vacant street, when yet a fourth police cruiser, more lights flashing, slid to a sideways stop right in front of her, blocking the street to all traffic. Two officers jumped out with guns drawn, leaving their respective doors wide open. One stayed by the cruiser while the other, a muscular man with blackish brown eyes as serious as a heart attack, ran towards her.

"Ma'am, get back in the house, please. NOW!" In one involuntary reaction, Marci jumped back inside the front door.

"Are you alone?" was the next question in a long line of questions to follow. Marci could only nod. Her voice had lost its footing. The short, stocky officer, nevertheless, with gun still drawn, searched the house carefully, including closets, while closing each room's door behind him and locking each exit. Only then did he holster his gun and turn to face her, drawing out his notebook and pen as he did.

Marci barely registered that his name tag was Dredd.

"How long have you been at this Open House?"

"What time did you get here?"

"Was the other sign out when you got here?"

"How many people came through your Open House?"

"Was there anything suspicious about the one couple? Please describe them."

"Did you notice anything suspicious about street traffic? Any cars driving slowly by, for instance?"

"Any foot traffic on the street since you've been here?"

"Any dogs barking; any yelling or screaming?"

All of Marci's attempts to ask what happened, after answering each of the officer's questions, were interrupted with more staccato interrogative questions. The more questions he asked, the more frightened Marci got; the more frightened she got, the more her hands and voice shook, triggering an urgent need to visit the nearest toilet. An ice-cold knot of fear, as large as a softball, filled her stomach, chilling her to the bone.

"Stop. What happened? No more questions until you tell me what happened."

Finally, Officer Dredd told her the few scraps of information he knew, which was: The body of a young woman was found in the Open House down the street when the owners came home early, and initial reports were that several rooms in the house were quite gruesome.

Marci wished she hadn't insisted on knowing. Now she REALLY had to go to the bathroom, and barely made it.

Later that evening, after the tied baseball game was halted because of rain, Marci's husband got home to find three police messages on the recorder. "Please call the station immediately," they said. His wife was okay, but he needed to come pick her up.

As reality set in, Marci realized what a close call she had had that afternoon. A sympathetic policewoman gave her a shot of Jim Beam to steady her worsening nerves as she waited and waited for her husband to arrive. She correctly surmised that the murderer had seen Tom Little's name and face on his sign and thought a man was holding her Open House. The other sign, with the face of the young, blonde, smiling agent, alone and at the end of the street, must have magnetized him.

As soon as she was safely back at her home, she broke down sobbing in earnest and promptly threw up the shot of Jim Beam she'd tossed down an hour ago in an effort to calm her nerves, not making the bathroom this time.

When Ginger called a few days later to check on her, Marci told Ginger that she had been having recurring nightmares in which she saw her own name on the Open House signs that day. She never stepped foot back at Fakke & Co. Her husband brought in her lockboxes to give to Tom Little and took only her personal photos from her desk, tactfully avoiding her framed business license and real estate license. He took a job transfer to Portland, Oregon where we heard that Marci found safe work as a loan processor inside a national bank with lots of employees.

After that first call with Ginger, Marci never returned any of our calls. Personally, I had never been too crazy about holding Open Houses anyway, since national statistics show they account for less than 5% of all sales. After hearing Marci's story, unless the owners of a new listing insisted, I rarely did them from then on.

TWENTY

MIRIAM'S SOAP OPERA LIFE

Miriam was looking so stressed lately, I called an emergency Fab Five meeting. We all convened that night at Miriam's home with four bottles of wine after her girls were in bed.

We already knew that Miriam had been living her life on a roller coaster. Her trophy client from South Africa, Willems, had bought two homes and sold one within seventy-five days of bringing his family to San Marea. All three homes were well over $1.5 million each, so with her commissions in excess of $110,000, she and Claude had the down payment to buy a house. Their house was due east of San Marea, next to the polo fields in a very chic neighborhood. Miriam added to her Nordstrom wardrobe, acquiring expensive shoes and designer pantyhose and tights, everything still in black.

Claude had decided to quit his life as a strolling minstrel and opened a mortgage loan business in partnership with one of his drinking buddies. Even though neither one had a background in loans, none was seemingly needed. Miriam was making around $200,000 annually by her third year (nearly $500,000 in today's dollars), and she handed over every check to Claude, since he was a financial man now. He kept track of the money, paid the bills, got the girls to school, and she was free to just work and make more money. He drank almost nightly at Murphys with the other crowd of locals, and she joined many of those nights. That's how the Good Life looked to this hippy couple.

The smoke-and-mirror loan operation of Claude's lasted just two years before ending in bankruptcy. Its bankruptcy marked the end of their nine-year marriage also, when he left Miriam and her girls for his twenty-two-year-old secretary. Not only was the secretary slightly older than Miriam's oldest daughter, but she was pregnant with his child. These basic details were all she had told us before I remembered seeing her jump up from her desk in the office last week to go outside to pick up a discarded, still-live cigarette off the sidewalk and finish smoking it.

Instantly, I understood the enormity of her situation and was glad I had called the emergency meeting. Miriam was always a very private person and rarely shared anything without a bottle of wine or two to grease the wheels.

Miriam disclosed that in the two months since her husband had left, her attorney had pieced together the backstory, and it wasn't pretty.

Claude had left with everything they had in their joint bank account, except for fifty dollars. There had been over $115,000 in that account. The attorney said Claude had not only not paid IRS taxes for four years; he had not paid the first mortgage or the home equity mortgage for six months. He had failed to pay the minimum payment on the twenty-seven credit cards he'd opened with her income statements; or the lease payments on their two cars. They were all jointly-owned credit cards, and all were maxed out—some even above their limits.

The foreclosure sale for the house was imminent. Because California is a community property state and Claude had disappeared, Miriam was informed by her attorney that she owed almost $270,000 in IRS back taxes ($685,000 in today's dollars), another $350,000 ($885,000 today) from all the credit cards and the leases on her late model Mercedes and his brand-new Porsche, even though he had taken the Porsche when he left.

One day, right after Claude left, Miriam had received a call from a woman whose husband had worked for Claude. She told Miriam that Claude had actually taken his entire staff of four loan officers, their wives (including her), and his secretary to Hawaii on the week he was supposed to be at a convention. She overhead Claude joking at the bar that he had used up all the remaining credit card balances, and that he would be leaving Miriam as soon as he got back.

Mariam was sobbing by now. "Claude even waited a couple of extra days to put his plan into action, knowing I was due a big escrow commission, but the closing had gotten delayed. When it finally closed, I gave him my $27,000 commission check late on a Friday. He gave me a quick kiss, left for the bank, and never came back."

Lolly, Krista, Ginger, and I were stunned. We realized what a deep pit she was in—that her credit would be ruined for all time, probably, and we had no idea how to help. Miriam said she had a small escrow closing shortly and would have about $4,500 to find a place for her and the girls so they wouldn't see the sheriff coming when the foreclosure finalized next week.

The attorney told Miriam she would have to declare bankruptcy right away. He told her to anticipate her commissions to be garnished by the bankruptcy court as soon as she filed, but that hadn't happened yet. She had another escrow pending, with a $10,000 commission that she planned to have Granny hold for her so it couldn't be taken from her bank account. That way, she could have him distribute it to her little by little, so she could feed her girls and pay her rent.

Then the pendulum that was Miriam's life swung the other way.

The confessional door was open, and Miriam seemed relieved to be able to unburden herself. She had taken a new lover—a regionally famous artist. He was tall and ruggedly handsome with rumpled medium-length, dark, slightly curly hair, looking always like he had just gotten out of bed (to the delight of his groupies). She had met him at Murphys and began an 'affair to remember' with him.

My mind felt like it had been whiplashed from jerking from one extreme story to the next so quickly. Our regular Fab Five sharing of intimacies would normally have taken several sessions to cover these widely ranging stories, but Miriam was on a roll.

The four of us were still trying to wrap our minds around the mess Claude had left her in when she segued seamlessly into more about her new lover and her ultimate embarrassment just a few weeks ago

This embarrassing event involved an early 6 a.m. booty call with this famous artist at his studio. Other than guitar players, Miriam was attracted to artists—and they to her. Although she still practiced her free love religion while married, she confided that this artist was probably her soul mate. Until his untimely death a few years later from brain cancer, he repeatedly used Miriam to represent him in listing and selling several high-priced houses, further debunking my 'don't sleep with them first' theory. He had no family or children, so she cared for him in his final days.

This famous artist/lover (whose name and reputation we all knew, but never had found reason to discuss) had a small pottery studio in the adjoining city of Cardin. Even though it was small, he created enough product to supply six high-priced galleries around Southern California that sold his work.

An eight-foot rough, wooden stake fence surrounded his studio to afford him privacy from his groupies and from people wanting to steal his work instead of buying it. He kept the gate padlocked on the inside at all times. His front door could only be opened with a key, and he had the only one. Three short knocks were her arrival notice, but he usually opened the door on the second knock, she said.

After this particular early morning quickie, Miriam got into the shower and Mr. Famous Artist left for a 7 a.m. gallery meeting. Fifteen minutes later, a fully-dressed Miriam was confronted with a locked front door inside the studio and an eight-foot fence with a padlocked gate on the side yard. She was trapped and was supposed to meet a client to write an offer in ten minutes at the office. As always, the best real estate agents are the best problem solvers, so Miriam had to figure this out quickly.

Not having a key to the front door, going over the fence was her only escape. She stacked up some of her lover's wooden shipping boxes next to a barrel next to the gate. However, her slim black skirt was too tight to step up on them, and the rough wood of the fence was going to snag her thirty-eight dollar black Donna Karen tights that she had just bought yesterday.

(If you remember me saying that one of Miriam's dress codes didn't include wearing underwear, you have a mental image of what was to come next.)

So, like any real-estate-agent-with-no-other-expensive-Donna-Karen-tights-to-wear-to-her-meeting would have done, she took a quick look over the fence to make sure the street was clear this early in the morning. Then she tossed her Day Timer appointment book over the fence, took off her tights, and stuffed them into one shoe.

After tossing her shoes onto the street after her Day Timer, she hiked her tight black skirt up around her waist, stepped carefully up on top of two stacked wooden boxes in her bare feet, then the barrel, and threw both long legs over top of the fence like she was in a high jump competition.

She'd started to drop onto the sidewalk in her bare feet when she noticed an elderly man standing below her with his eyes wide in disbelief and his mouth hanging open. He had been taking his morning walk with his little white fluffy dog when Miriam's bare legs popped over the fence into view at his eye level.

In less than two hours and three bottles of wine, Lolly, Krista, Ginger, and I had run the emotional gamut from sympathy for Claude's betrayal of her to shock at the identity of her new lover, ending now with comic relief. We were all gasping for breath from laughing and trying not to wet our pants while an intensely red-faced Miriam ended her story with:

"I didn't know what to do. I was half over the fence, hanging with my bare naked everythings displayed for all the world to see, and I wasn't strong enough to pull myself back over the fence, so I had to drop onto the sidewalk right in front of the dog. I pulled down my skirt, picked up my scattered belongings, and muttered, "Have a nice day" to him as I walked The Walk of Shame as nonchalantly as I could, over to my car."

TWENTY-ONE

SUNDOWNER II —
MORE WHY AGENTS DRINK

I had a great story for tonight. Just a few hours earlier, I had been standing on the back deck of the new house that Tom and Nan had just bought. Nan was ecstatic because, from their deck, she could actually see the Nordstrom sign on the shopping center across the canyon. She and I made a toast to Nordstrom with our plastic glasses of celebratory champagne I had brought.

Tom casually said to me, "So, how much commission did you earn on this sale?"

I was so caught off guard, I couldn't say anything. I thought that they might think I made too much for just showing them one house.

But Tom finally said, "It looks like you don't remember me." Instantly, it dawned on me how I had met him, and then his question made sense.

About five months earlier on a holiday Monday, Tom had walked into our office. He needed to get a copy made before he put something in the mail and couldn't find any businesses open. On floor duty was the same lazy agent that had been there the day Jamison walked in. Same pose—with his legs on top of the desk, ankles crossed, reading a paperback.

Jon, the lazy agent, said, "Try the bank across the street".

Tom replied, "It's a holiday, the bank isn't open."

"Then try the copy place two blocks up the street."

"I've already been there, and to two other real estate offices on this street. No one is open today. I'll be glad to pay for a copy, it's just a few pages."

Jon's reply was to shrug and glance back down at his riveting paperback, signaling the end of this conversation.

Tom was already out on the sidewalk before I could grab the front door and invite him back inside.

"Please come back, I'll be glad to make copies for you."

I led him past lazy Jon to the copy room at the back of our office. He handed me some legal-looking papers that were way more than a few pages, so we chatted amiably while we waited as our cheap copier slowly made copies, one . . . at . . . a . . . time.

Tom told me he and his wife were living in a rental in the Beach Colony of San Marea, enjoying a nice relaxing summer before purchasing a home at the end of the year when their lease was up. He wanted to know what the real estate market was like these days, so I gladly shared my opinion.

When the copies were done, I took a 9 x 12-inch brown envelope and placed the original and the copies inside for him to keep them together. Tom said, "I really, really appreciate your help. How much do I owe you for the copies?"

I smiled and said kiddingly, *"You don't owe me anything. I'm glad I was here to help. But when you're ready to buy a home, come back to me. I'll be your agent, and these will be the most expensive copies you've ever made!"*

A few months later, the phone rang at my desk. A woman's voice excitedly said, "We're finally ready to buy a home, and my husband says we need to work with you. He found an ad for a perfect house in the area we want. It's $535,000, and we want to see it as soon as possible." As I always do, I asked her how they heard about me, but she said she didn't know. Her husband just gave her my name and told her to call me.

Tom and Nan were dream clients. I showed them the house they found in that ad, and they put it in escrow. The showing and their offer went so quickly, I never thought to ask Tom how he had found me. They paid cash and the house was vacant, so it was a quick close.

Tom's question this afternoon was not about how much commission I'd made—he wanted to know the cost of the copies I had made for him five months ago. He and Nan both seemed pleased to hear that his copies cost *$634 per page.*

Ginger leaned forward to refill her wine glass and said, "We haven't heard from you yet, Krista. How did your date go this weekend, to meet your boyfriend's parents? You said they lived in Washington D.C. Were they out here?"

Thus prompted, Krista blushed a bright crimson, leaned over, and started to whisper conspiratorially, even though there was no one else in the office. "His parents live in Washington D.C., so we had to fly to meet them. When he picked me up in his jeep on Friday morning, we went to the San Diego Airport, but he drove around back to a private parking lot. You aren't going to believe this, and you absolutely can't tell anyone—we flew on *Air Force One*—his parents live in the White House!

"Lolly, I have to tell you, for the first time in my life, I wished I taken your advice and had better clothes to wear so I didn't look so much like a surfer chick. But his parents were gracious. His mom and I had a great time talking about real estate and dancing. Her mother had been a real estate agent at one time after her father died, and you know how much I love to dance. I met his sister, and we actually stayed upstairs in the private quarters."

Our mouths were hanging so far open, it was a wonder our tonsils didn't fall out. The details were sketchy, as Krista didn't want to talk too much about it, although we could tell she had been dying to tell someone. (For those of you wondering who the boyfriend was, the answer is *Yes!*)

Leave it to Ginger to inquire bluntly, "So, Krista, are you a member of the Mile High Club, now?" Silently, Krista's raised eyebrows, lowered eyelashes, and increased blushing answered Ginger's question.

Lolly closed us out that night with an update on a story that had started in January. Granny had run a sales contest for the last six months of the year. Any client who bought or sold a home with a Fakke agent would be entered into a grand prize drawing to win a pair of darling yellow Volkswagen Foxes, as seen in his ads. One car was for the winning client(s) and the other for their agent.

After all his advertising and showmanship in drawing the

winning client's name from a giant rotating metal drum (like a church might use in a bingo game), the winner was Robb, an attorney, and his agent, Marie. Marie was the office hardship case. Her car had been repossessed right before Thanksgiving, and her clients had to drive when she showed them houses. Every agent there had been thrilled that Marie's luck was turning around—until Granny added that they had both won a *one-year lease* on the yellow Foxes.

Lease? There had been no mention in the advertising that the prize was two *leased* cars. All the TV and newspaper ads said the prize was two cars, period.

Lolly's update was that Marie's attorney client, Robb, had gone into Granny's office on Monday after the drawing with a copy of the ads Granny had been running. When Granny didn't budge on the prize suddenly being a year's lease, Robb had taken both cars and put them in storage somewhere. Marie didn't know where, but in a year when Granny would have to buy them because he couldn't turn them in, she would have her car.

TWENTY-TWO

WHEN THE WRONG HOUSE IS THE RIGHT HOUSE

Sam and Sandy were one of my best success stories, in a very serendipitous way.

Sandy was a librarian and Sam was a new engineer at a large company with even larger government contracts. He had survived polio as a child and, at age twenty-nine, still wore leg braces to help himself walk. He must have had a severe case of polio, as he had to swing his hips forward to be able to walk. Obviously they needed a one-story home, but their income was hampering their ability to buy in San Marea. So they chose La Casa, a good area about ten miles north of San Marea, and we started looking one sunny Spring Sunday.

At 11%, the interest rates were down from the 14% of two years ago but were still high enough to hamper a buyer's ability to get a loan. Even though I tried to show them only single level homes, I never knew how many stairs existed in everyday life until I saw it through Sam's eyes.

The first house we looked at, Sandy fell in love with, and they made an offer. Theirs was one offer of eight so I padded the accompanying exhibits with a heartfelt letter from them about why they loved what the sellers had done, a copy of their bank statement, a pre-approval loan commitment from their credit union, and a cover letter from me.

But they required 90% financing, so they were passed over for an all-cash, non-contingent offer. To console Sandy, I assured her that every time I had ever seen someone lose out on a bid for a house, a better one always appeared. Always. But she wasn't to believe me for several months.

After another three weeks of weekends looking, nothing compared to the one they lost. On our way to the last home on today's tour, we drove past a new Open House listing that looked one-level. Once inside, it was a disappointment. It had a sunken living room and a raised dining area. I didn't know the agent, Margie, but chatted with her about the house while Sandy and Sam looked in the bedrooms.

Suddenly, Margie froze and her eyes widened. She grabbed my arm and whispered in a panic, "Don't leave me. That's my husband coming up the driveway. We're getting divorced, and I have a restraining order to keep him away. He's not supposed to be here. I'm frightened. I need to call the police—talk to him; do *something*—just please don't leave me."

I had never met Margie's husband, but it wasn't unusual for a husband to come visit with his wife at an Open House if he was bored being alone on a Sunday. I greeted him at the door to give her some time to make her call. Her husband introduced himself as Ron before asking about Margie. He was about 5'9" with a military-style haircut, wearing shorts and a Guns N' Roses Tour tee shirt. Because I wasn't a psychic, I didn't see the subliminal message of his wearing that tee. He was pleasant and spoke nonchalantly with me.

I didn't sense any anger or anything 'off' about him, so I figured Margie was being over-reactive because of their divorce. Sam and Sandy were already swinging their way down the sidewalk towards my car, so I yelled down the hall toward Margi, *"Your husband is here. I've got to go"*. Then I excused myself to Ron by saying, *"Why don't you take a seat on the couch? Margie is in the bathroom and will be right with you."*

The three of us sat in the car for a few minutes, looking at the MLS printout and map on the final home of the day. As I pulled away from the curb, I heard police sirens in the distance. Simultaneously, in the rearview mirror, I saw Margie running in a zigzag pattern from the house out into the street and towards the cul-de-sac. Sam and Sandy were quietly discussing the next home as this unfolded two houses away behind us.

Concurrently, I head a 'pop' and Margie seemed to trip and fall face down in the street. My buyers were oblivious to her fall, although they had looked around when they heard me say 'ouch', but they didn't look behind us.

The sirens were very loud, now. Oh my God, that sounded like a gunshot. It spurred me forward. I floored the gas pedal and almost hit the police car coming around the corner. I was so rattled that I drove right past the last home on today's tour and was back at my office in San Marea before everything started to sink in. I told Sam and Sandy that I didn't stop at the last house because it had sold yesterday, and I forgot to tell them. I was worried about Margie and was anxious to get back in the car and go see if I could give her some moral support with her husband and the police. I desperately wanted to apologize for leaving her when she had asked me to stay.

When I got close to Margie's Open House, the street was cordoned off two blocks away. I could see several police cars, an ambulance, and a fire truck in the distance when, suddenly, a Life-Flight helicopter rose up above the roof tops and flew away.

The lead news story on TV that night said, "Estranged husband shoots wife and then commits suicide in La Casa. Wife is in critical condition at a local hospital." I didn't want to hear the story; I already knew most of it, and I couldn't have felt worse for misjudging the situation and leaving her than I already did.

The following weekend, I took Sam and Sandy, who were fast becoming my good 'weekend' friends, down into San Diego to try a different neighborhood. We looked at several cute bungalows, but Sandy had really, really liked the second house we had seen that day.

It was a storybook little white stucco home with a red tile roof. It was situated on a canyon rim, and the back of the house overlooked the canyon, which dropped off precipitously behind the rear fence. By lowering the rear fence about three feet, it would open up a panoramic view over the San Diego River and city lights would twinkle at night, she thought. It was a little pricey for a small two-bedroom with hardwood floors, arched doorways, shutters, and an original fifties kitchen, but it could be in their price range if I could negotiate about a $25k lower price.

We were at the final house for the day when I started hearing sirens in the distance. We stood on the balcony of this house and could see smoke in the sky back over the neighborhood where we had seen the little white house. Sandy wanted to take a second look at that home before we called it a day. We had all seen the smoke and heard the sirens, but I couldn't tell specifically where the fire was. However, I started to worry it might be close to the little house when I had to drive over a fat fire hose laying across the street right before I got to it. People were running down the street, kids were crying, moms were yelling. A fire truck was stationed a little past the house and a fireman with a bull horn was broadcasting something I couldn't understand.

I told Sam and Sandy we had to make this one quick, as one of the other houses in the neighborhood must be on fire and we didn't want to be in the way. Sam tried to hurry, but obviously couldn't, with his heavy leg braces.

Sandy loved the house, loved the kitchen, and started making mental notes about what furniture she might ask for in the offer. Just one more thing before we left—she wanted to take another quick look at the view, so she asked me to give her one more minute. I was still inside the house, so hadn't seen the smoke rising behind the fence. Sandy was very short, so the fence must have blocked it from her view. She stepped out the back door in the kitchen, took four steps, and unlatched the gate.

The view was of a wall of flames so thick, you couldn't even see the smoke behind it, and it was just about to attach itself to the fence when she opened the gate. I heard someone scream at the top of their lungs, and very close by, *"OH MY GOD, RUN!"*

It wasn't SOMEONE screaming— it was ME—and we ran so fast, my words were left hanging in the air. Sam ran, too, and I swear he beat Sandy and me to my car, parked at the curb.

Of course, being the good real estate agent even in the face of Death by Fire, after slamming the back door shut, I locked the front door, got the key back into the lockbox, and was driving back over the fire hose to safety in maybe ten seconds flat.

The next day on Monday morning, my buyers still wanted to make an offer on the house, if it was still standing. The evening news had said the fire started in a homeless camp under a freeway overpass and was fanned up the hillside by Santa Ana winds. Twenty-seven homes were lost and one right in the middle, for some unknown reason, lost only part of its fence.

That was my first encounter with Brian Buffini, who was the listing agent. (In later years, he would become a world-famous 'By Referral' real estate coach.) Brian confirmed the house was still standing but was adamant I come look at it before I sent him an offer.

I drove back down to San Diego to do what he asked before sending him my offer. As I sat in my car and looked at the carnage on the street, my hands started shaking so badly, I couldn't even drive. The little house Sandy loved was the ONLY house left standing on the block. At least five houses were burnt to the ground on both sides of it and part of the rear fence was blackened and gone. It looked like a marshmallow that had been burned on one side while being roasted. But it was standing.

Granny had taught us agents to never get in the way of someone wanting to buy a home. It was to be their choice, not ours. Just set our own personal judgement aside and do what they asked, even if their choice was under power lines, even if it was on a busy street or next to a freeway. Our job was to help them buy whatever house they choose.

I had never taken Granny's advice before, and I wasn't about to now. I pointed out that, yes, Sam and Sandy could buy it and probably get a great deal given the circumstances. However, there would be a couple years of noisy demolition and construction ahead, and then their house would be the only old one in a brand spanking new neighborhood. Bad for them. Very bad. Very, very bad. Finally, albeit reluctantly, they agreed.

We had seen all the homes in their price range within fifteen miles north of San Marea, and all the ones within fifteen miles south, so the only area left was inland and due East of San Marea. There was a Navy air base in between them, and much of that area had jet airplane noise to contend with. I was also quite nervous, as we had had two close calls. I was beginning to wonder if perhaps we had bad Karma together. Maybe we'd live longer by not working together? I swore to myself that if we had even one more remotely close call, as nice as Sam and Sandy were, I would have to save myself and let another agent find them a home.

On Sunday, the three of us drove by the easterly neighborhood known as Silverwood. Sam and Sandy's tongues were hanging out. All the homes were on half acre lots, and many were Spanish hacienda one-story style with white stucco, red clay tile roofs, and dark brown wood trim. Many had three-car garages.

We passed one so beautiful that they asked me to stop just so they could look at it. It had a split rail fence around it, abundant fruit trees, and a colorful rose garden. It was manicured and serene—a dream come true. At the corner of its lot where two streets intersected was a for sale sign. I looked it up in my MLS Blue Book and was not surprised to see that it was already in escrow, according to the book. At $355,000, it was above their price range anyway. I drove down to the local Mini Mart to use the pay phone to call the agent, just going through the motions for the heartbroken couple in my car.

The listing agent wasn't in the office, but the secretary said it had just fallen out of escrow, and yes, that was the correct price, and here was the tenant's phone number to make an appointment. The lady who answered the phone said to give her ten minutes to tidy up the house before we came in, so we drove back up the street, parked outside the front walkway, and sat in the car to check out the sizable front yard, the fruit trees, and the rose bushes.

In ten minutes, a car pulled out of the garage and left, so we walked up to the front door. The man who answered the door looked perplexed. He didn't know the house was back on the market, and his wife had just left for the store without telling him someone was coming to look at it. I assured him that I had checked with the listing agent's company, and they'd said for sure it was back on the market, so he graciously allowed us in.

The house was more unbelievable inside than outside. The ceilings were low and had exposed beams, and the kitchen had old fashioned handmade white tile with blue and white Mexican designs on the counters and back splash. The cabinetry was yellowed knotty pine with handmade wrought iron hinges and pulls. I just kept shaking my head. This house should be way more expensive. I couldn't believe my clients' good fortune. Sam had overcome adversity and polio with cheerfulness and love, and I was convinced this was his reward. I was a HERO to find it had just fallen out of escrow. PERFECT, I thought!

Back at the office, I told them I would write the offer and contact the seller tonight after I looked up the ownership on our microfiche (film formatted) library. The MLS showed the listing date had expired while it was in escrow, and since the agent was out of town, it probably hadn't been renewed. I would be sure to ask first thing when I got the owner on the phone.

I realized this offer would take longer to get accepted when I read that the owner's name was Robertson, and their address was in St Louis. But the occupant was a tenant, so the fact that the owner didn't live locally meant I would have to send the offer via overnight mail. I called the Missouri phone number listed in the microfiche.

A woman answered and I told her I had an offer on her home in Silverwood from a delightful and deserving young couple and asked how I could present it.

There was a pregnant pause on the other end that got more and more pregnant as the minutes passed. Finally, Mrs. Robertson said, "The market is so bad out there that when it fell out of escrow, we just decided to rent it out until next year. I'm surprised the listing agent's office didn't tell you our listing expired while we were in escrow, and we didn't renew it. But, we are interested in selling it, so let me ask my husband; and will you please call me back tomorrow?"

I'm sure all three of us had our fingers crossed, prayers said, and candles lit all evening. When I called back the following day and gave them my clients' best offer of $300,000, it was again noticeably quiet on the phone. Finally, a small, sad voice said that they had over $325,000 in it. They had bought the lot and custom build package six years ago. It only looked old because they paid the architect and builder to make it that way. They just couldn't sell at $300,000. $325,000 was as low as they could go. I imagined both Sam and Sandy cried themselves to sleep that night. They were really, really in love with that house.

Ever the enterprising agent and ex-mortgage officer, I had been watching the interest rates coming down over the past couple of weeks, and if they would just come down another half of one percent, I told Sandy they could qualify for the payments at $325,000. It was like throwing a life jacket to a drowning person. They called me every evening at 5 p.m. to see what the rates had done that day. And, sure enough, about ten days later, The Universe aligned, the interest rate dropped into the target range, and we re-wrote the offer for $325,000 and sent it by overnight mail to the waiting Robertsons.

After an eternity of nail biting, the signed offer came back in the mail five days later. I called the number I still had for Robertson's tenants, and this time the man answered. I told him I wanted to bring the buyers back to look again. I didn't mention the sale, as I wanted Mrs. Robertson to deliver that news.

Sandy cried tears of joy all the way from the front door through the kitchen and into the living room. The drapes had been drawn, before, making the living room very dark, so she drew back the drapes and gasped.

There was a wonderful view of local Lake Hodges. I couldn't believe my eyes; this house should have been priced at $500,000, not $325,000.

After dropping a glowing Sam and Sandy off at their car, I retrieved a hostile message from the Silverwood listing agent who had been on vacation this past week. Her sellers were FURIOUS. I had made two appointments to show their house and never shown up, either time. What kind of agent was I, anyway? I gave agents everywhere a bad reputation, etc. etc. etc. After a five-minute tirade, I was able to respond. I said "I have no idea what you are talking about. Your listing was expired, you were out of town, I called the Robertsons in Missouri, and the tenants had let me in. Twice. You must be mad at the wrong agent."

She informed me in her most nasty voice, her sellers did not live in Missouri and were not named Robertson. Was I talking about the Spanish house on the corner, priced at $550,000, that fell out of escrow last month? That wasn't her listing anymore, and those weren't her sellers. With that, she hung up on me.

I found an old MLS Blue Book from five months ago. There was the house I had just sold for $325,000 but it was listed at $550,000. And, on a different page, there was her listing, priced at $355,000. But, instead of being **5525** Silverwood, it was **5255** Silverwood. Both were Spanish architecture, but side by side, they were obviously different. Hers was a three-bedroom tract home at 2,000 square feet. I suddenly realized I had been talking to the owners of her listing while selling an entirely different house that was larger and priced $200,000 higher.

No wonder the woman was mad, as I had done that to her owners twice. Tenants were occupying the custom house we actually looked at, and didn't question that I kept showing up unannounced. So it was understandable that they didn't know what was going on. All they knew was that the house had been for sale and the escrow had fallen through, and different buyers were now looking at it.

Neither my buyers nor myself realized there were two totally different homes with similar stories, whose addresses were almost identical, and both were on Silverwood Street. I laughingly told myself this entire chain of events was all the listing agent's fault for taking a vacation and not being available to answer my initial questions when I was first trying to gain access for my buyers

Yes, The Universe aligned for Sam and Sandy. I didn't tell them the real story until the day they closed escrow, as I was embarrassed about the mix-up. I thought it made me look like I didn't know what I was doing—because—I didn't. But when we sat in their living room with glasses of wine and watched the sun set over Lake Hodges, the story just came out of my mouth, with the help of a little wine.

PS. The story of Margie, the Open House agent, continued for some time. Although Margie had been shot in the head, she survived with some memory and motor skill loss. She moved to Oregon about five months after the shooting to recover at her sister's house, so I never got the opportunity to apologize. Her husband had committed suicide in her client's Open House right before the police arrived. I couldn't even imagine how the poor owners of that house disclosed that series of events.

TWENTY-THREE

ONE BLACK DOG AND TWO PSYCHOS

I really needed to take a day off. I had been working for almost an entire month without a break. In this real estate sales business, if you left a buyer to themselves for even a day when they were in the buying mood, you might wake up to find that they bought with another agent. An agent who DIDN'T take the day off and was holding an Open House. I only felt safe taking a day off if it was raining. Then, after educating my buyers on the perils of a rainy day, they wouldn't risk going out with another agent and falling down on slippery wet floors or sidewalks.

But, today it didn't rain, so I was left to show houses to my clients Mildred, a psychologist, and her fiancé Shelby, who was a psychiatrist. Mildred was excited to see the house I described to her over the phone; it sounded perfect to her. She'd been looking for two years off and on and was tired of looking. She wanted a house and wanted to be married to Shelby—in that order.

Mildred was a short, Plain Jane brainiac in her fifties with wire-rimmed glasses, non-descript straight mousy brown hair that she cut herself, and sensible sandals. She had no sense of fashion, as is stereotypical of someone who has been practicing psychology for twenty-five years. Her sensible, wrinkled cotton clothes usually blended with her hair. This was to be her first marriage and she was in the nesting mood big time, so I was calling to check in with her every day.

Shelby was a seventy-ish Maxi-Me (the plus-sized polar opposite of a Mini-Me). He embodied a proper British butler. He had a ruddy complexion, thick black framed glasses, distinguished silver hair with matching bushy eyebrows, mustache and a goatee. He had four other marriages under his belt ('under his belt' had he worn a belt instead of suspenders).

The few times I'd seen Shelby, he was dressed in a psychiatrist's uniform—tweed jacket, black turtleneck sweater, corduroy slacks, and a black beret. His face was so camouflaged under the beret, facial hair, and glasses, he looked like he was hiding from something or someone. Witness protection, perhaps? I assumed he smoked a pipe at home because that was all that was missing to identify him as a distinguished Doctor of Psychiatry who had been practicing for over forty years (both at his profession and also at being distinguished).

Shelby didn't show up again today, as usual, because, as he informed me on the day we met, he didn't like to look at houses. Plus, he preferred to stroll while contemplating other people's stuff in preparation for analyzing their motive for selling, and Mildred always prodded him to hurry along.

So, Mildred flew solo into the office and off we went. When we drove up to the house, it was already 'perfect' (according to Mildred's pronouncement). They had been looking, most recently now, for three months—the average time it takes a buyer to locate and buy a home—and she was READY!

The house was a charming (meaning smallish, in real estate jargon), single-story, wood-shingled home with a wood shake roof and a brick chimney. The brown and tan color palette was offset by Forest Service green wood casement windows. There was a low wood fence around the front yard that would have been painted white, had it been pickets. However, it was only two horizontal poles high, and made of wood which had silvered-out by years of coastal weathering. In other words, this house conjured up a vision of the charming house described in The Three Little Pigs.

There were flower beds in bloom. There were pansies, snap-dragons, bachelor buttons, and sea pinks, with a gardenia bush here and there lining the brick walk-way to the glass-paned single French door entrance. This pastorally charming picture was complete with a small, compact, black Labrador-type dog sitting on the walk, wagging its tail in welcome as we approached.

Perfect, I mistakenly thought to myself (it was still early in my career).

Mildred had been so hard to please, I held my breath as we stepped into the house. From the first step inside the front door, the house measured up to both of our expectations. "Perfect!" she exclaimed while clapping her hands together for emphasis.

There was one slight problem—today was Broker Caravan Open House for agents. The house was so small, agents were bumping into each other everywhere as we all tried to move around. If you have ever stuck a stick into an ant hill and poked it a few times to make the ants swarm out looking for a fight—that's the sight in store for you on Caravan Day. It was a seller's market as commission-hungry agents previewed the new listings—especially the charming ones in good neighborhoods that were well priced like this one. Every agent gave each other the 'stink eye' so the house wouldn't be sold before they had a chance to show it to THEIR client.

But I had them all beat, this time. I had my client WITH me today, and she was looking for her checkbook, but was not finding it.

Since this was the age prior to cell phones or pagers, we were in a quandary as to how to get ahold of Shelby so he could come put his seal of approval on the house and bring the checkbook. If we used the phone in the house, it would alert the other agents, so stealth and discretion were in order. My office was a good eight minutes away, and every minute was precious with all these agents potentially competing for this easy sale.

I prayed and The Universe answered. I had sold the house across the street a few years ago, and as good fortune would have it, my old client was just getting home. Mildred and I scurried across the street to use her phone to call Shelby, followed good-naturedly by the overly friendly black lab dog. *Perfect*, I thought again. *Today, The Universe is on my side.*

Shelby only had a short time open between clients, he said. But he was pressured by Mildred to jump in his car, follow these easy directions to meet us, and bring the checkbook—and make sure that it had checks in it.

While we waited, I sat in my car with Mildred and started filling out the Contract to Purchase. She took the opportunity to walk back through to see if there were any items to include in the offer, like the refrigerator, washer and dryer, patio furniture, or other furnishings that caught her eye.

I always encouraged clients to ask for extras so they would have something to give up during negotiations. Depending on what was important to each individual, everyone wanted to feel like they'd negotiated something in the sale for themselves—both buyers and sellers. So, if my clients asked for things they didn't even want, then gave those things up during the counter offers, they ended up with everything they DID want, and the sellers felt good at having deprived the new buyers of something.

The time was dragging by—where was Shelby? I ran back across the street to call him again. He was still at home, looking for a map, as he wasn't sure he could find the house using my directions. Now he was feeling the time pinch; he had used up ten precious minutes looking for the map, so I told him to drive to my office and wait on the sidewalk in front so he could jump in with us as we drove by.

Mildred and I sped off to the office where Shelby was waiting outside with a black checkbook in his hand—a checkbook that matched his beret, I noted. Shelby was looking perturbed. Although his body language showed he was disgruntled that he was not in charge of the new life he and Mildred were embarking on, I was falsely encouraged because he had brought the checkbook.

Back to the little Perfect House with the Black Dog, as Mildred and I were now calling it. This is a universal habit among buyers and agents, to nickname a house as they struggle to keep them straight in their head. So, you might have the Smelly House, the House with the Red Bathroom, the House with the Pink Shag Carpet, etc. But today, it was the Perfect House with the Black Dog, who was still there to greet us, happily wagging his tail.

Shelby didn't like the house.

A crestfallen Mildred had tears in her eyes that were starting to arc into sparks as she demanded to know why. Shelby didn't want to discuss it, he just needed to quickly get back to his car and his next client, saying that they would discuss it tonight.

But when Shelby opened the back door to the car for Mildred, the friendly black lab jumped in first. It was funny, initially, until we realized the dog was not about to get out of the back seat. The more we tried to coax him out, the more he just looked away and ignored us. It didn't take a dog whisperer to translate his intentions. When Shelby tried to reach for him, he slowly curled his upper lip into a not-so-friendly sneer—which translates as a snarl without the sound—and asserted himself as a not-so-friendly Top (black) Dog.

I suggested that maybe the dog just wanted to go for a ride, and why didn't I take him around the block while they took another quick look at the house. I'd be right back. All Shelby did was keep looking at his watch. He was avoiding all eye contact with Mildred, me, or the dog, but nevertheless was petulantly conveying his irritations. He didn't like the house, and he was going to be late for his next appointment. His ruddy complexion darkened and reddened down his neck into his black turtleneck sweater.

I quickly drove the dog around the block—three stop signs, of course, just to irritate me—and came back. By this time, even though I had the windows closed, I could hear Mildred and Shelby yelling at each other in the driveway of the Perfect House, with amused agents coming and going around them. The black lab quickly jumped out as soon as I opened the door and gave me a grateful wink as he ambled down the street, sniffing and peeing on bushes as he went.

Just as quickly, Shelby got in the back seat, with Mildred getting in right next to him to continue the fight. As I chauffeured them back to my office, the shouting and fighting between them escalated. Mildred wanted that house, and if he really loved her, he would buy it for her. Shelby's counter was it needed too much work; he wanted a brand-new house (something he had never mentioned in the past twelve weeks) with an office upstairs where he could counsel clients (something else he had never mentioned, as we had been looking at a single-level homes these past two years in preparation for their retirement years). And, besides, he was a cat person. He detested dogs. He said this as though he assumed the black lab would come with the house.

I didn't quite know what to do. I was mentally debating on whether to turn on the radio and pretend they weren't there, or try to overcome some of Shelby's objections before we got back to the office. However, I lost my chance to talk to my captive audience when I had to obey yet another stop sign.

It happened in the blink of an eye, and, thank heavens, I was completely stopped: Mildred reached across Shelby to the door handle, opened up the rear door, and proceeded to use both her feet and other hand to try to push Shelby out onto the street. Concurrently, at the top of her lungs, she profanely informed him that if he did not buy her this house, not only was he going to walk back to his car, but the wedding was off.

Here's the visual I caught in a glimpse over my shoulder: Shelby's distinguished face was bright red and upside down, making his silver, bushy eyebrows (now centered in his glasses lenses), mustache, and goatee almost iridescent in contrast. His little black beret was the only thing between his head and the asphalt, as he was holding on for dear life with one hand to the inside door handle. His size fifteen feet were wedged on the floor underneath the back of the front seat while little mousy Mildred had both feet against his shoulder and butt.

She was straining to push him out of the car into the world as though she were birthing him, by using her hands to hold on to the seat for leverage. Her face was equally bright red, with the veins on her neck standing out. It was an Andy Warhol-type of warped, post-menopausal birth scene—Freud could have had fun with that dream, if only it had been a dream.

Mildred was winning the battle, but ultimately I knew, she would not win the fight. Any potential commission was already history. Amidst the chaos in my back seat, in a moment of lucidity, I realized that neither of them was using any psychological arguments to persuade the other. Their sixty-five years of combined training was expressed in profanity, physical, and verbal abuse. They had both reverted into a primal state to get what they wanted! (If only their patients could had been present to watch and learn from their conflict resolution example.)

Out went Shelby on his distinguished head, hands, and knees in downtown San Mario, while Mildred turned her fury at me, instructing me to drive off and leave the Bastard. So I did.

While I never saw them again, a week later, Mildred did call extremely late one night, making sure I wouldn't be there to answer. She left a message on my work answering machine to apologize for Shelby's behavior, ending with, "Thank you so much for your time."

TWENTY-FOUR

THE DAY MY TOENAILS FELL OFF

We all know about Mondays—it's the day after two weekend days of relaxation when normal people are jerked into a reality full of issues, problems, and disasters at work.

In the world of real estate agents, however, we rarely get a few days off together for relaxation, and NEVER on a weekend. Agents rarely even get one day, and even more rarely do they ever feel relaxed. A real estate agent's life is one continuing sequence of issues, problems, and disasters that don't take time off. If an agent is *not* experiencing that, they don't have any business.

Even though it was Thursday, my week was continuing to be a week of Mondays. I had been on the run every minute of every day, starting with getting out of bed to take the first phone call at 7 a.m. until I collapsed back into it at midnight after trying to catch up on my paperwork.

I put all my clients' needs first, even at my own inconvenience. I have postponed vacations, missed friend's birthdays, missed the first half of plays or concerts, rescheduled hard to get doctor appointments just to get a client's offer written, or presented, or accepted. I hadn't had a day off in several months, but I was also selling up a storm. It looked like I might open eleven escrows this month, raising my star yet another notch in the office.

Granny was adamant that the real estate industry had expectations of professional dress. If it weren't for him and Ginger's urgings, I wouldn't be wearing gel-coated fingernails, or letting my toenails grow long and painting them bright red to look beautiful in stylish, open-toed shoes. I wouldn't be getting my legs, armpits, and crotch waxed. I wouldn't be putting on weight from all the fast food I downed while driving. Some days (usually Mondays, for me), real estate was just not my friend, and today promised to be yet another Monday.

I had ten new sales in escrow this month so far, and was concentrating this past week on getting an offer out of Sherry and Dave, who were looking at million-dollar homes in Rancho de Rio (a less expensive subdivision adjacent to The Ranch). My other possibility would be Rob and Theresa, who were looking for the perfect lot to build their dream home. These two clients were my best chance of hitting at least eleven escrows (eleven has always been my lucky number), with only five days left in the month.

I mentally compared myself to a car salesman working feverishly to hit a dealership quota to win a $500 bonus for his production. But I wasn't a car salesman, I didn't work for a dealership, and Fakke & Co. didn't have quotas. The bonuses I would receive from those two extra sales would total more like $20,000.

Like all high-producing agents, I had built-in goals that fueled my drive. Sometimes it was just for the satisfaction of achieving a personal goal, but most of the time it was the looming bottom of an empty checkbook that was setting the pace.

Granny had once said in an office meeting that the lament of real estate agents everywhere was, "God, please give me one more large commission and I promise I won't p-ss it away this time." I could, and still can, relate.

This morning, before meeting Sherry and Dave at 10 a.m., I had already made a dozen phone calls, met one physical inspector and one appraiser, solved world hunger and created peace in the Middle East. I was looking forward to showing Sherry and Dave a wonderfully unique house in Rancho. I was 99% sure this was destined to be my eleventh escrow.

The middle of this fascinating house was a geodesic dome. The listing comments said, "A geodesic dome has a spherical form composed of triangular facets, birthed from Buckminster Fuller's goal of creating a structure to reflect nature's own designs." This unusual structure was hidden inside an innocuous exterior that the Rancho architectural committee had easily approved. The sellers were concert musicians who adored the acoustically perfect orb of a living room, which contained their two baby grand pianos.

The off-shoot of being acoustically perfect is that if you are standing anywhere in it, even a whisper can be heard distinctly by everyone present. The house had two wings opposite each other, with Romeo and Juliet balconies facing each other at the point where each wing joined the dome's middle. The balconies over-looked the pianos, and Sherry had fallen in love with them. She said Dave was soooo romantic, and she could stand on one of the balconies while he whispered love sonnets to her and be able to hear his every word. Of course, the sellers overhead her every word, so they silently eased onto a bench and softly played the love theme from the Romeo and Juliet opera to hasten the offer. We spent almost two hours at that house, so I rushed off, trying not to be late for my next appointment.

I had been showing land, off and on, for a month to Rob and Theresa, necessitating that I wear boots or sturdy shoes to tramp around unimproved property looking for boundary pins. I always carried boots in my car to be ready for tramping, but I really wasn't looking forward to showing land today. Today, my feet hurt, my head hurt, even my hair hurt like it does with a hangover. But I didn't have an alcohol inspired hangover, I had a too-much-work inspired hangover.

After looking for two months, today Rob and Theresa had spent three hours looking at the four lots, and then we wrote an offer on the first lot I ever showed them sixty days earlier. It was less than the asking price, but I had hopes of turning it into my twelfth escrow before the end of the month. I had hopes it would solidify my elusive perception of myself as truly being a Top Agent.

I still had several hours of phone calls and paperwork in the office before I could head home. It was after 9 p.m. when I drug myself through the front door of my house. I was too exhausted to eat. Like a horse heading to its barn, all I wanted was to get into my Jacuzzi-type tub of bubbling hot water with a glass of red wine, then collapse into bed.

As I got out of the tub thirty minutes later, after a good long soak, the phone rang. Dripping wet and wrapped only in a towel, I tried not to slip on the bathroom tile as I rushed to the phone beside my bed. It was Sherry (as in Sherry and Dave, my million-dollar buyers). Sherry needed to talk, she whispered, while Dave was in the living room watching the end of the Thursday Night football game on TV. His birthday was coming up in a couple of weeks, and she needed a favor. A big favor, she said.

They hadn't bought a house yet, but we'd looked almost every day this week, and they were close. Even though I was rapidly getting chilled, sitting on my bed wrapped in a wet towel, I said to myself, *Perfect*. I do a favor for them, and they'll owe me a favor— like the maybe twelfth escrow I had in mind.

"Sure, I'd be glad to do a favor for you, just name it."

"Well, I want you to know that Dave and I really like you."

"Yes, I like you, too."

"I mean, Dave and I really, REALLY like you. Dave, especially, REALLY likes you."

"Ok," I said. *"I appreciate you guys, too. I've been really enjoying working with you—and I don't just say that to everyone."* But on my side of the phone, I was thinking—*I would really, REALLY like you better if you cut this call short and buy that $1.2 million house we looked at today.*

"So, here's the favor. Dave's birthday is next week, and I wanted to give him something special. We, um, have a great sex life. Um, and sometimes we film ourselves having sex so we can watch it later, um. Have you ever done that?"

"No, I can't say that I have. Why do you ask?"

"Well, um, Dave was mentioning the other day that he wishes we had some closeups of us kissing, and closeups of our faces as we have our orgasms. The camera we use is on a tripod, and we can only have one shot of us on the bed. There's no way to stop and get closeups.

"Um, so here is the favor—we really, really like you, and Dave really really, REALLY likes you . . . would you come over here on his birthday and take closeups of us making love? You know we trust you, and you know everything about us anyway, from all the questions you've been asking as we look at homes. This is not that big of a thing, is it? Please say you'll do it. It would really make Dave's birthday incredibly special."

As I sat speechless on the bed, shivering in the cool night air, I was trying to think of a quick excuse to decline while still keeping them as clients. I heard myself say, *"I don't think I even know how to run a camera."* Then, after mentally visualizing the million-dol-lar sale commission wing its way to heaven, I followed with, *"Well, I appreciate you trusting me so much. Let me think about it and get back to you. What day is his birthday?"*

After a few more details from Sherry, I hung up and sat in disbe-lief on the edge of the bed with my head down in my hands, staring unseeingly at my bright red toenails against the fluffy white area rug next to my bed. I no longer even noticed I was freezing. As my eyes started to focus on my toenails, something weird about them caught my attention. The red nail on my big toe wasn't straight. It looked tilted. Looking closer—yes, it was definitely tilted.

As I reached down to touch it, the phone rang again. It was Dave. His voice was bursting with enthusiasm as he said, "Sherry just told me you agreed to film us having sex for my birthday. That is so great! I'm already excited. But what I would really, REALLY like is for you to join us on the bed. I think she forgot to ask you about that. So, what do you think? The three of us. We both really, REALLY like you; it'll be fun."

I'm sure I gasped. Not at his invitation, but as I touched my big toenail, the entire nail literally fell off onto the rug. It looked like a large dead ladybug with no spots. I have no idea what I said after that, or when I hung up. I was watching in growing horror as all ten of my beautiful bright red toenails fell off, one at a time, as I touched them. My fluffy white rug was littered with dead red toenail bodies.

I was not only chilled to the bone AND still stunned by Dave's proposition, but I was hysterical looking at my naileless toes when

Ginger answered my panicked call. Between sobs and shivers on my end, she started to laugh. Leave it to Ginger to find humor in human tragedy.

She asked me, "Did you buy a couple of closed-toe shoes in a half size larger when you let your toenails grow out? You have to do that. With long toenails, your regular shoes will rub and bump the tops so fungus can get under the nails to make them fall off. With all the red polish, you wouldn't see it growing.

"Don't worry, it happens to all of us; they'll grow back." And she hung up, still chuckling.

Yes, my toenails grew back; and No, Sherry and Dave never bought a house from me. That's the same answer to the other obvious question.

TWENTY-FIVE

A DEATHBED PROMISE

Nelson called me one Wednesday about two months after he and his wife, Louise, had moved into their new home in Skyloft. "I need to see you immediately," he said without preamble. "When can you come by?"

I was booked solid that day and asked if I could come on Friday.

"No," he said. "I need to see you TODAY." So, at 6:30 p.m., after my last appointment, I went to see him.

I had met them about ten weeks earlier when Nelson and his wife had dropped into an Open House I was holding. He had told me he was in a big hurry to find a new home and wanted to buy the home I was holding open. I then listed their house, and it sold immediately. Within two weeks, I had two quick, all-cash closings. A rare occurrence in the life of a real estate agent, but a welcome one for sure.

That Wednesday evening, Louise greeted me warmly and took me upstairs to the main bedroom where I found Nelson propped up on pillows in bed, looking very wan and very grey. I was shocked. Eight weeks ago he'd appeared tired, but not deathly ill like he did tonight.

He reached for my right hand, saying, "I'm dying, and I need you to promise that you'll look out for Louise after I'm gone." His two-handed grip on my hand was strong, and they kept squeezing mine as he made his pressing request.

This was a Deathbed Promise, he said, and he needed me to know that it couldn't be broken. I was moved to tears and promised. Twice he made me repeat my promise, and on Friday evening, he was dead.

Over the next few years, I would call Louise occasionally to chat or ask if she needed a referral for a handyman or plumber. I was too busy to notice, but six years went by when I didn't call her or hear from her.

One Wednesday, I came back from Broker Caravan to find fifteen messages from Louise. The receptionist said she had been calling every few minutes for the past hour and seemed distressed that I hadn't called her back yet.

I called her immediately. Louise said she wanted to sell her home and move up north by Santa Barbara to be closer to her son. She remembered that Nelson had said to call me if she ever needed anything with the house. Could I come over right away?

"Of course," I said.

The house was two levels, with a nice ocean view from almost every room. The prices had gone up generously since she and Nelson had bought it, so I knew it would be an easy sale. Until I stepped into the house.

The house looked like it had been burglarized. Piles of clothing, full bags of garbage, and counters covered with dirty dishes of rotting food greeted me. Unopened mail was piled so high on the dining table, it had been sliding off onto the floor on all sides. I picked a handful off the floor to put back on the table and noticed they were all bills. Several had red-stamped "Final Notice" on them.

Upstairs was equally bad, if not worse. Plates of old food covered with fuzz were stacked willy-nilly all over her bathroom counters and her nightstand. Piles of clothes on the floor were so high, it was hard to walk in a straight line. Her adult daughter, Nancy (whom I had never met and never even remembered hearing about), was living in one of the guest bedrooms. When I opened her door to introduce myself, overpowering fumes from empty and almost empty liquor bottles greeted me. At 4 p.m. in the afternoon, Nancy was too drunk to stand up.

Louise was apologetic, but insistent on getting her house on the market immediately so she could move closer to her son. Just when I thought I'd seen the worst, I went to use the powder bathroom on the main floor and saw black fuzzy stuff growing up the wallpaper behind the toilet. (In real estate, we hope to never use that four-letter word—MOLD—to describe black fuzzy stuff.)

"Oh," was Louise's response. "I forgot that that toilet doesn't work. It overflows every time you flush it."

I sat down at the dining room table that was groaning under the weight of all the unopened mail. I looked Louise right in the eye. *"Louise, what is going on here? Do you think you are depressed?"*

Louise allowed that yes, she probably was depressed.

I put my hand on her arm and asked, *"Do you have a doctor that you could call for some anti-depressant pills?"*

"Yes," she said. She did. She could ask her cancer doctor.

"Cancer doctor? When did you have cancer, Louise?"

Louise said she had just completed an eight-week course of radiation last week after stomach surgery three months earlier for a stage three cancer tumor.

I put my head down with my hands covering my face for a moment, to process all I was seeing and hearing. I felt awful that I hadn't talked to her in years after my promise to Nelson.

"OK, Louise, let's talk about selling the house. I'll need to get a cleaning crew in here and a plumber to fix that powder room toilet. Are you okay with them going through your bedroom and Nancy's bedroom to pick things up and clean? It's probably going to cost $400, is that okay?" (In today's dollar, that's $700.)

Louise said it would be fine, but no one could come before 11 a.m. as she was not an early riser. She had a hard time sleeping and roamed around a lot at night, so she slept mainly in the mornings.

I continued my normal pre-listing counseling: *"You need to put any jewelry, small items of value, or loose coins away when the house is shown. You don't want to have anything out to tempt a theft."*

The next bomb hit when Louise said, "Well, I have some money in my bedroom and in Nancy's bedroom. Should I put that away?"

I inquired as to how much money and where was it exactly, and she said she didn't know.

I said, *"Show me please."*

We went back upstairs where she opened her nightstand drawer. It was stuffed with loose twenties, fifties, and 100 dollar bills, mixed in with some more uneaten food.

"Yes," I said. *"Yes, Louise. You absolutely have to put this money away. Is there any more?"*

At which time Louise reached under her bed and pulled out two huge black plastic trash bags. They were the size normally stuffed with leaves, but hers were stuffed full of more loose, crumpled, assorted denominations of bills.

"Louise, how much money is in here?"

She didn't know. She said she didn't trust banks, so wanted to keep some money handy in case she needed to buy food or gas.

I pressed on, *"Is this all?"*

Then she lifted up the edge of her mattress, and underneath were stacks of 100 dollar bills. They were encased in bank wrapper bands and neatly laid out, side by side and end to end, to cover the area below where she slept. There were many thousands of dollars just quietly lying there.

"Is THIS all? Louise, this is especially important—please remember where you have more money."

Now she opened the walk-in closet and pulled out four more brown paper grocery bags with paper handles and a large suitcase—yup—full of loose bills in a variety of denominations.

"You said there was money in Nancy's room too."

"Yes," said Louise, "but we can't go in there while she's home because she doesn't know about it. Next time she goes out, I'll call you."

"Louise, where do you bank? We need to put this money back there so it's safe while you're selling the house."

She didn't know the name of the bank but was able to find her checkbook from Bank of America.

I called B of A and asked for the manager to apprise her of the situation. After first asking to speak to Louise, the manager then confirmed that, yes, Louise was a customer. They were open until 6 p.m., and please come right in. She would be watching for us.

I consolidated all the mattress, the nightstand and the four grocery bags of bills into three king-size pillowcases. Money can be heavy and it took two trips for Louise and I to portage them and then the suitcase and the two black plastic trash bags down to my car. At B of A, the kindly manager took Louise into a room to count the bills and put the money back into her account. All $63,520 of it, according to the deposit receipt from the bank.

We got back to her house after 7 p.m. and there was a taxi double-parked by the front door. Louise had said that every time she left, Nancy would call a taxi to bring her more liquor, so that's what was happening since we had gone to the bank.

"Louise, I need to go, but I'll come back tomorrow so we can go through the mail to see if there is anything important. I also need you to call your son and tell him that you're putting the house on the market. Please give him my name and number in case he wants to talk to me. I'll see you tomorrow at 11 a.m."

At this point, I still thought Louise was depressed. I could see she needed help, and even without a Death Bed Promise, I would have helped her. (Louise's story illustrates one of the main differences between a classic one-to-one agent/client relationship and a multiple-person real estate team where every step is handled by a different person after the lead agent takes the listing. Louise would have likely been a casualty in a team scenario, where no single person saw the whole picture.)

After a couple hours at my office to do paperwork and reschedule the day's appointments, at 11 a.m. I was back at the Skyloft home. I rang the doorbell at least a dozen times before a sleepy Louise let me in. We sat at the dining room table, and I sorted through the mail for over an hour. I tossed the junk mail and started piles for gas and electricity bills, water and trash bills, property tax bills, doctor bills, hospital bills, HOA dues, with one last pile for credit cards and miscellaneous items.

The earliest dates on the bills started four months earlier, so Louise must have quit opening her mail when she found out about the stomach cancer. But the most current ones on the top of each pile had "Final Notice" printed in giant letters and stamped in red ink.

The first bill I called on was for the water company, to apologize for the late payments and explain the reason. The lady informed me that the man who was to cut off Louise's water was due to arrive sometime today. After hearing Louise's story, the lady was kind enough to take Louise's credit card over the phone although she really wanted me to bring in a cashier's check. There wasn't time.

That galvanized me to look for the most recent bills in all the other stacks. As I called each one, they were all in various stages of being disconnected or sent for collection in the next couple of days. I paid each bill over the phone and then went outside with my handwritten notes: *"Don't turn off service—this bill was paid today."* Before I could even finish, the man from the gas and electric company drove up. Talk about being in the nick of time (or, perhaps, the Nico of time!).

Two hours later, Mary Ann arrived unexpectedly. When Louise had called her son late last night, his wife, Mary Ann, had jumped in her car first thing this morning for the seven-hour trip from their home in Paso Robles to Louise's. I'm not sure what she expected to find, but after an hour of talking to her, showing her the deposit slip and the stacks of unopened mail while outlining what we were doing, she visibly relaxed.

About that time, Nancy left in another taxi for some appointment, so we were able to access her room. Under the mattress was a raft of 100 dollar bills in bank wrappers, so Mary Ann took that over to B of A, increasing Louise's account by another almost $30,000.

Those immediate disasters averted for the time being, the Same Day Emergency plumber showed up next. He pulled the toilet to find the wall behind it full of black fuzzy stuff and the floor rotted out underneath it. The cleaning company I had called sent three ladies, who worked a full eight hours and only got the kitchen and family room cleaned. They took sixteen large black trash bags out to the garbage bin that serviced Louise's neighborhood. They would have to come back another day for the upstairs.

Given the state of the house and Louise trying to recover from cancer, I discussed with Mary Ann about selling Louise's home "as is" to an investor I knew who bought fixers. Mary Ann agreed, so I called the investor, who took one look at the ocean view and bought it at the discounted 'fixer' price I had suggested.

The next step was to send Louise up to San Luis Obispo to look at homes. To research a good real estate agent to help Louise, I had called a San Luis Obispo escrow company and was referred to Donna, a local Coldwell Banker agent.

The following Tuesday, Louise started out for the Coldwell Banker office in San Luis Obispo. About four hours later, she called me from a pay phone somewhere around Los Angeles. It was a miracle I was in the office when she called. She had forgotten where she was going. She sounded very frightened on the phone. From her description of the freeway ramp next to the pay phone, I figured out she was still south of Los Angeles, and told her how to get back on the freeway to come back south to her house.

That was also when it actually sunk in that Louise had some form of dementia and wasn't just depressed. In the late eighties, Alzheimer's and dementia had not hit mainstream media, so I didn't consider it when I first went to her house.

I called the Coldwell Banker agent, Donna, to reschedule Louise's appointment for house hunting to the following Friday. After telling her that I would be bringing Louise, she agreed we would split the commission 50/50 if Louise bought something while we were there for the three days. Otherwise, she would pay me a 25% referral fee after this weekend. Donna recommended we stay at the Seaside Bed and Breakfast and that turned out to be a huge blessing.

The six-hour trip up to San Luis Obispo was uneventful. The Bed & Breakfast owner's mother had just passed away from dementia, so she was well versed in Louise's issues. She put me in a room next to the stairs and under Louise's so I could hear if she came down the stairs during the night. She told me that, based on her experience, Louise was well along in the middle stages of dementia. I called Mary Ann to share the info. She was not surprised.

On Friday, Mary Ann joined us as we looked at five houses carefully chosen by that lovely, ultra-professional agent Donna. She really listened to what I described. Louise found the one she liked first thing and Donna put in an offer. We worked on it Friday and Saturday, then opened an escrow with a kind escrow officer who came into her office on her day off to accommodate Louise and me.

I had hardly slept a wink for two nights as Louise paced each night in the room above me, but she never came down the stairs. We got back in the car slightly before 7 a.m. on Sunday morning for the long trip south back to Skyloft so I could hold an Open House at 1 p.m.

I hadn't planned for the return trip to take *fifteen hours.*

According to the news on my car radio, a gasoline tanker truck had overturned just after midnight south of Carpinteria. The accident happened in a narrow neck of Coast Highway One above the ocean, and it had closed the freeway both directions since 2 a.m. We sat for hour upon hour on the hot August freeway, waiting for the traffic to start up again.

As luck would have it, our southbound traffic had stopped close to an off-ramp. Louise and I were among the first to see the porta-potties being delivered and we both jumped out to use them. I went first, and two ladies behind me kept an eye on Louise. I knew from past conversations that Louise had an extreme hatred of policemen and might actually attack them. There were several of them standing on the ramp by the potties, so I asked the ladies to stand in front of Louise to talk to her so she would have her back to the officers.

Louise was hungry and increasingly restless. I had to do something to get us off the freeway. After asking some people in a large motorhome next to us to talk to Louise while I ran an errand, I walked back to the officers stationed at the off ramp and explained why I needed to get off the freeway.

I went to fetch Louise, and from the doorway, briefly recounted what the policeman had told me to the motorhome occupants. The freeway would be closed for at least four more hours, maybe as much at ten, and cars were backed up for over 100 miles behind us. I turned around moments later to find Louise missing. She had just vanished.

One of the people in the motorhome spotted Louise approaching the same policemen posted at the bottom of the off-ramp ahead. I sprinted to catch her just a few yards short of her target. The police were making people scrunch their cars over so I could drive on the shoulder to the ramp and didn't notice her approach, thank heavens.

We spent the subsequent four hours at a restaurant close to the freeway, and finally our waitress told us it had been re-opened. We got back to Skyloft at 11 p.m.

Three weeks later, Louise was ready to move north. She kept raving that she had bought a house with an ocean view but I didn't remember seeing that. It had been really foggy the whole time we were there, so I called Donna about an ocean view.

No view, she said, but the owners had a painting of the ocean over their fireplace. A little more negotiation, and the owners left it for Louise, who seemingly never knew the difference.

TWENTY-SIX

THE RETURN OF ROBERT REDFORD

Meeting Jamison was a turning point in my life, and I knew it the moment I first saw him. Foreigner had a new song out, "*I Want to Know What Love Is,*" and today the cassette tape broke in my car, worn thin from being played over and over and over and over. I had been obsessing about Jamison in that context ever since he walked into my office less than a year ago. Every moment that didn't involve showing or selling property, I thought of him. He might never buy a house from me, but I didn't care.

My emotional wellbeing had vaulted from ecstatic peaks of happiness to abysmal valleys filled with despair in the months since I came back from Washington D.C. We had 'gone around the corner' in the trajectory of our lives, and neither of us would ever be the same. But he had someone at home and I didn't. I had too much time to think and wallow in my dark thoughts about the likely-inevitable outcome of loving him so passionately. He was just too good to be true. He was coming back to San Diego soon for business, and we planned to spend the weekend together before he went back to Texas.

I read Cosmopolitan magazine and I listened to talk shows. I knew how affairs ended, but like every other woman involved with a married man, I hoped our affair would be different. What I didn't know was whether he was still feeling the same cataclysmic emotions as I was, after D.C. To make matters worse, all this week I had been struggling with the Escrow from Hell, and the possibility of getting it closed by Friday before Jamison came to pick me up was looking more and more remote. Not even like a long shot—more like a Going, Going, Gone shot.

This particular Escrow from Hell was a condo sale. It was being sold mostly furnished, meaning the buyer wanted all the toys like the TV, stereo, blenders, espresso machine, expensive bottles of booze, and boogie boards; but everything else was to be taken out prior to closing. The combustible ingredients consisted of my listing with a seller who lived out of state, and a nervous, first-time fireman buyer who had Trixie as his agent.

It all broke loose on Tuesday, two days before we were scheduled to close, fueled by Trixie's continuing jealously for me being Fakke's top agent every month. The reputation she was curating was to find any opportunity to stage a drama of some sort, right before closing. Personally, I found it, and her, annoying.

When Janine, the escrow officer handling the condo sale, accidentally told Trixie she didn't have all the seller's paperwork yet, Trixie's expected meltdown instead turned into a nuclear mushroom cloud, one that only Trixie could conjure up.

I resented this drama right before Jamison arrived. I didn't want to miss a precious minute with him, so I vowed to not take Trixie's bait to start a fight. I would just put my head down to get my seller's side completed and close this escrow on time.

At least Janine had not told Trixie that she had the paperwork, but the notarization was missing on an important piece called the Grant Deed—the one that transferred the ownership. I knew the notary was missing, having been tipped off by Janine last week. I called my seller, who, thankfully, was coming to town the day before closing to attend opening day at the Tijuana Racetrack. His limo was picking him up at 1 p.m., but if I could come to Oceantown and pick him up, he said, I could take him to the escrow office in San Marea, and he would have the limo pick him up there. *What luck*, I thought. *Perfect. Crap*, I reminded myself. *I've got to quit using that word. It always portends disaster.*

When I reached Oceantown at 11:30 a.m., there was a security gate into the condo project where he was staying—something he forgot to mention. I waited and waited, hoping someone else would come through so I could sneak in the open gate behind them. After twenty minutes of sitting helplessly outside the gate, I was getting nervous. There was absolutely no one around.

I drove back to a Mini-Mart about a mile away to use the pay phone to call the escrow company. I could have Janine call my seller's office in Arizona to get me a gate code or the phone number where he was staying (or a blasting cap to use on the damn gate). I anxiously waited on hold, putting quarters, dimes, and then nickels into the hungry payphone while praying that Janine would come back on the line before I ran out of change.

Finally, she came back. She had reached his secretary. I was to go back to the gate. The secretary was calling her boss, my seller, to tell him I was outside because she couldn't find the gate code either. And, please hurry, added Janine. Once she had notarized the grant deed, it still had to be taken down to the County Recorder in San Diego before 4 p.m. to record, and it was already a little past noon.

Outside the gate, I waited and waited and waited. (After it had taken him three years to find a house, one of my clients told me I had the patience of Death—and I did.) I had no more change to call Janine again, and finally, FINALLY, the limo pulled up with a gate code. My seller, it seems, had not changed the pickup place (which seemed odd, as he was an attorney and very detailed-oriented).

I followed the limo through the gate and stood at the foot of the entry steps while the driver rang the doorbell and knocked on the door. And knocked on the door. And knocked on the door.

Finally, he used the dispatch phone in the limo to call his office to check the address. The address was correct, but there was no seller for me and no passenger for him. As we just stood there looking at each other and hoping some idea we hadn't thought of yet would appear out of the sunshine, a property manager from the rental office pulled up. Alerted by my seller's capable secretary in Arizona, he came over with a key to the unit. I was thrilled. We still had time to get to escrow before 4 p.m.

Until we found Mr. Dead Man, nee my seller, at the bottom of the stairs just inside the door.

Color me gone—I took one look at the grey hand lying stretched out from behind the door and left it to the limo driver and the property manager to figure it out.

Death is generally not a problem in an escrow. If all the paperwork is in order, it will just close as usual. However, without the notary acknowledgement under a signature on the paper that transfers title (the Grant Deed), everything stops until the probate gets to court. That might be months or years from now. It certainly wasn't going to be in two days.

I was so rattled I hadn't thought of Jamison in almost ten minutes. I drove directly to the escrow company since that was the original plan, and I was on autopilot. Janine jumped out of her chair when she saw my face, thinking I was about to faint—and I could have been. I felt a hopeless dread seeping into my consciousness. Dread at my seller's unexpected death, dread at not being able to close escrow and dealing with Trixie, and dread that my time with Jamison would not happen.

I used Janine's phone and called Mr. Dead Man's secretary to give her the news. When she asked if the escrow had closed today, I said no, explaining that the Grant Deed had come back without being notarized. Now it could possibly be months before it could close, depending on the will and the probate time. I also asked her what should be done with all the furnishings in the condo that were supposed to be removed prior to closing.

That probably sounded like a silly question, given that we wouldn't be closing any time soon, but without hesitation, the secretary said, "Overnight the deed back to me. He signed in front of me, and I'm the one who forgot to notarize it. Don't tell anyone, just get the deed back to me and I'll handle it. I suggest you donate the furnishings to your favorite charity—that's what my boss was going to do anyway."

On Thursday, the Grant Deed was back, properly notarized and dated pre-death. That same morning, I sat nervously in the County Coroner's office in downtown San Diego, humming "I Want to Know What Love Is' to keep myself from biting the gel coat off my nails. The last thing needed to close was an official copy of the death certificate, which I would then rush back to escrow so everything could be recorded, and we could close on time. And I could finally get on with my life.

I was meeting Jamison tomorrow at 1 p.m. He said I would be attending a company dinner with him before he would be free for the rest of the night, and that he intended to introduce me as his real estate agent. I hadn't asked for any details and I didn't care. I was waxed and polished, had a large purse full of perfume, lipstick, and mascara, clean underwear, a 100 dollar negligee, a toothbrush, and floss.

Floss? Yes, floss. I wasn't going to take any chances of having some food particle in my teeth to ruin this date. It would be a *perfect* ending to a perfectly awful week. I would be celebrating being with Jamison and being rid of this Escrow from Hell (and Trixie too, as a bonus).

But it was not to be. After I had been sitting for four hours in the County Coroner's reception area, waiting (impatiently) for the death certificate, I was called to the front counter. The person who needed to sign the certificate had felt ill, and went home early. So sorry, come back tomorrow (Friday) after 1 p.m.

The saga continues:

Trixie did a final walk through with her buyer on Wednesday evening and the Second World War started again on Thursday when she left a message in my office that the items the buyer did NOT want were still in the condo. Furthermore, Trixie dramatically informed me, they had to be out before closing or her buyer would be canceling.

This was a typical last-minute power play I had seen Trixie inflict on other agents given the opportunity. No matter the issue, this was how she acted so she felt in charge. It always ended with "and we're not closing until it's done", or "my client will be canceling." There are some agents who have to have drama in their transactions, maybe to help them feel like they are earning their commission, and she led the pack.

At that moment, I was numb. I felt emotionally drained,

devastated, and totally defeated. Jamison was picking me up at
1 p.m. for lunch before we drove out to his partner's place for his
company dinner, but now it was looking like I wouldn't be able to
go. I had to get this escrow closed and didn't know if he would, or
could, wait for me.

It's a handicap, being the first born—your DNA makes you
responsible. To me, that responsibility meant my clients *always*
came first, and MY wants, needs, and desires came later. There
wasn't even the slightest hesitation—you don't argue with DNA.

I had to tell Jamison, when he called after his plane landed in
the morning, that I couldn't meet him at 1 p.m. I hoped against
hope that he would be understanding, but somehow, in the meantime, I also had to get the unwanted stuff out of the condo. I had
called several charities like Goodwill, Father Joe's, and the Veter-
ans of America, but no one could come for at least a week. As with
all problems, I always reviewed them before I went to bed at night,
expecting that upon waking in the morning, I would know the
answer. It always worked for me, so I woke up early Friday morning
knowing exactly what to do. The secretary had told me to give to
MY favorite charity, so I told myself I had discretion in selecting it.

There were three blocks of side-by-side oceanfront condo
complexes on the same street as my listing, so there were
always gardeners and workers around somewhere. I found four
strong-looking Mexican gardeners in front of a complex in the next
block. I told them I had some free things for them if they could
come pick them up at noon during their lunch break.

I'm not sure how much English they spoke, but the word 'free'
mobilized them. They dropped their gardening equipment where
they were working and followed me down the street in their pickup
truck. They were so enthusiastic about the barely used furnishings
and food from a $500,000 condo that they sounded like little bees
buzzing happily in a hive.

Even though the condo was on the third floor of the building
and only accessed by stairs, in ten minutes, they had filled up their
pickup. Then two other pickup trucks with five more gardeners

magically appeared to finish the job. It was like watching a Tarzan movie where he thumped his chest, yelled out into the jungle, and all sorts of critters came out of the foliage to help.

I had to make them bring back the TV and the booze about three different times, but in less than an hour, all the offending furniture and food was gone. Another obstacle to closing removed, I hoped Trixie would stew in her own juices at my ingenuity.

Yay, Team Nico!

At 12:55 p.m. on Friday, I was sitting in the Coroner's Office praying to get the certificate just a little early, but my prayers went unheeded. The Coroner's Office was having a going-away party for one of the retirees during lunch, and everyone was running late. Did The Universe not want me to be happy? That debilitating thought did occur to me as I sat forlornly in the empty waiting room.

Jamison had called at 11 a.m. when his plane arrived. He pretended to understand my explanation that The Curse of the First-Born means being responsible for everyone else before yourself. I could feel myself slowly turning blue from holding my breath while waiting for his reaction.

After a disquieting pause that seemed to me to last hours rather than moments, he said, "I can't be late either, so I will have the driver take me to the meeting and I'll send him back to your office for you. Try to be ready when he gets there so you don't miss dinner at 6 p.m." He hung up, and four heartbeats later, called back.

"I'm sorry, I'm sounding like a jerk. I've really been looking forward to seeing you again, and I'm disappointed to have to wait some more. I'll get over it; just get your work done as quickly as you can. Okay?"

"I promise."

TWENTY-SEVEN

THE $41,000 FLUSH

The call came in at 5 p.m. just as Krista was leaving the office for the day. She was exhausted from working six months non-stop with no sales. She hadn't discussed it with us, but we all were worried she was about to go back to waiting tables. While that wasn't a bad thing (other than coming to work smelling like grilled burgers), every single person in our office adored her and wanted her to make a sale soon. She never had a bad thing to say about anyone—not even Trixie.

The secretary said out loud to the few agents left in the office, "Does anyone speak German or French?" It was a question that changed Krista's life. Her dad had been Swiss, and she could speak a limited amount of each.

Two hours later, Krista was still talking to The Lady from Luxembourg, Monique Marie. It was 7 p.m. in San Marea and 4 a.m. in Luxembourg. It appeared that Monique was either drunk, or lonely, or both.

Great—another nut job who has seen the Torrey Pines Open golf tournament on TV. We get lots of calls like that, this time of year. People are living in an area with snow and cold, and they watch everyone at Torrey Pines wearing shorts in the sunshine. The calls come in flurries, like the snow outside the callers' windows. They want to move, how much does a house cost around San Marea? The answer usually results in a short phone call, but that didn't seem to deter Monique Marie.

In spite of being tired, kind and compassionate Krista seemed to be enjoying herself. Among other items of mutual interest, they constantly argued about whether Swiss or Belgian chocolate was the best in the world, and French versus California wines. Monique

Marie did speak English; she was just fishing for someone she could relate to by starting out asking for a German or French-speaking agent. And please, just call her Monique.

For three days in a row, Krista was at the office at 5 p.m. to talk to Monique for several hours. The rest of us Fab Five were also in attendance the first two days to revel in the newest chapter of Krista's new client, but then we drifted off to get the shorter version the following day.

Germaine to all good client/agent relationships is the sharing of confidences. It seems that Monique had just found out her husband was having an affair with her sister, and she was contemplating divorce. She wouldn't mention her husband by name, but Krista started believing he was Luxembourg royalty from the hints Monique dropped here and there. Monique wanted to buy a home around San Marea where she could come to be in hiding when the divorce was announced.

There was an area of The Ranch that was gated and guarded 24/7, but the houses started at $1.8 million ($3.7 million today's value) and went up to $4 million ($12 million now).

"That is no problem," said Monique. Would Krista go see some for her and describe them to her? She was interested in buying one. Of course she would pay cash.

Ever the optimist, Krista rose to the challenge. We all tried to gently cushion the road to disappointment for her, but she was having no part of our pessimism. She went day after day to The Ranch and reported back to Monique in hour-long conversations. She wasn't paying attention to the fact that Monique was now calling the office when she knew Krista wasn't in, so Krista would have to call her back. Thus, the one- to two-hour phone calls were on Krista (or Fakke & Co)'s phone bill mostly.

Until Granny got the first Fakke & Co. phone bill that was over $2,000 for the office. Almost half of the long-distance phone calls were out of the country to one particular phone number, and who the hell was calling Europe every day? This was a business and no place for personal calls, and if someone didn't fess up and pay that bill, they were FIRED. That was until sweet Krista stepped forward and told him the story of Monique and the impending divorce and The Ranch and her conviction that she would earn a big enough commission to cover the phone costs.

Granny's disbelief was evident in the snort and the "You'd better" response, but Krista started making some of the calls from her house to marginalize a portion of Granny's anger while the weeks dragged on.

Krista was now taking a full roll of thirty-six photos of the most promising houses and sending them via international mail to Monique. Lolly was giving Krista money to support the expenses she was incurring in hopes of making this huge sale. She had put all her other clients on the back burner as she worked and networked, looking for the perfect house for Monique.

One finally caught Monique's eye. The house was a huge grey stone French Colonial centered on an acre. It was seven bedrooms and ten bathrooms, with twenty-foot ceilings, and was priced at $2.3 million. It had been on the market for almost a year. It was vacant, dusty, full of floral wallpaper, ornate gold plumbing fixtures, and twenty-foot drops of frilly curtains. In other words, not the style of any buyer to date.

In the foreground, you could see a large gold lion crest above the front door. At three feet in height, it was quite gaudy, but to Monique, the lion was a selling point. Her husband had some type of Order of the Golden Lion medal in Luxembourg (kind of like becoming a Knight in England), and Monique took that as a sign from The Universe that this was her house.

Now Monique required a video of the interior and exterior of the house, the grounds, both ways on the street (so she could see the neighbors' proximity), and a close-up of the lion. Additionally, she wanted footage of the community pool, golf course, stables, and security-gated entrance to this exclusive area in order to make her decision.

The videographer's cost was $800, so we four pitched in $200 each for Krista with the understanding that we would be unlikely to get it back. We all agreed that it was worth the cost to be involved in such an outlandish client story and at this point, it didn't matter to us if she bought or not—it was already a great story.

Especially since the week before, a forty-pound box of Swiss truffle chocolates, encased in their delicate shells, showed up at the office. It was courtesy of Monique Marie, to settle the ongoing chocolate argument with Krista. The chocolate was hard to describe, other than each piece was an oral orgasm.

Oh my God. Monique Marie wanted to buy the French colonial house. She would only pay $2.1 million cash, however—take it or leave it.

Krista's hands shook as she wrote up the offer and went to the post office to overnight it by international mail with a prepaid overnight return mail envelope. It was truly unbelievable that this might actually happen. With the hour-long, almost daily phone calls over the past three months, the photo developing, the video cost and postage, Krista had probably spent at least $2,500—money that she really didn't have. Plus, it was for a stranger on the phone in a foreign country who sent her a forty-pound box of Swiss chocolates and who *MIGHT* (or *MIGHT NOT*) buy an expensive home. God bless our friend and optimistic agents everywhere!

One week later the signed offer came back, and one day after that, the desperate seller of the French colonial had signed it. Then the REAL fun started.

Monique didn't like the inspection report about the gold fixtures having corrosion on them. Or the stains inside the toilets from having water sitting and evaporating. Yuk. And, what in heaven's name were termites? Bugs? Double yuk.

Because Krista was of the successful agents' mindset that her job had no job description, she cleaned the inside of the toilets herself, found a company to come soak the corrosion off the fixtures, and initiated a termite inspector's letter on letterhead. It stated that because the house was stone, the bugs were only in a few of the decorative shutters along three of the exterior windows.

Although the normal treatment was to spray some powerful

bug poison on the wood infestation, the seller had already agreed to replace and repaint those three shutters, so the problem was totally erased. And, for $99 per month, the inspector's company would do a monthly inspection inside and out to keep any and all bugs annihilated.

When it was all completed, Krista sent by overnight mail the new photos of each plumbing fixture back in place and shiny, and the three shutters installed and newly painted.

And Monique Marie sent a Swiss bank cheque for $2.11 million, to include closing costs, back to Krista. We all stood looking over Krista's shoulder with our mouths hanging open, fascinated by seeing a check with that many zeros laying casually on her desk. To all of us, a sale of $500,000 was a huge event, so we were living vicariously, looking at Monique's check. Krista wanted to take a picture of it before driving it over to the title company. She finally had to hand the camera to Ginger for one last picture. Her hands were shaking so hard, she was afraid it might be blurry when she developed the film. Then she had Ginger take several more. We all wanted to be sure to have a legible picture of the check for $2.11 million U.S. dollars to hang over our desks too, in hopes of attracting that for ourselves.

Finally, four and one-half months after the first phone call, Krista had a commission check. For $34,750, because Granny took his normal 30% and kept an additional $2,750 for the phone bill. Krista didn't care: this was more money than she made all last year. She blew it up to 150% on the copy machine and framed it for her office cubicle.

But this wasn't the end of the story, either. Monique Marie was coming at the end of the month to inspect the house. She wanted Krista to find her a live-in housekeeper, a gardener, a handyman, and to get the termite company under contract for their monthly inspections. She needed a phone and cable TV installed. She wanted flowers and an assortment of mature fruit trees planted before she arrived. She wanted to be sure the flower gardens would be full and blooming when she got there.

Next on her list was for Krista to supply the kitchen so she could cook; put towels and rugs in all the bathrooms; get queen-size linens and bedding for her bed (in a gold or silver motif); and stock cleaning supplies. Monique had called Neiman Marcus, who would be delivering new furniture that she had ordered for the main bedroom, living, and dining rooms. Neimans had been instructed to call Krista to schedule the delivery.

Here's a good visual of what transpired: Krista came into the office with six gigantic plastic bags from Target with two or three sets of bed linens, five bathroom rugs, seven towel sets, and two Bedspreads-In-A-Bag with matching shams so we could help her chose for Monique's $2.1 million home.

We were collectively so horrified that only Lolly could respond in her nicest, kindest way by saying, "These are all very nice, Krista, but the sale tags are still on them and I don't think Monique would be pleased to only reimburse you $140 for all of them. I bet she's expecting you to spend $400-500 for her queen-sized bed linens alone."

Krista tended to shop for her clothes at the grocery store or the drugstore while getting groceries or beauty items. We all had tried talking to her, putting peer pressure on her, and even shaming her to buy high quality clothing. She had taken the semi-annual self-improvement classes provided by Granny that stressed the importance of dressing like our clients, but it was like talking to a wall. Expensive clients dressed expensively and would recognize if you didn't, especially in the shoe or car department. The most successful agents drove Mercedes, Jaguars, or BMWs and shopped at Nordstrom, Saks, or Neiman Marcus. Krista shopped at the grocery store and still drove her old gray Nissan. She thought she dressed 'cute'.

Socially adept Lolly helped Krista re-bag all her sale items but could only talk her into Macy's as an upgrade. Two credit cards and $1,800 later, there were some reasonably luxurious items in the French colonial awaiting Monique Marie's arrival.

On the day Monique was to arrive in San Marea, Krista borrowed

Lolly's black BMW to pick her up. She was dressed in a black and gold silk pants suit with real leather black heels that Lolly had picked out for her from Nordstrom's sale rack. Two hours before Monique's plane was to arrive, we Fab Five were sitting in the office with Krista for moral support. We were a collective bundle of nerves as we counted down the minutes. Until the phone rang for her.

It was Monique. She was still in Luxembourg. Her husband had come crawling home with a forty-carat emerald necklace and a cocktail ring. He profusely apologized for his indiscretions and begged her to take him back. What was she to do but accept his apology and his gift?

"So, I want to sell the house right away. I'm not getting divorced now, so I won't be needing it.

"I'm so sorry, Krista, that we won't get to meet, but I love emeralds. I'll be putting a check in the mail to cover the things you bought for me, with a little extra something for your trouble. Keep anything you like for yourself. I'll have Neiman Marcus pick up the furniture next week. Please overnight me the paperwork for $2.8 million."

We were in collective shock. Not only had Krista scored an impression $34,750 commission ($77,000 in today's value), but if she sold it anywhere close to $2.8 million, her share would be another $49,000 ($109,000 today). At that moment, we all wanted to be Krista.

Infrequently, we agents will get an escrow closed and the buyers either change their minds or their hearts and it comes back immediately on the market. But none of us had expected this from Monique.

But the story doesn't end here, either.

Two weeks later, Krista had gotten the signed listing paperwork back along with a 'small' $5,000 check for her 'trouble'. The office was touring her new listing after the Tuesday morning office meeting. She had purchased a six-year-old white Mercedes sedan in anticipation of her continued good fortune.

Even nine hours away, Monique knew when the office tour was to happen, and she was checking that we were on time. We thirty-plus agents had spread out as we toured this huge, mostly vacant, home when the phone rang in the kitchen. Because the home was still largely unfurnished with its twenty-foot ceilings and stone floors, it was an echo chamber downstairs. The live-in housekeeper of a month, Ms. Gomez, answered it and passed the phone to Krista. Monique wanted to know how the tour was going, if the agents liked it, and what they thought of the price.

However, the faint sound of a toilet flushing somewhere upstairs could be heard. I was standing close to Krista and could hear Monique scream, "Was that a toilet flushing? In *my* house? Did someone use the toilet in MY house? WITHOUT ASKING?"

Even as Krista stuttered and stumbled, trying to calm Monique down, saying that the agent HAD asked, and had only used the powder room toilet by the media room upstairs, she was losing the battle. She turned white and handed the phone back to Ms. Gomez.

With one flush, Krista's $2.8 million listing and $49,000 commission were history.

TWENTY-EIGHT

COLLECT CALL FROM LAS COLINAS PRISON

Johnnie was my new idol. She oozed money and confidence. I had pre-qualified her bank statements. I knew she had several million dollars liquid in the bank, with annual tax returns showing her net earnings in the million-dollar range also. I wanted to be just like her. In retrospect, I *could* have been earning that kind of income had I bought for myself the fabulous real estate bargains I'd found, instead of selling them to my clients.

Johnnie was a financial advisor from Santa Monica who invested money in real estate for very, very wealthy people who never saw the properties or questioned what she did to give them a 20% return on their money. She flew her own Beechcraft Bonanza luxury plane down to Palomar Airport after she discovered how cheap our oceanfront properties were compared to the ones in Malibu and Santa Barbara.

Wren-the-Pervert and I sourced oceanfront homes to remodel and flip. Johnnie provided the purchase money and got excellent returns on the resales as a result. Wren was her project manager, and I was her real estate agent. We both earned good incomes too. I should have known Johnnie was likely to be a problem somewhere in the future, as clients always refer their like-minded friends. She had been referred by Wren. (This is why I never ask for referrals unless I still enjoy my Sellers or Buyers when the sale has closed.)

Johnnie had 'star power'. She was an intimidating woman who wore cowboy boots with her designer skirts and smoked cigars. Not regular cigars, but thin, hand-rolled cigarillos a.k.a. 'Rum-Soaked Crooks.' (The name of those cigarillos alone should have tipped me off.) Johnnie knew what she wanted, and she wanted only the best. She had a firm handshake, a Janis Joplin raspy voice from chain smoking, and a deep belly laugh reminiscent of Santa Claus.

Her husband, K.C., was a private detective who specialized in photographing the suspected wandering spouses of Johnnie's clientele. He was moderately good-looking, expensively but casually dressed, younger than Johnnie, and had just given her a 5.5-carat diamond solitaire ring on their fifth anniversary. As a precaution, he had also given her a small derringer with a pink grip and was teaching her how to shoot it in case someone ever attempted to steal her diamond ring. He wasn't so much an oily-looking dark-haired gigolo as more of a cleaner-cut 'boy toy' version of one.

Predictably, K.C. was ever the gentleman. With impeccable manners, the moment the Bonanza taxied to a stop, he jumped out to rush efficiently around the tail and open the cockpit door so Johnnie could make her decent onto our commuter airport tarmac. He lit her Crooks as they appeared one after another. He would remove her boots and massage her feet that rested in his lap while she and I talked business and pushed papers back and forth across my desk. He treated her like the royalty she personified.

Yes, I wanted to be successful like Johnnie; possibly even emulating the cachet of the rum-soaked Crooks, even though I hated smoking and was afraid of small airplanes.

During the third house transaction she was about to fund for Wren's new purchase, Johnnie taxied up to me at Palomar Airport and, uncharacteristically, opened her own door. It was Thursday, she was two hours late, and her star power wattage was visibly dimmer as she got into my Mercedes. In the presence of a good listening agent like myself, Johnnie was quick to burst into tears, and start unburdening herself.

She told me K.C. was having an affair with his secretary, an ex-masseuse in training to be a private detective under him.

"Under him," she scoffed as she lit up a new Crook.

I would never allow a client, rich or poor, to smoke in my car, but for some reason I didn't want to interrupt Johnnie. Instead,

I drove quickly to the airport bar to minimize the smoke damage inside my Mercedes 'office'.

Johnnie had a couple shots of Glenfiddich Scotch whiskey 'neat', and I had a glass of red wine. We commiserated over men in general and her man in particular. She was working hard to please K.C. with her earning power, her social network, her lifestyle, and he'd left her for a 'nothing' (not to mention an 'ugly nothing in Birkenstocks', no less). She was beside herself with what to do. She couldn't eat, and she didn't want to work. What she really wanted was to do something to make him realize how much he needed her, but she didn't know yet what that was.

Johnnie was in no mood to sign the papers for the oceanfront property she and The Pervert had just bought. With all the upset, she had forgotten to bring the cashier's check for $2.3 million, also. After two hours of drinking, she was in no shape to fly the Bonanza back to Santa Monica, so I took her home with me for the night. Since she had probably drunk seven or eight whiskeys without eating, she spent the night crying and throwing up in my guest bathroom.

Like I've said before, we agents have no job description. If I had one, I definitely would have crossed this situation out of that description.

Early the next morning, with bloated face and swollen eyes, Johnnie was ready to swing by my Fakke & Co.office to quickly sign the papers and get back to Santa Monica. She had a plan, she said, and needed to find K.C. right away. She would overnight the check to me later that day.

Three days went by without the closing check and everyone from the listing agent and the sellers, down to the title officer and escrow officer, were screaming at me like it was my fault the $2.3 million check was not in escrow yet. I had made thirty or forty calls to both Johnnie's office and her house that had not been acknowledged. Both answering machines were full after the tenth call, and I couldn't leave any more messages.

On Tuesday (and on probably the fiftieth phone call), K.C.

answered the phone. "Sorry," he said. "I've been in the hospital, and I think Johnnie's probably still in jail. I'm packing to go on vacation to Peru, so I can only talk a moment."

"WHAT? In jail? Are you ok? Is Johnnie ok? Peru? What happened?", I said, all in one breath

"Yes, I'm going to be ok," said K.C. "Johnnie shot me—did she tell you I was leaving her? I can't stand being a kept man. I hate all the fake movie star clients she has. I hate all the pretexts about the money, that ridiculous fake diamond ring, and the plane. I want a simple, unfettered life having massages, meditating, going to yoga, and wearing sandals instead of Cole Haans.

"Listen, there was a priority mail envelope in the car with a title company address and your name referenced on it. I found it when I left the hospital late yesterday, so I dropped it in the mail on my way home. I hope you get a good commission on this last deal; you've certainly earned it."

"Well, thanks for putting that in the mail," I said, trying to sound matter-of-fact when in reality, my stomach was churning, trying to digest his story.

"I'm so sorry you're getting divorced, you seemed like such a perfect couple. And I'm glad you're ok. You must be okay if you're on your way to Peru. Where did she shoot you?" (I've found that when I'm matter-of-fact with my questions, I get matter-of-fact answers back.)

"She shot one of my testicles off. It was hanging by a thread, and although I had a couple of operations immediately, the doctors weren't able to save it. It's probably okay, I don't really want to have kids anyway."

I stupidly wondered as I hung up: Is it possible that I was having one of my infamous early-morning-Monday-phone-call-curses on a midday Tuesday? What do I tell everyone now? I've always said the best real estate agents are the ones who are the best problem solvers, but I don't think sleeping on it was going to offer up a solution this time. So, after calling escrow to tell them 'the check is in the mail'; I rescheduled all my appointments for the rest of the day and went to the beach. I watched the colorful sunset, then treated myself to a nice dinner and several glasses of wine at Murphys because I couldn't think of anything else to do.

The following morning, I got two unexpected phone calls at my office. The first one was from the title company, confirming that they'd received the cashier's check in the morning mail and had just received confirmation that the transaction had recorded. "Congratulations and thank you for the business."

The second one came a couple of hours later. The receptionist yelled from the front desk that I had a collect call from Las Colinas Women's Prison, and did I want to accept it? All eyes were on me as I told her to put it through.

Johnnie's signature rasp sounded like she was still right beside me in the Mercedes. "Bet you didn't think you'd be hearing from me again so soon. K.C. said he told you what happened. Did you get the check; did the escrow close? That house was such a great deal, I'll make a lot of money on it, thanks to you. Please find me another one right away. Mail my papers to my regular P.O. Box. I'm getting it forwarded through my attorney. I only get five minutes—is there anything you need to tell me? I can't call again for another week."

"Yes, one more question. K.C. told me you shot him in one of his balls. I think we know each other well enough for me to ask you—did you hit what you were aiming for?"

She was still laughing as the line went dead.

A court order came into my office a few weeks later, ordering the sale of that house. At closing, I had to hire an attorney, who cost me $6,000, to appear in court in Santa Monica to separate my court-reduced commission from the proceeds of the house. It would have been pennies on the dollar if it had been combined with monies which were to be distributed for creditors, investors, and attorneys to finalize her divorce.

TWENTY-NINE

THE RETURN OF ROBERT REDFORD — PART II

"Yes, Jamison," I said. "Yes, it will be okay. I'll get this escrow done and it will absolutely be okay. I'll see you as soon as I can."

My whole body started smiling again inside and out as I sat in the San Diego Coroner's reception area, reliving over and over the conversation from a couple of hours ago. Yes, absolutely okay, this weekend still had a chance to be perfect.

I was barely able to be civil at 2:30 p.m. when my name was finally called. I was handed a single certified copy of my seller's death certificate (I needed, and had paid for, five.). Fifteen minutes later, I was on my way back north to take them to the escrow. An hour later, I was still twenty minutes away from the escrow office. Friday traffic had started early today, probably because of the horse races, and a twenty-minute quick trip was looking to be ninety minutes. The snarled traffic appeared to be on both sides of the freeway. Which meant that the runner for the title company would have to wade through it to get all the deeds recorded.

My resolve to spend time with Jamison was being tested by The Universe, and my resolve never wavered. A ray of sunshine finally appeared when I arrived at the escrow at 3:45 p.m. The original death certificate did not need to be recorded, but it did have to be in the escrow's possession. Janine could fax a copy of it to her main office in San Diego, who already had the other Grant Deed (that transferred ownership) and the Deed of Trust (that secured the mortgage on the condo) ready to run across the street to the County Recorder's office for recording, thereby closing this escrow.

I was done. I was free for the weekend. I drove quickly on all the side roads I knew back to my office in San Marea and, hallelujah, the town car and the driver were still patiently parked in front. I was on my way to my destiny with Jamison. The driver came into the office to make a quick call to tell Jamison we were leaving and promised he would be delivering me in a couple of hours.

Of course, he hadn't taken into account the slow-moving Friday traffic that had stacked up while he was waiting outside my office. I realized I didn't know where we were going, and I was barely able to resist saying "Are we there yet?" every ten minutes for the next four hours. Jamison had left a soft suede jacket in the back seat, so I sat with it in my lap, my arms through the sleeves backwards and my face in the fabric, re-acquainting myself with his smell as darkness fell.

When we finally got off the eastbound freeway, seemingly halfway to Arizona, we drove on a frontage road, then on a side road, then on a dirt road. I had no idea where we were. In the clean air, the stars looked close enough to touch and the Milky Way was a ribbon of light.

Out of the quiet night, a limo bus came towards us as the driver announced, "We're here." He turned left down a block-long, sloping gravel driveway. Sentinel palms stood guard every fifty-feet on both sides as a border between the driveway and vast expanses of lawn. A full moon rose into view over the horizon much like an English muffin might rise out of a toaster. A large, mirror-still lake reflected the moon, the stars, and the solar lights under each palm. It was a very magical approach to a sprawling, territorial-style hacienda, with a solitary man backlit by the open front door behind him. I had already dry-brushed my teeth in the car several times during the drive, so, with my overnight case in hand, I stepped from the car.

My mouth dropped open. I had only been looking at Jamison as we approached, but there in front of me was a full-size carousel with an amazing array of elaborate horses, camels, rabbits, giraffes, and elephants softly glistening in the moonlight. The lead animal was a glorious white unicorn with a twisted golden horn. Jamison's arms encircled me from behind.

He softly inquired, "That unicorn is as unique and beautiful as you. Would you like to ride her?" I was so mesmerized by both the carousel and his presence that I could only nod.

The driver disappeared, and a few moments later, the carousel lit up softly and without music, as befitted the solitude of its surroundings. I pulled myself onto the unicorn side saddle instead of straddling the seat. Jamison stood beside me, leaning against a zebra, without taking his eyes off me. It was a comfortably warm night, but his look sent shivers down my spine.

The carousel started up, and out of the night came the driver, now dressed in a tailless black tuxedo jacket with a white pleated shirt and black bowtie. With a steady hand, he balanced a glass of red wine and a snifter of brandy on a serving tray as he slipped between the undulating carved animals to deliver the drinks. The stress that had accumulated in my shoulders melted more and more away with each revolution.

Wordlessly, through tears inspired by the beauty of the night, I watched the lake, the full moon, the mountains, and the hacienda twirl slowly around inside a world inhabited solely by Jamison and myself. I picked the biggest star above us and made a wish—I wished that this night with Jamison would never end. Even now, years later, the scene defies the words to adequately describe it, but the tears always reappear effortlessly.

Eventually, the carousel slowed to a stop. Jamison took a step, put his arms around me, and rested his chin on my shoulder while we gazed a little longer at the moon's reflection in the lake.

Without turning to face me, he said in a low voice into my ear, "Nico, I've missed you more than you can ever realize. I was so glad to see my driver coming down the driveway. I was afraid you might not come. Let's go into the house. I had the cook leave a plate of her most excellent food in the oven for you." His hand found mine and he walked beside me into the house and into yet another jaw-dropping world.

Inside the front door was a great room containing a kitchen, a dining area, and a living room. The enormous living room was full of large Sergio Bustamante papier mache animal figures— some as big as pieces of furniture. The baby giraffe lay with its legs folded under its body, but its head was still above mine. Even though it was tempting to sit on its back, I had seen smaller ones at a high-end art gallery in Laguna Beach and knew how expensive they were.

Bustamante was an internationally famous Mexican artist known for both his papier mache and his ceramic sculptures. I speculated that these life-sized animals cost at least $10,000 apiece back in the late 1980s. I counted fourteen of them.

Fingers still entwined, we walked across the room to a fire, which was burning low in the cavernous fireplace centered on the far wall. I do believe the eyes are the windows to the soul, for as I finally was able to truly look at Jamison's face and his eyes in the firelight, we needed no conversation. We sank as one onto the soft alpaca rug on the floor in front of the fireplace. There would be no dinner for me tonight.

Early morning found us in a king-size bed under a cloud-like natural white cotton duvet. There were pillows everywhere that we had flung off the bed in our haste to make love again. There was a diaphanous fog outside the bedroom windows that was rapidly dissipating in the morning light. I've loved fog ever since our time in Gettysburg, so Jamison got up to open the bedroom door to the outside, and the friendly fog sneaked in along the floor towards us. I could hear the muffled sounds of monkeys and parrots outside. As the love-induced cobwebs cleared inside my brain, I really did hear monkeys.

Where the bleep were we? The world of the rich does sometimes include their own private zoos—was that what I was hearing? I had read stories about the exotic animals at Michael Jackson's Never-land Ranch, and asked Jamison if that's where we were.

In his soothing baritone laugh that I will never tire of hearing as long as I live, he said, "No, we're not at Michael Jackson's ranch. We're about two hours east of San Diego. The zoo and this property belong to my business partner, who hosts seminars and dinners here for his investors on a quarterly basis. It allows him to deduct the cost of the entertaining, along with part of this property maintenance and expense, from his income taxes. It's all legal, and he can mix business and pleasure here."

I was starving. After a quick shower and change of clothes, we went into the kitchen where fresh coffee, cream, a medley of cut-up fruit and rolls had been laid out invitingly on the counter by some invisible cook. All the empty glasses and used napkins left carelessly on the Bustamante animals last night by the earlier crowd had been cleared.

Rays of sunlight broke through the canopy of trees, dappling the path towards the private zoo. We walked, with steaming mugs of Mexican cinnamon coffee in our hands, towards the cacophony of jungle sounds. A jungle it was—there were large cages full of screaming black and gray lemurs, macaques, and capuchins. Another cage housed blue and yellow macaws; another was full of rainbow-colored lorikeets. There was a mother and baby alpaca, a full-sized two-humped camel named George, a small giraffe, and a pair of zebras. No meat eaters, which I appreciated on several levels.

Jamison and I had started to talk on a deeper level of confidence made possible by our intimacy. He told me about his wife and teenage daughter. When he was in high school, his family had encouraged his dating the daughter of another prominent Texas family. He felt she had deliberately gotten pregnant to force the loveless marriage he still endured. He needed some time to think about what he wanted to do. What he felt with me, he had never felt before. He knew he was in love for the first time in his life, he would never give me up as long as I would have him, but he had to really reconcile his obligations with his desires. The Curse of the First Born was upon Jamison too.

Being patient to a fault was one of my specialties. In a voice cracking with emotion, I said, *"Jamison, I will wait for you for as long as it takes—even if you are married. I want whatever you can give me—I just want you in my life."*

I could see the relief written on his face as he gave me a giant hug. But as he released me, his face had clouded over as he told me he had to catch a plane later today and couldn't spend the whole weekend, as we had planned. We walked back to the house in silence and tidied up the master bedroom area after one last languid lovemaking session—one that forever will always be imprinted on my soul.

There was a pedal boat tethered to a small dock that I hadn't noticed in last night's moonlight, so we took it for a twenty-minute tour of the private lake's meandering shoreline. There were fish jumping, birds singing, even a muskrat sunning on a log at the far end. It felt too good to be true, and I suddenly despaired that I might never see Jamison again, let alone spend the rest of my life with him. I believed in Karma, but I was so hopelessly in love with him that my normal optimism was fading.

We chatted amiably about houses and about work for the two-hour ride to the San Diego airport. Unexpectedly, Jamison stopped mid-sentence as we approached the airport and took a long, long look at me. The intensity of his gaze conjured up a vision of a camel storing up water before crossing a desert.

"Nico, I need to go to Orlando in about a month. I have a series of meetings on Thursday and Friday with a bank that might be financing one of my new businesses, but I'll be free in the evenings and through the weekend. I've already got my suite reserved at the Marriott, and we could definitely have a full weekend together then. Will you join me if I send you tickets? If you need to think about it, you can let me know next time we talk."

I didn't even consider saying 'No'. In retrospect, I probably should have, but without hesitation I said YES. YES, I would meet him in Orlando. Then, after one long last lingering, soulful kiss, he disappeared into the crowd outside the airport just as Foreigner's new hit "I Want To Know What Love Is" came over the limo's radio.

THIRTY

SUNDOWNER III —
WHY AGENTS DRINK MORE

Miriam started tonight's Sundowner with sobering news. She had overheard our office manager, Miguel, talking to his doctor. She sat closest to Miguel's private office, but he didn't have the door closed, and she heard him talking about not being able to take time off work for his cancer treatments.

Cancer? Miguel?

We were all fond of Miguel and were collectively horrified to hear the news. Miriam had gone into Miguel's office and closed the door. Miguel said yes, he had stage III cancer in his left salivary gland, and the doctor was going to use chemotherapy to reduce its size so it could surgically be removed. Miguel expected to have trouble swallowing until the course of chemo was over. He admitted that he couldn't afford to take time off work, since his wife had lost her job and its paycheck last week. Luckily, her employer's medical insurance would still cover him, since the cancer was diagnosed while she was still working.

What a mess. Miriam said both she and Miguel were in tears.

Serendipitously, one of Ginger's clients was a well-known naturopathic doctor in San Marea. His dietary methods were strict but known to be very effective in fighting cancer. She immediately called Dr. C. to find the cost of his therapy regime was $5,000; however, for her friend, it would be $2,800.

We knew Miguel couldn't afford even the lesser amount, but Lolly thought that if we would all chip in $560 apiece, together we could help him. Ginger thought we should do it anonymously, and we Fab Five sisters immediately agreed. (Although it was anonymous, eight or nine years later, in the late 90s, Miguel thanked me for helping him survive cancer. In 2022, he is still alive.)

Ginger went next with a story about her client, who'd just paid $1.1 million cash for his new home in San Marea. He'd invited her to dinner at Antonio's, a five-star restaurant on San Diego Bay, and had told her to order anything she wanted. Ginger had loaded up on shrimp appetizers, Caesar salad, lobster entrée, finishing up with their famous tiramisu for dessert.

Her client had been a real nitpicky buyer and had driven her crazy through the entire escrow, so she felt she deserved this reward. She even got his permission to order her new favorite Dom Pérignon rosé wine. She felt that by racking up a good $200 dinner just on her side, that evened out the nitpicky aspect of their transaction. He had ordered about the same and shared the Dom Pérignon until he got almost to end of his meal.

Then he leaned over and said to her quietly, "Do you know how I keep most of my money? Watch this, and don't say anything."

At which time, he calmly pulled out his wallet and unfolded a stamp-sized piece of wax paper. Ginger didn't even have time to react as she watched her client take a sip of Dom Pérignon, then pop the generous size shard of glass that had been hidden in the wax paper into his mouth, and bite down.

He yelped and pushed back from the table so fast, his chair tipped over. Blood started oozing out from between his lips. Any amount of blood can look like a lot, and especially when it was mixed with a mouthful of fizzy champagne, it WAS a lot.

Ginger said, "I didn't know how I could even get in the car with him to go back to the office. He made a big show about saying he was suing them for negligence in causing him bodily harm. Of course, the restaurant manager was properly horrified and the entire dinner for us both was free. I was mortified."

And we were all mortified along with her.

Lolly's restaurant story took a different tack: Polo season in San Marea brought in the nationally and internationally wealthy, beautiful people. People who stood out in couture hats, clothing, astonishing jewelry, limos, and who owned polo ponies. People who were shadowed and imitated by scam artists who followed them like hyenas follow herds of gazelles.

Lolly had run into Joyce on Caravan. Joyce was a long-time agent at a competing brokerage a block away from Fakke & Co., and she warned Lolly about a new scam artist in town. About a week earlier, a very tan, very gorgeous man with a great accent and dark curly hair came into her office on Joyce's floor time. He was dressed expensively (you always look at their shoes to judge *how* expensively) and continually gestured with a hand circum-navigated by a diamond-encrusted Rolex.

His name was Paolo, he said. He was from Argentina, where he owned a string of polo ponies. He and his ponies competed on the polo circuit, and he'd always liked the San Marea area. So, this year, Paolo said, he was interested in purchasing a condo he could live in while competing on the polo circuit, then stay in off-season during the winter.

Joyce was excited by the prospect of selling him a pricey ocean view condo for his vacation and winter home.

"First, before we look" Paolo said, "I haven't eaten breakfast, so please join me. We can eat and also talk about what my needs are."

While Joyce politely had a cup of coffee and a muffin, Paolo enjoyed a full three-course breakfast and several mimosas. He ate with such gusto, it almost appeared like he hadn't eaten recently. It's a quick story, because after they ate, he started looking for his wallet and, unbelievably, he was so embarrassed. "This has never happened before, so sorry; please pay, and I'll have my driver bring me some money to reimburse you. So sorry, let me go find my driver. I'll meet you back at your office," he said. "So sorry."

Of course, Joyce paid the $53 breakfast bill, but after two weeks, she was still waiting for him to come back to reimburse her and buy a million-dollar condo.

Fast forward to this week. Lolly had been on the 9 a.m.-12 noon time slot for floor duty two days ago, and had a man walk in who met the same general description from Joyce's story, except that his name, now, was Gianni from Venezuela. He invited her to breakfast first, but when Lolly sat down, she said she had already eaten and didn't drink coffee; but go ahead. She would take notes on what his needs were.

However, when the same ("Oops, so sorry, no wallet") blustering started, Lolly said she just reached over and patted his arm, saying "I feel so bad for you; how embarrassing. I left my purse in the office. Let me go get it, and I'll be right back."

When Lolly went home at 5 p.m., she walked by the restaurant, but Gianni wasn't there anymore.

"But, yesterday," Lolly said with a twinkle in her eye, "I think I saw him getting into Trixie's Mercedes after they came out of the same restaurant."

Oops. So sorry.

It was my turn for one last story since we were on our last glass of wine and the bottles were empty. I told my story of The Vampire Seller. Only Lolly had heard it before.

I had gone down to San Diego for a listing. The owner, Simon, was the after-hours County Coroner. His pale, almost transparent skin was due probably from working nights and sleeping days. (Lolly interjected that it was more likely 'coffin pallor', to peals of wine-induced laughter.)

Simon had worked nights for many years for the County of San Diego and was selling his house because he was getting divorced. He and his wife never spent any time together, and she accused him of loving the roses more than he loved her.

I mentally had already decided to use a picture of his spectacular front yard rose garden for the marketing brochure. His roses were stunning. The flowers were the most vivid colors of the rose rainbow, their leaves, the waxiest emerald green. There was not a blemish of rust or evidence of bug damage anywhere. These roses were Best of Show quality award-winners, and worthy of decorating catalog covers.

At the initial Open House, the first couple was extremely interested in the house. He was opening cupboards and closet doors, and she was inspecting the appliances. That is, until she opened the refrigerator. Following a large yelp, she shut the door and they quickly left the house. Of course, I had to look to see what prompted that reaction. The refrigerator contained at least a dozen pints of whole blood, all uniformly lined up on the bottom shelf above the crisper with stickers identifying the blood types of the contents and a 'use before' date.

With a sigh, I closed the refrigerator and sat back at the table with my face in my hands. What had I ever done to attract such unusual clients? Was this guy a vampire? I don't believe in vampires; but then, were the jars of blood somehow connected to his unusual pallor? Did I even want to know?

When Simon came back after the Open House, I didn't admit we had opened his refrigerator. Instead, I relayed all the compliments about his roses and that people wanted to just buy the front yard or know his secret for their care.

He just quietly nodded his head and said, "I might as well tell you before you hear it from a neighbor. As I told you, I work for the County at night, in the coroner's office. Instead of pouring expired blood down the drains there, from time to time I bring the pints home instead and pour it on the roses.

"That's what makes them look so outstanding; but the general public doesn't need to know that, so please don't tell anyone. I would probably lose my job if the County knew what I was doing. Tell them to use blood meal that they can buy at the store."

Simon continued, "A couple of the early morning neighbors saw me pouring blood on the roses, which started the whole neighborhood discussing whether I'd killed my wife and poured her blood in the yard to disguise the crime, or if I was a vampire and put leftover blood on my roses when I was full.

"I guess that's what I should expect for never going to neighborhood parties or telling them what my career is. I'm photosensitive, meaning I'm allergic to sun—it gives me hives—so that's why I work nights.

"As to my wife, she moved out several weeks ago when she filed for the divorce."

I told this story over the uncontrolled laughter from my fellow agents, but I had to admit I never did meet the wife during the sale or the move-out.

THIRTY-ONE

THE MAYOR'S GHOST

The Mayor had been dead for 107 years, but that didn't keep him from sitting in his rocking chair on the porch (where the porch used to be) and smoking his cigar from time to time, just to spite his wife.

I understand that time is not relevant to those in other dimensions, which perhaps explains why my young clients didn't smell the cigar smoke or hear the rocker creaking, in the beginning. Still, even several times a week over the past three years got to be too much finally.

Faith was now pregnant, and the smell of cigar smoke, albeit ghostly, nauseated her, and the creaking of the rocker had gotten on her frayed nerves. She was blaming Pat, which is a spouse's privilege, said clause contained somewhere on the marriage license.

I represented Faith and her husband Pat when they purchased this absolutely charming, whitewashed adobe hacienda on an oversized lot in a desirable area of Ocean Hills called Fire Mountain. (Oversized meant 10,000 square feet instead of the standard 7,500.) The house looked like a baby owl in the neighborhood of larger two-story models that had fledged up around it. It must have been a whitewashed jewel when it was built in the late 1890s. There were a pair of hundred-year-old pineapple palm trees standing sentinel-style in each corner of the front yard, and a real red clay tile roof. It oozed charm and history.

The old porch had been enclosed sometime in the past to be a formal sitting room adjacent to the tiny foyer and front door, and a half bath had been installed off the kitchen. The doorways between rooms were rounded at the top and demonstrated the foot-wide thickness of the adobe interior walls. With the porch enclosure, the little hacienda had mushroomed overnight from 900 square feet to its current magnificent 1100 square feet.

The interior of the home had been recently remodeled by the departing owners, Graciela and Jesus Mendoza. Under the Mendozas' thoughtful vision, the kitchen cabinets had morphed back to the original finish, showcasing its rich, golden-colored, old-stand pine panels with hand-forged wrought iron handles and hinges. The stove was a new version designed to look like the classic old-time stoves our grandmas had cooked on. It was black porcelain with silver trim, stylishly standing on four graceful silver legs with a warming oven on top. The top freezer-style refrigerator matched, but there was no room for a dishwasher. (My grandma had a stove and refrigerator like that in the fifties, but, likely her house then cost as much as these appliances did now.)

With a lot of elbow grease, the hardwood floors throughout the home gleamed with the graceful dark patina of age. The Mendozas had replaced the floor with quarter-sized hexagonal black and white 1920s vintage tiles to properly display the clawfoot tub in the full bathroom. The tub was complete with the shower curtain suspended from the ceiling encircling it from above. The half bath matched the full bath, including the pedestal sink but sans the tub.

It was a very cool first home for the newlyweds, and even though the house had no central heating system and rested on hardscrabble dirt (foundations hadn't been invented 100-plus years ago), it was HOME.

The sellers had said, in parting, while turning over their keys to the new young owners, "We hope you don't mind ghosts. Everyone told us the house was haunted by the old mayor of Ocean Hills, but we never believed it."

That probably would have been a good time to ask why they were moving after only living there for seven months and having spent all that money to remodel, but the moment was lost. This was also about four years before Seller Disclosures were required by law to be given to new buyers prior to closing, but Faith and Pat were in love with their first home, so it wouldn't have mattered anyway.

They adorned the home with overstuffed leather furniture, colorful Southwestern area rugs, and made the formal sitting room into an office complete with a desk, a space heater, and a rocking chair.

It started with Mister Kitty. Mister Kitty had been an orphan grey tabby kitten, able to curl up in a teacup when Faith adopted him from the Humane Society two years ago. (He was originally named Miss Kitty, but a trip to the vet for his first vaccinations initiated the need for a different name.) He followed Faith absolutely everywhere—except to the front door.

At first, they assumed he didn't want them to leave and was pouting, but then they started noticing him sitting at the edge of the foyer across from formal sitting room addition and staring at seemingly nothing, even when they weren't leaving.

Then he laid there by the hour, intently watching the enclosed sitting room as though he were watching a mouse hole. Sometimes he hissed and backed away with his back arched and his hackles at attention, but since they both worked full time, they only noticed this on the weekends. It took a while for Mister Kitty's unusual pastime to become puzzling.

The other puzzling thing was that the door into the formal sitting room wouldn't stay closed. Pat had started closing it for Mister Kitty, to lessen his fixation, but if he closed it at night, it was always open in the morning. When they closed it in the morning before they left for work, it was ajar when they got home. It was becoming increasingly the subject of arguments where Faith and Pat accused each other of deliberately opening it when the other wasn't looking, just to drive one another crazy.

These arguments accelerated when Faith started accusing Pat of sneaking a cigar and smoking in the formal sitting room when the door was closed. How else could the smell of smoke linger there occasionally? They both could definitely smell it from time to time, and Faith was appalled that Pat wouldn't admit it.

"It's not me, Faith. It's probably that ghost that the old owners mentioned when they left."

"Don't make me laugh. Just admit it, Pat; don't blame it on the old mayor's ghost. I thought you didn't believe in ghosts, anyway."

She was hard pressed to blame him for the faint rocker sounds, as sometimes he wasn't even home, but she was determined to figure out how he did it. She just needed to catch him once, for her own peace of mind.

Finally, Faith decided to check out the Mendoza's parting comment and went down to the Ocean Hills Historical Society. Upon stepping into the museum area, the first thing she saw was a four-foot square sepia photo of their house taking up prominent wall space opposite the entrance. The house was surrounded by a white picket fence, and she thought they should really do that again—it looked perfect. The porch with its rocker was easily identifiable, even though it was the enclosed sitting room now. A wide dusty dirt road ambled by in front, and empty lots covered with brush represented the neighborhood. The two pineapple palms that towered over her house now, looked to be about shoulder high in the photo.

Sitting in his rocking chair on the porch was The Mayor himself, cigar in hand. He was casually dressed in an open neck unbleached cotton shirt with a stand-up collar, wearing a hat.

The Mayor was Col. Tom Horne, the driving force to incorporate Ocean Hills from an old Spanish land grant. He sported a dark walrus mustache under bushy eyebrows, and a soft shapeless cowboy hat. (That type of hat was destined to be marketed as the Tom Horne hat.)

Seeing that photo turned Faith into a believer. The rocker and the porch were exactly where she heard the creaking noise—The Mayor's ghost must still be in her house.

At this point, I was called back to relist the house. Armed with the Historical Society information, Faith had forgiven Pat, but determined that she really needed some peace and quiet for herself, Mister Kitty, and the coming baby.

To my growing index of normal sources for listings—marriage, death, divorce, job loss or job transfer, fires or flood, more kids and less kids—I was able to add a new source—ghosts.

THIRTY-TWO

THE UNWRITTEN 'DEAD MAN RULE'

There are just some REALLY BAD stories in the life of a real estate agent that you couldn't make up even if you were trying to. Death is usually not a bad word in real estate—it's one of our best sources of listings. Four-letter words like MOLD or LEAK or RATS cause problems. Another four-letter word, DEAD, is also a problem. D-E-A-D almost always kills the sale. Always.

Ron and Rosie were so excited that Meadowlark Lane was to be their first house. Rosie wanted to start a family, and it was so appropriate that their nesting urges got them to a house on a lane named after a bird. They were an adorable couple, but nervous ad nauseum. I had looked at close to eighty houses with them, and engineer-minded Ron found fault in every single one to date.

Rosie was always looking for a 'feng-shui sign' that this was the right house. So, lingering odors or staircases facing the front door all had bad connotations, as did dead plants in the front yard. You name it: it was a potential bad omen to Rosie. The bigger problem for them was they couldn't afford a price range higher than $200,000 to get the house they envisioned. Even in real estate, that syndrome is called Beer Budget—Champagne Taste.

Finally, finally, just as I was getting ready to give up on them, they found this house. After lengthy negotiations involving six counteroffers between this sweet young couple and a difficult, morbidly obese, belligerent, beer-swilling seller, I got their offer accepted.

Then came the home inspection. My fingers were crossed that there were no problems discovered, other than the obvious need for paint and carpet. I had promised myself that if this sale didn't go through, Ron and Rosie would have to find another agent.

I had asked the listing agent to make sure the seller was out of the house so my buyers could look through it uninterrupted. I was taken aback when I unlocked the door and the TV was on.

I yelled, *"Hello—Agent!"* (When I open someone's door, I always yell "Hello, Agent!" as loud as I can, so I don't surprise a naked person getting out of the shower, or someone cleaning his gun.)

As I walked back towards the family room, I could see Mr. Beer Drinker's head leaning back against the headrest of his medium blue-grey Big Man recliner, like he'd fallen asleep watching the TV. Crap, he wasn't supposed to be home.

I turned back and put up my *Stay* hand, palm out, to Ron and Rosie to tell them to wait. Again, I yelled, *"Hello, Agent!"* loud enough to wake the dead, and still got no response.

I took a wide turn around the side of his chair so I didn't startle him too much. The first thing I noticed was that he was clutching the 32-oz beer can so tightly that it was dented in his hand; and second, that his face color matched his chair. As my brain caught up with my eyes, I registered that yelling loud enough to wake the dead was truly a euphemism—you can't wake the dead no matter how loud you yell.

Rosie went around me in her haste to thank the seller for accepting their offer. I in turn bumped the arm holding the beer can, which dropped to the carpet. By the time it hit the floor, Rosie had left the building. I could hear her screams coming from the driveway.

The home inspector had gotten his ladder down off his truck and was about to come inside. He quickly stepped aside to let Rosie shoot past. As he walked towards me, he said, "Were those your clients?" At which, I could only nod and sigh. He took a long look at the Blue Man Group reject in the chair and added, "Guess I won't need to inspect; they're probably not going to buy this house, huh?"

Yup, probably not.

THIRTY-THREE

THE MURRIETTA HOT SPRINGS CAPER

In my sixth year at Fakke & Co., I sold world famous Murrieta Hot Springs and Spa! While I have tried to disguise the identities of my clients and locales for obvious reasons, this story wouldn't be so noteworthy without naming it.

It was a Friday morning, the start of an epic day, to say the least. I had used all my problem-solving, detective investigation, and mortgage evaluation skills over the past ten days to unravel the myriad of entangled loans against Murrieta Hot Springs, and today I had presented an Offer to Purchase for $14,000,000 (that's FOURTEEN MILLION), all CASH, forty-day escrow, to the managing partner for the corporation that owned it.

I was The Wonder Woman real estate agent of my era already. I had sold seventy-five homes in my first thirty months at Fakke & Co., but my average sale was less than $300,000. I knew my commission would be over $223,000 ((that's TWO HUNDRED TWENTY-THREE THOUSAND DOLLARS—MY SHARE) when Murrieta closed. I was afraid I might jinx it by calculating exactly how much before the offer was even accepted, so I stopped myself every time I started to calculate it. (This began a lifelong avoidance of looking at my commission until the day before closing—a habit that drove all my brokers nuts. Brokers want paperwork completed a week prior to closing so THEY knew how much THEY were getting.)

But in order to build the suspense leading up to this epic day, let me start a month earlier when I was first contacted by Bernard and his manservant, David. They had heavy British accents and said they were from Madagascar. At the first opportunity I asked Bernard if he had ever seen a Tasmanian Devil. To which, he laughingly informed me that Madagascar and Tasmania are not the same, and no, he had never seen one of those vicious, nocturnal, smelly pests. It certainly was an embarrassing question (because no, I didn't know they were different places).

Granny had been running one of his come-steal-this ads on a three-house compound listing of Miriam's, and I happened to be the only agent in the office when David called. He announced that his employer, Bernard, wanted some more information on an ad he had seen for the compound in the coastal newspaper.

Bernard got on the phone and said he was looking to buy a large house with at least ten bedrooms. He wanted to open a private spa/retreat for women recovering from cosmetic surgery. The three-house listing was priced at $975,000, but as I described it as a big fixer-upper, I quickly established that it wouldn't work for him. I moved on to questioning him to see what else I might bring to his attention.

I've always been a good listener, and I was paying close attention to Bernard's answers to my initial list of qualifying questions.

I started with, *"How long have you been in the U.S.?"*

"A month."

"Are you a U.S. citizen?"

"No."

"Because you can't get a jumbo commercial loan without being a citizen, are you prepared to pay cash?"

"Yes."

"Where else have you been looking?"

"Los Angeles, Irvine, and Orange County."

"Are you working with other agents?"

"Yes, but not in your area."

"Could you pay more than $975,000 for the right property?"

"Yes."

"What might be the upper limit dollar amount, so I can only bring you properties that could work for you?"

"Money is no problem, but it needs to be the right property."

"Could you go as high as $3 million?"

"Of course." (At this response, I raised one eyebrow and decided to test the waters.)

"I know of one house that is still under construction, located on top of a large coastal hill. It's very private and has fabulous views. It will be about 20,000 square feet with eight bedrooms and ten bathrooms, when it's finished. It's not currently on the market, but it will be around $10 to $11,000,000. Would that be of interest?"

"Yes, tell me more about it." (Now both eyebrows were raised.)

"How long will you be available here in the U.S? I need to do some research on larger properties for you."

"I'm here one more month. I'm staying at a friend's home in Beverly Hills, but you can't call me here. I'll have to call you back."

Of course you are, Bernard! I was now starting to suspect I was wasting my time on someone calling different real estate offices to entertain themselves. That happens all the time in our area, when people want to entertain themselves anonymously on the phone, pretending they can buy big expensive homes in California and taking up a lot of an agent's time.

But, I'm also definitely a proponent of positive thinking, so on the off-chance that Bernard was real (he sounded real), I took the address of where he was staying. I said I'd mail him the listing information on properties that I found, and would he please call me back when he looked them over.

What the heck, I reasoned. Nothing ventured, etc.

Before two days passed, there was an article in the local real estate industry newspaper, The Transcript, about Murrieta Hot Springs. The Hot Springs was for sale, and after almost a year on the market, had just had a large price drop from $25,000,000 to $20,000,000. My eyes lit up. It was a potential steal, and maybe with Bernard's unlimited checkbook, it could happen!

Earlier articles that I had read in the newspaper outlined Murrieta's fall from grace. There had been rumors the mud baths were not sterilized every day, as touted, and the imagined grossness of that was hard to overcome. I didn't care. All of that could be fixed, and for a private spa selling to a cash buyer, those details could be ignored, as there would be no lenders, no appraisers, and no deal-killers.

In order to be able to answer detailed questions from Bernard on a huge property like this, and to make sure there were no lawsuits that might prevent a sale to him, I ordered the preliminary listing title report (the 'prelim') from First American Title, which was (and still is) touted as the title company to use for land deals or complex transactions. The prelim weighed in at five pounds and came in an oversized brown envelope about six inches thick.

The front summary of the prelim was twelve pages; eight pages of which were title exceptions of recorded mortgage loans, deeds, unpaid taxes, and lawsuit filings—easily forty, in all. (Normal prelims on homes have a page or two with a few exceptions—*not eight* **pages** *of them*.)

Having come from a mortgage loan background in previous careers, I understood all these items and knew what wasn't important and what could be deal-killers. Initially, I didn't see any deal-killers, except that the final tally of the mortgage loans was almost $24,000,000 or $4 million *more* than the asking price. That made my brow furrow. That was weird; but loving a good mystery, I dug deeper into the paperwork.

The copies of the dozen mortgage loans constituted the rest of the five pounds. *Each* of the mortgages had eight to ten *pages* of notarized signatures of people who held a fractional ownership of that particular mortgage. With six individually notarized signatures to a page x ten pages x twelve mortgages—was it possible that there were over 800 investors?

I was getting really confused, so I arranged my stack with the mortgage with the oldest date on top. As I read down through them, I started recognizing some of the same names over and over. By using a package of colored highlighter pens, I found the names came in groups on each mortgage.

By the time I looked at the most recent mortgage, all the names from all the other mortgages were attached, along with one last group of new names. The notarized list of signatures on the most recent mortgage was eighteen pages, or almost 120 people. One-hundred-twenty is a huge amount of fractional investors for one large loan, but it wasn't 820.

It still didn't make sense—all the mortgages with most of the same people on them, over and over. So, as I'm wont to do, I went to sleep pondering the problem and woke up with a solution in the morning.

The only mortgage that mattered was the largest, most recent one. The others had just not ever been reported as being paid off (reconveyed) by the managing partner because he *didn't* pay them off, he just added more money on top of (around) them. He hadn't paid them off, in real estate vocabulary, he was 'wrapping' them. In other words, think of a dart board. The smallest loan was in the middle and all the other loans were the rings around it and they were all *included* in the newest loan. The biggest loan was the outside ring and that mortgage was only for $12 million. (ONLY $12 million, seriously? ONLY?)

I tested this theory by comparing the original document signatures and realizing that, on each new mortgage, they were there in the same sequence, and some new signatures had been added.

Bingo, we have a winner! Or, at least I had a grasp of what the mortgage picture actually was.

So, when Bernard called, I told him about Murrieta Hot Springs. He said he'd already looked at it with an L.A. real estate Broker, but the owners owed $24,000,000, and he wasn't about to pay that.

"Tell me, Bernard—if I told you I think it could be bought for around $14 million, would you want and be able to buy it?"

"Yes, I would definitely buy it at $14 million."

I filled out the Offer to Purchase and headed for Beverly Hills on Saturday. In Beverly Hills, I had been instructed to go around back of the mansion at a particular address and find the service entrance, to meet Bernard and David by the pool.

It was such an outrageous scenario with the mansion, the manservant, and the service entrance that I decided I would just go forward and hope for the best, but that the story in itself was enough of a reward for my time.

It took me several minutes to drive the entire length of the driveway from the gate marked "*Service Entrance*" to a parking area big enough to hold ten catering trucks. The parking area was next to the outdoor kitchen and pool, and at its edge, a tall, thin man was standing. I could barely see the house further up the hill—it looked to be a stone monster of a castle, right out of a Gothic movie set in England. I had never seen a home like this, or been on a Beverly Hills tour. Too bad Ginger wasn't with me. I'll bet she knew who lived there or knew someone who did know.

David was the tall, strikingly handsome older Englishman with graying hair, a somber demeanor, and chiseled features who met me at the parking area. He escorted me up to the pool to meet Bernard. In contrast, Bernard was a short, paunchy, youngish man wearing a muted Hawaiian shirt and cream-colored linen shorts. He wasn't black but looked more like a very dark man of Pakistani or Indian origin.

"What would you like to drink, my dear? David will bring you anything you want to drink or eat. The cook doesn't leave for another half hour."

Although I was so excited that I was afraid I might throw up anything I ate or drank, I ordered a lemonade, as that is what Bernard looked to be drinking and I had just had a class on 'mirroring' as a way of bonding with clients.

Bernard wanted to chat, initially, about me and about real estate, probably to size me up. I had had enough training by this time to let him take the lead. This is especially important when buyers are from outside the United States, in case they aren't used to doing business with women. It's easier to avoid offending them that way. I'd learned in class that foreign business people think Americans are too direct in business transactions and I didn't want to waste this opportunity to make a huge sale by appearing too rushed.

After twenty minutes or so of chatting, I was relaxing a little and enjoying the delicious fresh lemonade. Bernard then asked me to go ahead with my proposal for buying Murrieta Hot Springs. I briefly explained that all the mortgages had been replaced by bigger mortgages, so the only one that was really against the Spa was not quite $12 million. I reckoned that another $2 million would pay closing costs, commissions, and back taxes, leaving some extra money in case new liens came up during escrow.

He and David had some quiet conversation, and he said, "Okay, where do I sign?" With that, he signed six pages of my Offer to Purchase and wrote a personal check for $250,000 to First American Title as a deposit. Ever the thorough agent, I asked if there was enough money in this account to cover a check of this size. He just nodded twice to confirm that there was..

On Monday morning, I drove into San Diego to present the $14 million offer to Robb, the man whom First American had identified as the managing partner. I had to leave the envelope marked URGENT with the receptionist at the front desk. She told me Robb wasn't in yet, and she didn't know when to expect him.

On Tuesday, I called. He wasn't in.

On Wednesday, I called morning and afternoon—he still wasn't in.

On Thursday, I called, to be told he might be in on Friday morning.

On Friday, I stepped out of the elevator into Robb's lobby to find it was alive with fifty or sixty short, round grandmothers. They were surrounding the sole male, who was also quite short, rotund, and bespectacled.

Most of the grandmothers had grey hair cut short and tightly curled by a perm, sensible shoes, and wore glasses. Most were crying and reaching out their hands to him, as if beseeching him to touch them. They were saying things like, "We love you, Robb", "We know you'll take care of us, Robb", and "We are praying for you, Robb." Except for one extra-loud, extra-mad-sounding voice. "I want my money back *right now*, Robb. Right now."

He looked like a meek, mild-mannered, somewhat perplexed man who wasn't sure what the fuss was all about. I recognized him from the gallery of directors photos on the wall facing the elevator. I don't know what I expected, but he didn't look like the president of a large financial company in that chaotic scene.

I took a seat at the edge of the lobby hoping to be the 'fly on the wall'. When things quieted down, Robb ushered the flock of grandmothers to the elevator. As the door to the elevator closed, he leaned forward in earnest and waved goodbye to them, saying, with all sincerity, "Everything will be alright, you'll see."

But when Robb turned around to come back into the lobby, he wore a different face, and it wasn't that of an earnest or sincere man. It was a hard, I-couldn't-care-less face. I was somewhat surprised, and instantly felt bad for those little old ladies.

The receptionist pointed at me, saying I was there to see him about Murrieta Hot Springs. As he walked towards me, I noticed how unkempt he looked. He had a day or two's growth of beard, his shirt looked un-ironed, and the lowest button on his shirt was unbuttoned, allowing a hairy part of his generous belly to hang over his belt. He slouched into the chair across an end table from me.

Quite frankly, for an instant, I wondered if he were mentally impaired. He looked at me distractedly and myopically through his coke bottle glasses, saying tersely and with authority, "You have five minutes."

I had prepared and practiced my sales speech to explain the offer and convince him to accept it, but when he said five minutes and started picking his nose and wiping his finger on a magazine on the end table, I was caught off guard. There was no one else in the lobby except for the receptionist, so I just blurted out, in one breath, *"I've read through all the mortgages and see you haven't been reporting the older ones as paid off because you've been wrapping them, and I know you only have about $12 million against it, not $24 million; and my cash offer is for $14 million, forty days close, and you can be done with this mess."*

At that, he quit picking his nose, buttoned his lower shirt button, and actually looked at me. He sat up straight, gave a wry smile, and said calmly, "You've done your homework. Give me a pen."

And, with that, I had a $14 million signed offer!

On Monday, I opened escrow at my favorite First American Title. However, that same day, headlines in 24-point type graced the front of The Transcript. It broke the story that Robb was being investigated for orchestrating a Ponzi scheme with Murrieta Hot Springs at the center. The article said he had over 200 investors, mostly older divorced and widowed Jewish women, who were his victims.

I still optimistically continued with the escrow at First American, but they needed some information from Robb, and he wasn't returning their calls. All the major newspapers in Southern California and Arizona picked up the story, so after almost two weeks without any progress, Granny gave me his attorney to try to find out what had happened to my accepted offer.

The attorney couldn't make any progress either; except one day, almost a month later, he called me to say that a court-appointed attorney had called him saying that Murrieta Hot Springs could not be sold at this time. That attorney had told him that it didn't matter anyway, $14 million was way too low; there was $24 million owed against it. Except for Robb and I, no one else yet understood the mortgage conundrum.

Three years later, the headline in The Transcript newspaper said that Murrieta Hot Springs had been sold for $6,000,000 (SIX MILLION), or less than half of what Bernard had offered.

THIRTY-FOUR

FROM MODEL TO MODEL PRISONER

When Becca Snively walked into Fakke & Co. to interview, my first thought was, "Here comes another Fakke & Co. beautiful agent." I couldn't have known then that, while still in high school, Becca had been a successful teen model. She had appeared in many national beauty product ads, culminating with being on the cover of Seventeen Magazine. I grew up in such poverty, I had never bought any magazines, or any beauty products for that matter, so I wasn't awed by her accomplishments.

All of us agents were initially impressed by Becca's stunning good looks—until she opened her mouth. She had the dirtiest potty mouth of anyone I've ever heard—before or since.

If you could hear her talking in another room without seeing her, you would think she could teach profanity to longshoremen. She could string together more swear words and expletives than should be legally allowed. Which, in turn, certainly promoted an expanded vocabulary within our office for expressing anger and frustration.

When she ran out of nasty words, she just made some up that sounded nasty, and kept going.

All I knew was that this newcomer looked so model-perfect as to not be real. Every time she appeared in the office, at the beach, or in public, her makeup was perfect, as were her strawberry blonde hair, her lacquered nails, her matching lipstick, and her stylish clothing. She even looked perfect in short shorts before Granny forbade everyone from wearing them in the office.

Becca's road from Seventeen model to model prisoner ran right through our office. At age twenty-three, Becca blew into San Marea in a red Mustang convertible with the wind whipping her strawberry mane. She was considered too old to model anymore, so real estate sales were a perfect next step.

She was as blunt as she was beautiful. The first day after Granny had hired her, Becca announced to those of us in the office that she was looking for a rich boyfriend or husband and would appreciate being introduced to anyone fitting that description. Although she said she liked her men tall, she declared she would also accept a short man standing on a tall wallet. Becca Snively had arrived and was open for business.

Within two weeks, she had moved in with the owner of a local nightclub, a famous 'IT spot' halfway between San Diego and L.A.

Richard Hadley (aka Rich—of course) was arguably the most eligible bachelor in all of Southern California. He was tall, dark, and wealthy, with chiseled features crafted by the best plastic surgeon in Southern California. He dressed right out of GQ Magazine and was known to have any drug you might need, want, or desire. Even on a weeknight, his nightclub had lines two blocks long of people waiting to be evaluated by his bouncers. One needed to be at least an 8.5 in order to gain entry, at $8.50 per person. The name of the nightclub was Eight Point Five (of course). Any woman, or man, garnering a ten got free admission.

It was the era of sex, drugs, and rock and roll, and the club elevated Becca from model to arm candy for Rich. Her legs looked longer than a baby giraffe's because her skirts were amazingly skimpy; exposing the presence, or the absence, of panties when she sat down. She made Eight Point Five her real estate 'farm', and the parade of wealthy, gorgeous young clients trooping into our office after the weekend was impressive.

Even more impressive was the way she talked to them over the phone in her longshoreman lingo, as in, "You f--king better get your ass over here and see this whorehouse or I'm f--king going to sell it to another a-hole and cut off your balls." This was one of her milder sales pitches and was generally made while standing up and screaming into the phone. When Becca picked up her phone, the agents around her cut short their conversations so they could hang up before THEIR clients overheard the coming diatribe.

Enter Cass.

One day at about noon (which was early for Cass), a Hummer stretch limo capable of holding twenty-five partygoers pulled up in front of Fakke & Co. It was too long to park anywhere, so it just stopped mid-street. The doors opened, disgorging a 5'5" Cass with four towering Vegas showgirls framing him and taking up the entire sidewalk as they walked arm-in-arm abreast (pun intended) up to the front door of the office. Becca's newest client from Eight Point Five was making his grand entrance.

It was no problem for the forty-foot Hummer to stop in the street, as it wasn't blocking any cars. All the traffic both ways had halted to watch the girls strut their stuff, although I did notice a couple of nerdy-looking guys eyeballing the limo instead.

Cass was accompanied by a differing group of escorts, comprised of ladies in a wide spectrum of different colors of skin, of hair, and of micro-miniskirts. Each wore a matching lipstick red tube top over breasts unfettered by bras and emblazoned with one word—"SEXY." The word was written in silver sequins that shimmered and sparkled as it bounced up and down to the rhythm of their steps.

Cass was an uber-successful entrepreneur (under the age of thirty) from Las Vegas who carried at least $10,000 cash on his body at all times (according to Becca). He worked for a lady boss who did something with financing. He was never truly clear about what he did, except that he ran a bullpen containing over a hundred employees. They were raking in the money, and he was compensated accordingly. He was looking at homes in the $1 million range, which was the upper price tier, in those years, for San Marea.

The next time Cass came in, he only had two showgirls with him. The last time, when he came to sign his closing papers on a big white ultra-modern San Marea estate on a bluff overlooking the ocean, he flew solo. He was in love with Becca, and everyone, including both of them, knew it. The house had its own private free-form pool which sloped up to a real sand beach on one end. Cass wanted their kids to be safe when that time came.

Becca hadn't quite finished extracting herself from Rich's orbit, however. The ability to 'farm' all this beautiful cliental from Eight Point Five was heavy in her purse. She had gotten (or perhaps continued) into constant cocaine use. Ginger speculated that Becca's habit was up to $200 per day now. (Ginger was a never-ending fountain of off-the-wall tidbits of knowledge like this, and I never questioned their veracity.) Staying with Rich meant she never paid. At least she didn't have to pay in dollars.

Becca's habit seemed to be causing problems with her nose. She had always been vain and was spending more and more time in the office, looking in a pocket mirror at her nose every moment when she wasn't insulting someone on the phone. Sometimes even when she WAS on the phone. I wondered if Becca was so fixated on her nose that she didn't see what was really there—a wonderful Elizabeth Taylor snub nose—one ever so slightly freckled.

Then I heard that Becca had septoplasty surgery to repair a tiny hole in it from the cocaine. Right before the surgery, she confided to Ginger she was frightened at having the surgeon's knife so close to her face, so she promised herself to cut way back on her habit. She actually did cut back, which allowed her to leave Rich and move in with Cass at his 'beach" house.

Becca then told Ginger that she and Cass were going into business together and she wouldn't need to sell real estate anymore. Cass had figured out how his lady boss was making such an ocean liner full of money and had poached a couple of her major employees to come to San Marea and work with him. She had found her 'short man standing on a tall wallet', it seemed.

Before she could leave Fakke & Co., Becca had two more surgeries because she wasn't happy with the results of the first one. She'd had to change plastic surgeons twice by then, as after each surgery, that surgeon would not do any more. Ginger said that evidently Becca's septum collapsed entirely, and most of it had to be removed during the last surgery. That had changed her looks so drastically that we could see all the way up into the upper chamber of her nose when she looked directly at us. If she had had any brains, we certainly could have seen them, too.

Becca was devastated, as anyone would be, but even more devastated because of her vanity issues. Cass endeared himself to us all by telling her he only saw her as she was when he fell in love with her, so let's go make some money. This was in May.

The next time we saw Becca, we were invited to her new company office Christmas party a few days before Christmas. It was held at one of the most expensive beach hotels in San Diego. Knowing Becca's penchant for luxury, Lolly, Krista, Miriam, Ginger and I couldn't wait, and the party didn't disappoint. It was so 'out there and over the top', I speculated that this might reflect what the Playboy Mansion parties were like.

First of all, the hotel's top floor penthouse was likely 5,000 square feet on one level, plus the balcony deck. There was a well-known local band at one corner of the patio and a sea of beautiful, young, well-dressed women and men pulsating to the music. The buffet tables were groaning under enormous heaping bowls of seafood and caviar, accompanied by seemingly unlimited bottles of Dom Pérignon champagne. As the party progressed, many of their employees walked around drinking straight out of their very own bottle.

Also, as the party progressed, lead crystal bowls of white powder with tiny silver spoons appeared. Although Lolly and Krista wanted to dance some more, none of us was into drugs, and I wanted out of there before something bad happened.

Lolly needed to use the bathroom first, but there was a long line at the one by the front door Becca provided for the guests. Ever the resourceful, problem-solving agent, Lolly snuck through the closed door into the adjoining main bedroom to use the private bathroom. She immediately came back and got us. "You've got to see this before we go." She was insistent, and we were glad we looked.

The huge bedroom was all gold decor, including the ten-foot round bed which looked like it had been moved in fresh off a movie set. Above the bed was a one-piece gold-veined mirror, framed and mounted on the ceiling. A gigantic white hairy coverlet was thrown stylishly over it. It may have been real fur, but in trying to think of what is white and furry and that large, all I could come up with was 'polar bear.' Considering Becca, it was certainly possible.

In the car back to San Marea, Ginger confirmed that Becca and Cass had been making obscene amounts of money, as he had promised. The Christmas party had cost them $60,000 (today's equivalent of $152,000), and they were keeping the suite through New Year's Day. Ginger gave us a detailed version of Becca's business.

"It's so simple, it's genius' was Becca's introduction in explaining it to Ginger. It involved calling people to tell them they had won a Las Vegas vacation worth $2,500, but the winners had to pay a $495 service fee to collect their prize. However, Becca said the fine print on the prize voucher they mailed out had so many restrictions, a winner could never collect. And if the complaints got to be too many, she and Cass would just close down and move everyone to a new city.

Our mouths hung open so long, through the telling of Becca's escapades, that our tongues dried out as we digested what we had eaten, drunk, seen, and were now hearing.

Although we never saw Becca again, we read about her in the newspapers starting around Valentine's Day. The sordid tale had blossomed from a Federal investigation into the scam in Las Vegas. Seems that Cass's former lady boss was raided by the FBI. In a plea bargain to avoid prison, the lady boss had given him up as the Main Man—the one who had come up with the idea and was operating out of the San Diego area. As she pointed out, she was small potatoes, (just look around her bull pen), with less than ten employees. Cass was really the one they wanted.

We'd all heard there was no honor among thieves, and we watched it as this unfolded in real time. According to the local newspaper, Cass admitted under oath that the vacation scam was actually masterminded by Becca. Look at the paperwork, the bank statements—they were all in her name. (According to Ginger, Becca said she had to put everything in her name so the old lady boss couldn't accuse Cass of stealing 'industry secrets' and then competing with her.)

By tossing Becca under the bus, Cass got a one-year sentence reduced to time served, after which, we heard, he moved back to Las Vegas.

The only one who ultimately got a seven-year prison sentence was Becca. She called Ginger when she got an early release to tell her she'd married one of her prison guards and was living somewhere around Los Angeles.

THIRTY-FIVE

THE NAIL LADY AND THE BILLIONAIRE

The Painted Lady Nail Palace was the Top Ranked Hair and Nail Salon, according to the Best of the Best list published annually in San Diego Magazine. Accordingly, their prices reflected that, but Ginger had been going there since she moved to San Diego and was loyal to the cute young lady who did her weekly manicure.

Like me, Ginger was a nail biter, so with all the contracts we used, having to point out the lines for our buyers and sellers to initial or sign, many of us had standing weekly nail appointments. Ginger's favorite manicurist was Brandi, a pixie-like waif who resembled a young Audrey Hepburn and who considered Ginger to be her second mother. They became great confidents for one hour every week, with Brandi asking for, and Ginger giving, motherly advice.

Until Brandi went to Tucson with her best girlfriend for the weekend of her twenty-second birthday and came back a changed woman. A woman who was about to become the American mistress of a Frenchman from an ultra-famous French family (but none of us knew that yet, including Brandi).

One Valentine's Day, Brandi and her girlfriend had flown to Tucson on Saturday after work. They had reservations at a five-star restaurant on Saturday evening, where they had a great meal and a nice bottle of wine that someone had anonymously sent to their table. When her complementary piece of cake had appeared after dinner with a lit candle on top and the waiters had finished singing "Happy Birthday" to her, a gorgeous man, probably twice her age, came over to their table.

He was well-dressed in an obviously expensive custom suit that fit him impeccably, a white silk shirt, no tie, and with an even more gorgeous French accent. He asked if they had enjoyed the wine, adding that it was a special bottle that came from his vineyard in France. He declared himself 'enchanted' with Brandi, and after apologizing for not being able to spend any time with her this evening, asked if she and her friend would have brunch with him on Sunday.

Sweet, naïve Brandi had no choice but to say 'yes'. Their flight was at 6 p.m., so they had plenty of time tomorrow. He then gallantly offered to arrange a ride for the two back to their hotel. The ladies, thinking he was calling a taxi, thanked him and went out to a white stretch limo with a liveried driver holding one cream-colored rose that he presented to Brandi with a flourish.

The following morning, promptly at 11 a.m., Gerrard arrived at the hotel in the white limo with the same driver. He had a lavish picnic basket filled with brunch food and a selection of wines with the same label as last night. His driver drove them to a spot on a mountain just outside Tucson that had a 240-degree panoramic view of the city and the desert beyond. He was the consummate gentleman, laughing and teasing with Brandi and her friend while showing her the Tucson sights for four hours. He asked for Brandi's business card when he dropped them off, and arranged for his limo to come back in two hours to take them to the airport.

That was the initial weekly installment. It was a precursor to weekly installments that we grew to look forward to as Brandi's own private Cinderella-Prince Charming soap opera gathered steam.

The following week, Ginger came back all excited after her nail appointment. Gerard had been sending Brandi bouquets of a dozen roses to her work every day since she got back from Tucson. Every day, the bouquets were a single color, but always with one cream rose among them. He was coming to San Diego in a couple of weeks. Brandi, Ginger, and all the rest of us were looking forward to that.

That was the second installment, and we Fakke agents were hooked to the point where we always knew what day Ginger's nail appointment was and managed to schedule ourselves in the office to hear the Brandi-Gerrard update. Subsequent weeks' stories grew and improved.

After Gerrard's second visit to San Diego, he left Brandi a credit card for any of her needs. No monetary restrictions were mentioned. He told her that he never wanted to see her in the same clothes when he came. Everything from underwear to workout clothes to special occasion outfits had to be brand new.

He selected a personal shopper for her at Nordstrom Designer Shop and left instructions as to how he wanted Brandi to dress, even specifying the acceptable clothing designer's labels. She had to wear lots of leather clothing, and when she did, she had to wear matching leather gloves and have a matching leather clutch handbag. Had to be clutch—no handbags with handles or straps were to be purchased.

Two months later, Brandi and Ginger were shopping for a house for Gerrard. He wanted to arrive, stay, and leave San Diego in anonymity. His wife and children lived in France, but he wanted his private life with Brandi to stay private. He hobnobbed with the *crème de la crème* in local social circles, and he didn't want journalists or photographers taking photos of him to splash in newspapers or magazines. The house would be registered in a new corporation he set up specifically for the purchase.

This house had to be in a top neighborhood, under $1 million dollars, be in a private setting, and, when Brandi found what she wanted, she only need call his private secretary with the escrow information so he could have the purchase price wired for closing. Of course, Brandi relied on Ginger to make sure Gerrard would be pleased with the house.

It was common knowledge that Becca's old boyfriend, Rich, was needing a cash infusion to keep Eight Point Five afloat. Armed with that knowledge, Ginger got Brandi a sweet deal.

The house was a 4,500 square foot gracious white stucco, Spanish-style hacienda with a red tile roof. It was mostly one-story, with only the main bedroom and an office upstairs. It had been designed by an architect who was an award-winning local celebrity of sorts.

The hacienda was situated on two acres at the end of a cul-de-sac street that was considered one of the most sought after addresses in San Marea. There was an Olympic-sized pool with a state-of-the-art outdoor kitchen and bar (one that only a restaurant and bar owner would need) and a generously sized gazebo, tucked behind the house, out of sight of the street.

Both Ginger and Brandi were ecstatic. Ginger was especially ecstatic over the full 3% commission she earned on a $1.1 million dollar sale ($3.3 million today's dollar).

Then the opportunists that always seem to follow in herds behind money got their hands on sweet, naïve Brandi. Gerrard had approved of the house, but wanted it remodeled to meet his wealthy-person-with-excellent-taste specifications. He didn't specify what that was, so one of Brandi's nail customers, who professed to be an interior designer, took over.

Brandi had lots of nail customers at The Painted Lady Palace. Several of them with husbands or boyfriends needing work listened, learned, and lined up to take advantage of Brandi. The group of people who quickly got on the payroll behind the interior designer included a landscape designer, a sound system designer, a security system designer, a kitchen contractor, a pool contractor, the weekly maid, not to mention the weekly lawn and the pool maintenance people. The only person Gerrard actually hired himself was a bodyguard for Brandi.

Ginger watched in horror as slowly, very slowly (as in 'more time is more money' slowly), the posse sucked money out of Brandi's unlimited credit cards.

Brandi had no idea of how much things should cost. She was busy reading every social magazine that Gerrard had subscribed to for her 'education'. She was to memorize information about every person in photographs of the top social events of every season. Especially if there were only one or two people in the photos, and especially if they were the hosts or chairs of said events.

Gerrard's visits were now every other week, so he would quiz her to give him details of people whose names he recited for her.

He wasn't going to take her out in public with him until he was sure she wouldn't embarrass him in front of somebody important.

Finally, one day during Ginger's weekly appointment, Brandi confided that the interior designer/nail client she had hired was charging her $100,000 for her expertise, and that the sound people had just presented her with a bill for $240,000 to install a high-quality stereo system inside and out.

She was petrified that Gerrard may be mad at how much it was costing. She said he had given her an extra $1 million to remodel, after purchasing it for $1.1 million. That money was almost gone, and nothing was completed.

The interior designer had spent over $750,000 changing the house from a Spanish hacienda into a Turkish-Moorish habitat. Under her direction, the contractor changed the roof line itself, and the house, into a black and gold palette right out of 1,001 Arabian Nights. The interior designer assured Brandi that this was a prestigious Islamic-type design, currently popular in France.

After Ginger had driven by the house on her way back to the office, she was speechless at what she was seeing, and didn't know how to report back to Brandi. She bustled into Fakke & Co., saying she needed help. She wanted Krista, Lolly, Miriam and I to see if it was as bad as she thought it was. We had all been to parties there when Becca was still at Fakke & Co., so we were bursting with curiosity to see what was upsetting Ginger.

We jumped into Ginger's car, and what greeted us made us all speechless, as well. The red roof curved tiles had been replaced with flat black cement tiles and a black cupola. Gothic-looking peaks, accented inside with gold paint, had been added. Brandi had been assured the gold accents were paint with real gold in it.

The backyard gazebo had been painted black, as had the bottom of the pool. The pool rim had black and gold Moorish-looking tile under the coping. The three-year-old custom commercial outdoor kitchen had been ripped out and replaced with a cheaper version of itself. The new version cost more than the high-quality expensive one that was already there, yet it managed to look worse.

To me, the architecture of this monstrosity more resembled 'Hindu Hates Art Deco.' Brandi's interior designer probably made up the Turkish-Moorish description to sound more exotic.

The interior was worse than the exterior. It now had glossy black corbels and glossy black ornate doors to all the rooms. The coved ceiling in the living room on the left off the entry was black, with stars painted inside the dome in the real gold paint. The stars glowed when the recessed lighting strips that were hidden behind the rim of the coving were turned on.

The kitchen was unusable. The high-end commercially equipped kitchen had been gutted and, after a year, the contractor (who had already been paid) had yet to start the reconstruction.

Ginger said she felt like throwing up, as did we all. She had contacted some contractors and sub-contractors she knew who were honest and reliable, and found out the stereo system should have cost $80,000 and the designer's fee maybe $25,000.

But the work wasn't completed on anything. Like I said, it was going slowly, *v e r y   s l o w l y*. Brandi was reluctant to fire anyone. The interior designer instructed her to pay the contractor and all the sub-contractors in full, at the beginning and she didn't have more money to hire new workers.

This travesty continued to degenerate for almost two more years. The house eventually got finished and Ginger reported that it ended up costing $2.4 million ($6.1 million today), between the purchase price and remodel costs.

With $1 million being spent here and there, the next million came when Gerrard wanted Brandi to have his baby. She had grown smarter over the past two years, and she refused. He could leave at any time, and she'd have a child to raise by herself. Our Ginger should have been an attorney. With her counseling, Brandi negotiated $1 million cash to be put in a trust fund that was in her and the unborn baby's names only. That account showed up promptly, and within a few visits, Brandi was pregnant.

Here's the final installment of the saga of Brandi from The Painted Lady Nail Palace, the baby, and Gerrard with vineyards and a wife and kids in France and racehorses in San Marea. It was a spectacularly quick ending that felt much like an elevator falling from the fiftieth floor to the lobby in one minute or less.

When the baby was about one year old, Gerrard had been gone for almost two months. When he came to San Marea one week, he found that Brandi had been feeling neglected for an exceedingly long time now and had married her bodyguard a month ago. They were taking the baby and the $1.0 million trust fund, and that was that.

Ginger earned her final commission when Gerrard dumped the Turkish-Moorish-Hindu-Art-Deco house for $1.8 million. He then sold his string of thoroughbred racehorses that were stabled out by the polo fields and bought Brandi a home for the new family to live in. It modestly cost around $600,000, but Gerard still loved her and it was perfect for sweet, naïve Brandi.

THIRTY-SIX

HAPPINESS COMES BEFORE HEARTBREAK

Happiness comes before heartbreak both in Webster's Dictionary and in my life, it seems. Mahatma Gandhi is credited with saying, *"Happiness is when what you think, what you say, and what you do are in harmony."* But, having grown up in abject poverty with my alcoholic mother, I always thought happiness was money . . . as in—when I get enough money, I'll be happy. My personal earnings in the eighties were over $1 million total for the last five years. But candidly, even at age forty-three, I didn't have a clue as to how to be happy. My life looked like a great life, from some else's viewpoint. I'm reasonably good-looking with long, thick, blondish hair. I appeared successful with a personal shopper at Nordstrom, jewelry, and fake long fingernails. I owned matching yellow Mercedes—a sedan for work and a two-seater 450 SL convertible for single clients or for play. I was happening, and some of my closest agent friends told me everyone in the office wanted to be me.

While that looked impressive, behind the curtain, I was sad to the bone.

But when reality doesn't suck, it bites. Here I was, tonight, stylin' in a California ranch home with solid walls, real wall-to-wall thick cream carpet, a pool, and a fabulous ocean view. I hadn't closed an escrow in over four months; and was in one of these cyclical valleys that was complicated, in my case, by unrequited love. I was mentally in a black hole and feeling quite pathetic. What would Jamison think if he could see me now? I didn't even want THAT visual in my head.

Jamison had said goodbye to me three years ago at the end of a wonderful three-day weekend in Orlando. We were like carefree kids, enjoying each other, exploring all the different world country exhibits at Epcot Center while holding hands and eating junk food. We had shared about twenty trips and trysts, by then. Our routine was to take long weekends together, then fly home late Sunday night. No matter the time, he would call me when he knew my plane had landed to make sure my flight had gotten me safely back to San Marea. But that time it was different, and I remember that call like it was yesterday:

"Nico, I'm sorry, but I can't see you anymore. While I want to explore why I'm so attracted to you, I just can't keep doing this. I'm married. I have a young daughter to help raise and that's not going to change. I saw how devastated my Mother was when my Dad left us all for his secretary, and I promised myself I would never do that, no matter the personal price I might have to pay."

Jamison had told me in the beginning of our relationship if his wife had not gotten pregnant, he would never have married her in a million years. But his family and her family were staunch Christians, church elders, and well-connected in the Texas political scene, so he did the 'right' thing. Jamison could always be counted on to do the 'right' thing. That's probably one of his qualities that I admired the least, given our circumstances.

Jamison continued, "I'm like a moth to your candle, Nico (which were the same words I had used years earlier to describe my attraction to him.) I'm so attracted at a cellular level that I don't completely understand it. I realize I have fallen in love for the first time, but I am so, so sorry. I just can't continue. This has to stop."

After a long pause, he said "Please know I'll always love you, but I have to go. I'm sorry." With that, he was gone. He had hung up, but not before I heard him sigh loudly—a sigh that blew out my candle's flame and broke my heart.

In the days, weeks and years that followed, I translated his words to mean that I was the love of his life—and guess what? He was and ALWAYS WILL be the love of MY life. I had never known what it was to be in love until I met him. I had not dated a single man after our first meeting, but anyone who now comes after him won't have a chance—I will always be comparing them to Jamison.

During that last phone conversation when he imposed his decision on me, I said nothing. I didn't protest, and I didn't tell him I would always love him. Nothing. It is a regret that I wasn't able to tell him how I felt, the moment was lost as his words had struck me dumb. I just sat on my couch at home as the sun started to set. Along with it, I felt my soul slip down towards a very dark place. A place where no light and no love could ever find it.

But, as hard as it is to admit to myself even now, perhaps I wasn't able to say anything to Jamison because I was paralyzed by the sudden realization that he was walking away from me like both my father and my husband had done before him. Being abandoned by them both hadn't prepared me for this monumental loss of Jamison—I hadn't loved them like I loved Jamison.

Losing Jamison was losing the only man I loved MORE than I loved my own life. Because I wasn't willing to see myself as unlovable, I prepared instead to live in denial that Jamison might be gone forever. (And, as my favorite uncle used to say, Denial isn't a river in Egypt). I knew in my soul that he would someday come back to me. I just wanted it to be in this lifetime.

I had a pretend *IF* game I played when I felt abandoned. My father, my ex-husband, and now Jamison, would come back *if* he really wanted to, and everything would be 'perfect'. But I've finally learned that any time I said that something would be '*perfect*', it portended a disaster.

I had become fiercely independent after my phenomenal success selling real estate. I had insurance, money in the bank, and free time, so I didn't need anything from Jamison. Except, I would like my heart back please.

In the stillness of every night, right before I went to sleep, I always enjoyed feeling my heart beating and hearing the blood whooshing through my arteries. I didn't want to hear it beating anymore; there was no joy in there. There was no joy even in reaching an almost $3 million in earnings milestone. *That* was the cold realization that came out of my late-night reflections. In an epiphany moment, I suddenly realized happiness had nothing to do with having enough money. I was stunned. If happiness wasn't measured by money, what was it? Where would I find it?

As life is wont to do when you think you've figured it out, it all changed in an instant. The phone rang around 11 p.m. I didn't realize the time or I wouldn't have answered. I picked it up on the first ring.

A beloved, deep baritone with a Texas accent said, "Nico. It's me. I've missed you. More than you can ever know."

His voice hit me like a fist to my stomach. Something inside of me collapsed. It was like free-falling in an elevator. The enormity of my reaction to him, even on the phone, swept my breath away. Mascara was streaming down my face, but I couldn't say anything around the lump in my throat.

"Are you there?" I nodded my head and gurgled slightly.

"I have something important to talk to you about, but I need to do it in person. I'd like to come out to see you. Will I be welcome?"

The tears turned into stifled sobs on my end. *"Yes, yes, always"*.

"I'm planning my annual trip with three of my longtime friends to hike in the Grand Canyon, but I'll be in San Diego Sunday night, at the Marriott. So go shopping and buy something sexy to wear while you wait for me. I'll come as soon as we get in. Oh, and get some of my favorite brandy. I'm needing it. I'll see you late Sunday evening. Cancel all your appointments for the next few days, as we have some catching up to do. I sent you a registered package to your office. It should be there tomorrow, so tell the secretary to call you when it comes in, but don't open it. Wait 'til I'm there."

The last empty three years melted away when I heard myself use his pet name. *"Junior, I'm so awfully glad to hear your voice. I've regretted for years that the last time we spoke, I didn't tell you how much I loved you. I can hardly wait to see you. Have fun in the Grand Canyon and know I'll be waiting for you."*

My hands were shaking, and my tears flowed freely. But my breath was back, my heart was back, and my life was back. It felt like happiness was finally a recognizable, palpable entity. I told myself that happiness is when you get what you've asked for, and you still want it. Even through all my tears, it was sure looking like happiness was coming back on Sunday.

But, alphabetically speaking, as I said earlier, Happiness comes before Heartbreak in Webster's Dictionary.

I had been sitting in our Marriott Suite (it felt so good to say 'our' Marriott Suite that I said it every few minutes—since 3 p.m.). Every time someone came down the hall, my heart leapt back into my throat. I was showered, waxed, douched, coiffured, polished, and clad in the original unused stretchy sexy lacy red teddy with the snap crotch. I had gone by the office to get the small package he had sent me and it was sitting on the night table by the bed. I needed to eat, but didn't want to eat, couldn't eat, from the excitement of wanting to share room service with him 'afterwards'. I'd been watching TV since I arrived to allay the boredom and exhaustion of such high anticipation.

The candles I had brought bathed the spacious room in a soft light while the odor of bergamot floated aloft. Two dozen Sunset-colored roses were sitting in a beautiful cut crystal vase on the coffee table in the room when I arrived. An expensive bottle of his favorite Hennessey XO cognac and two elegant snifters were on a tray by the bed. I spritzed my wrists once more. My Obsession cologne was warm, sexy, and inviting. He frequently said he loved my smell.

Everything is perfect, I thought, as I surveyed the room with great satisfaction from the bed. Now I just need Jamison to arrive. The Ten O'clock News came on.

"Our breaking news story tonight concerns a prominent Texas businessman who fell to his death earlier today while hiking in the Grand Canyon. His name has not been released, pending notification of his family."

A prescient cold knot like a fist formed in my stomach. My nightmare was back. Was I yet again waiting for a man who would never come? No, No, NO, NO, NO.

The Eleven O'clock News came on—followed immediately by the sounds of a breaking heart reverberating through the suite.

"It has just been confirmed that the man killed in a fall in the Grand Canyon today is charismatic Texas millionaire businessman Jamison Rivers. Rivers recently announced he had filed for divorce from his wife of fifteen years. He is survived by his wife, his mother, two brothers, and his daughter Melody."

Before leaving the hotel in an emotional vacuum the next morning, I woodenly opened the small package still sitting on the nightstand. Inside it was a black velvet jewelry box that contained a stunning heavy gold ring. Centered in the ring was a Texas-sized green emerald guarded by two diamond baguettes on each side. I barely noticed the ring after reading the card on top, written in a familiar handwriting:

Always Know I love You

JR

THIRTY-SEVEN

FROM TEQUILA SUNSET TO HANGOVER SUNRISE

Jamison had been dead for over a year. I was depressed to the point of not caring about anything when Lolly, Miriam, Ginger and Krista enlisted my help with the annual Christmas party. They were trying to out-maneuver Granny at one of his own famous, yet pathetic, Granny Bleeps.

For years, every agent had been complaining about how bad our company Christmas parties were. Granny always hit the poor young title company or mortgage company reps up for our parties, luring them in with promises of business, so we had typical reps-with-an-expense-account company fare—cheddar cheese squares, crackers, baby carrots, celery sticks, and some horrible facsimile of ranch dressing for dips. Then there were always the desert special-ties—dry brownie squares and hard imitation grocery store sugar cookies, tasting faintly of Crisco, with colorful sprinkles. The wine came in gallon jugs or boxes with screw-off tops.

But this year would be different, they swore—it was the histor-ically best year ever in real estate. We had all been making a ton of money (so was Granny), and everyone felt that we earned and deserved a really, really great Christmas party. Of course, only the top agents could get Granny's attention without getting fired, that's why they needed me. Without advance notice, we four committed souls cornered him in his lair.

We could really have used Ginger's sharp tongue, but her pro-duction was still modest, so she had to wait in the wings. Granny, as he always did when his top agents teamed up on him, pretended to listen to our petition for $1,500 for the Christmas party, then, the-atrically, threw up his hands and shouted "Fine!" He dramatically pulled out his wallet and threw down his version of our budget in ten $50 bills to wine, dine, and entertain approximately one hundred plus people, then stalked out of the building.

You could always tell when Granny was about to erupt in anger: he stalked, rather than strolled. What you always looked out for in Granny is to make sure he didn't stomp! Stomping meant take cover, and the sooner, the better. Today, he just stalked.

Lolly, Krista and I assumed the leadership duties as we always did, along with Luis, who offered to carry the bags and boxes because he was secretly in love with Lolly. We were relying on Lolly, The Hostess Extraordinaire, to pull this off.

Lolly could throw a fabulous party like no one else—two years ago, she masterminded a "Doomed Lovers" costume party for Valentine's Day and was still getting the 'Stink Eye' nasty looks from those agents who hadn't been invited.

Bobby and Jon, our current Alcoholic-Agents-in-Residence, hovered closely to make sure enough of the budge got allocated for the booze—I think they had $450 in mind. Their theory, supported by Lolly, is that if everyone had enough to drink, the rest didn't matter.

The first shock was going to the local grocery store to find that a low-cost wine was $4 a bottle. Lolly calculated eight drinks in a bottle and four drinks per person (although plenty of agents would probably drink double that many glasses). For those challenged by math, that meant that $400 of our budget would MAYBE buy enough wine for most attendees—but what about hard liquor, beer, soft drinks, and food that the agents were expecting?

Everyone knew that even the weekly Broker Caravans were better attended, and those homes sold quicker if some really good food was proffered—like a taco bar, a dessert smorgasbord, or (best of all) a progressive lunch with all the above—coupled with wine and/or champagne.

There was no doubt in our minds that the future of us doing business with the other agents within our company depended on the party fare. After all, it WAS Christmas.

Typical Granny Bleep, giving us what we demanded while deliberately sabotaging our efforts from the first step. What to do? Go back and get more money? Like that was going to happen. Ask the agents to contribute to their own Christmas Party? Not if we ever planned on doing a deal with any of them ever again. No, with all of our healthy egos at stake, we had to figure out how to beat Granny at his own game.

I was still reeling from Jamison's death, so I was glad to start a huge project to distract me from my sadness and endless reruns of 'what-ifs?'.

It's likely I came up with the idea to go to Tijuana for the liquor, although we drank so much that night and killed so many brain cells, I really can't be sure. I loved Kahlua and knew it was $15 for a fifth bottle, here in the States, but only $3.25 for a quart in TJ. I figured everything else would be cheaper there, also. We could only bring two liter-size bottles apiece back over the border, but if we took enough people and made two trips, it could work. It was perfect! (Ever heard me say that before?)

The first decision came at the border—risk driving across without Mexican insurance, or park in the international parking lot and walk across? Given our budget and having two cars, buying astronomically priced Mexican insurance for a few hours exposure in Tijuana wasn't an option.

Undaunted, off we six amigos went on foot, accompanied by several more agent volunteers. Krista, with her normal three-inch heels, wasn't well equipped for the two-mile walk downtown, but typical Krista, who never complained regardless of the circumstances, led the pack.

Upon arriving in downtown Tijuana at 4 p.m. on a Thursday night, our thirst from the walk on uneven cement sidewalks littered with trash and potholes guided us directly to the infamous Tia Juana Tilly's. Tia Juana Tilly's was not just a hangout for tourists, it was a block-long, colorful watering hole for the in-the-know, young and adventurous people like us. Anyone, any age, could get a shot of Tequila with a green beer chaser for one dollar. If you were poor, you just stuck with the green beer for twenty-five cents. (Green beer doesn't refer to the color, it means it hasn't aged properly for six months. The ingredients are just mixed one day and served the next.)

We successful agents weren't poor, and although we started with the tequila shots and green beer chaser, we ended up drinking margaritas all night with the shots of tequila as a chaser. (And lived to tell about it amazingly enough!). Our dinner was a never-ending flow of chips and salsa. Krista loved to dance, and Luis was a fabulous dancer, so we ladies all danced with each other while we waited our turn to dance with him.

About 6 p.m., Ginger and Jon surprised us by joining us at the bar. They had closed up the office early and brought another agent, Carmen, with them. Ginger knew Tijuana well from her previous career as a prostitute (for a week) and figured she would find us here. Now the party could really begin. With three more agents, we could bring lots more liquor back across the Border, since each person was allowed two quarts duty-free per trip.

About 3 a.m., we were feeling so hilarious and so drunk, we figured we should buy our bottles for the party and hire a taxi to get us back to the border before something bad happened. It was a common occurrence in those days that drunk Americans trying to walk back to the border in the middle of the night were held up at gunpoint or knifepoint and relieved of any money they hadn't drunk away.

Ginger professed an interest in seeing a Dog and Pony Show. Jon corrected her ("It's a Donkey Show") while we all roared. I still had an ounce of sobriety in me, and that didn't interest me. We split up. Ginger, Miriam, Jon, and Bobby went to see if women really did have sex with donkeys while the rest of us concentrated on purchasing liters of liquid entertainment for the Christmas party.

It was a big score. Too drunk to find the Calimax store from my unemployed days, we ordered from Leyva's Liquor, a popular and reputedly honest liquor store on the north end of Avenida

Revolucion. After twenty minutes of negotiation for 'the best price', we ended up with a dozen liters of Cuervo Gold tequila, one liter of Kahlua (for me), four liters of Cuban rum, and a flask of Johnnie Walker scotch. At $12, the scotch was ridiculously expensive compared to the rest of the liquor, but that's what Granny drank, and we wanted to rub it in his face that we could buy it with the stingy amount of money he gave us. We had spent less than $120, so far.

The beer would have to wait for another trip. Jon, Luis, and Bobby had volunteered to come back in a couple of days and load up a dozen cases of assorted Mexican beer. That would cost another$100, so we were waaay under budget. The wine was to be Two Buck Chuck, so another $100 and the drinks were covered. (Two Buck Chuck was an urban legend about a divorce where the wife sold her ex-husband's entire vineyard inventory way below cost just to get even with him after he left her for a younger woman).

Lolly's brilliant plan was to have smaller plastic glasses so the four drinks per person limit was reduced by the glass size. The food was to be a Mexican buffet, and we eight decided to chip in $50 each to cover that without telling anyone (especially Granny) how we stretched his initial $500 budget.

Ginger, Miriam, and the guys had not shown up yet, so we left the bottles at Leyva's and went down the street to find them. Upon trying to enter the Donkey Bar, we were asked for $5 each entry fee. Not wanting to spend that $5 just to retrieve our fellow agents, we sat down on the unspeakably filthy curb in the squalor that was Tijuana and started sharing stories of our past week over the din of the drunks behind us.

The Curbside Sundowner began with my story of going to the San Marea fire station to get an offer signed. My favorite fireman Willy had just purchased a house from me. I was squeezed in at the table behind the station front door when one of Krista's clients came to the door, asking the firemen for help.

I recognized her from one of her many trips into the office to look at houses with Krista. I was trying to be invisible behind the door while her client was standing in the fire station threshold, handcuffed to a man who was not her husband. They said they had been playing with their young son, who was handcuffing them for fun, and ended by saying then they couldn't find the key for the handcuffs– did the firemen have a key? They didn't, but Willie told her the police hung out around the Mini Mart down the street, and to go wait down there. The firemen didn't start laughing until the car with the hapless couple in it had pulled away from the curb. I had held my breath the whole time, hoping her client wouldn't glance behind the door.

Krista said, "Oh my G-d, I bumped into that client a couple of weeks ago about 11 p.m. in the adult (meaning porn) section of Video Vault down the street. I know her husband travels a lot, and the man with her was not her husband. I wonder if that was the same guy you saw? I wasn't wearing a bra or any makeup. that night. I had on sweatpants and a tee shirt. with my hair in a pony tail. I knew I looked awful, but I didn't expect to see anyone I knew that late. We were both embarrassed, so we pretended not to see each other. She hasn't called me since that night, and I haven't called her either."

We were all getting giddy from being so tired. We had eaten poorly and were starting to sober up. Our grim curbside surroundings were looking worse now that daylight was creeping towards the horizon.

Although he had never attended any of the Sundowners in our office, Luis jumped right in. "Being on this impossibly gross curb is my Karma. This is what I get for not bailing my client out of jail when he called me at midnight a couple of months ago."

He was so sincere, as Luis tended to be, and so remorseful (as Luis tended to be), we had to really look sympathetic to coax the rest of story out of him.

"Well, do you all remember seeing on the local news about the series of bank robberies called The Freeway Heists that were occurring all up and down the Interstate-5 freeway? The clip always showed a photo of the robber with a hat pulled low over his face in the grainy security video being shown for the past two months on the news. He only hit banks next to the freeway, grabbing what he could and driving immediately onto the freeway for his getaway. I didn't recognize him from those grainy photos, but when the police had finally caught him and his mug shot was shown, I recognized my Buyer. Evidently, he had lost his job about six months ago, right after he bought his house, and was desperate for money to make his mortgage payments."

It took some friendly ribbing that, yes, it was indeed all Luis' fault that he'd turned his poor client into a criminal by selling him a house he couldn't afford, for us to get Luis to lighten up.

It was Lolly's turn to take center stage (er, center curb). Lolly's confession involved a dramatic couple from Brazil who were buying a million-dollar vacation home in San Marea with her. Both Fernando and Chaquita were model-beautiful. I noticed them immediately when they came into the office to meet Lolly a couple of weeks ago. The woman's three-inch heels made her over 6-feet and slightly taller than the man. She had a huge bouffant head of black hair, which put her closer to 6'4".I had admired her slim, shapely legs and was slightly surprised that she was wearing a bright red, expensive-looking dress with no back at 10 a.m. in the morning. The man had on gray silk shirt and pants, accessorized by a full head of black wavy hair and pencil-thin mustache.

Lolly had started to be intrigued by the woman's deep baritone voice and broken English as she was showing them homes. First she noticed her large hands, with their blunt fingers and red polished nails; and then she saw the prominent Adam's apple.

Lolly's eyes kept getting wider and her gestures wilder as she told the story. Chaquita saw that Lolly had probably put the puzzle pieces together, so, not unexpectedly, she took Lolly into her confidence to explain the reason she and Fernando were moving to San Marea.

Chaquita told Lolly she was a born a male, but had had the surgery to be anatomically a female now. She was a famous exotic dancer in Brazil. When she married Fernando, they became a focal point of all sorts of nastiness, so they came to San Marea to buy a place far away from South America, where they could just live quietly and be anonymous.

Lordy lordy, the things our clients tell us.

The beautiful couple had found a house, paid cash, and came into the office the previous week to get the keys from Lolly. They were pushing an expensive-looking stroller with silver wheels that was occupied by their two-month-old twins—a boy and a girl. After realizing the truth of Lolly's story, we turned up our laughing. But it wasn't for her story anymore, it was that we were so tired and had been laughing for so long, we couldn't quit.

As I sat on the curb between Lolly and Krista, I felt a hand on each of my arms when they heard me laughing. Krista said, "I haven't heard you laugh for a very long time. Since your sweetheart died."

Lolly followed with, "How long ago was that, now—a year, maybe?"

"No," I sighed. *"It will have been sixteen months next week. Ironically, it was also the anniversary of the first weekend I ever spent with him when I met him in Washington D.C.*

"And, Krista, you're right. I probably haven't laughed since that day. I thought I forgot how, until I heard myself laugh just now. I'm pretty much focused on going through the motions of living just to get through each day. I sell some houses, remind myself to eat, and try not to cry. I know that sounds so pathetic—sorry."

"It's been rough on all four of us, seeing you so sad and not knowing what to do," said Lolly softly. "Miriam says we should be patient; you'll start smiling again when you're ready. And Ginger— well, you know Ginger. She bluntly told us to leave you alone, period. She's so wise, she reminded us that grieving is different for every individual and might be a long process. When you're ready, you'll start hanging out with us again. So, we've all just been sitting by and worrying about you, in the meantime."

Krista snorted, "Sell a *few* houses? Nico, you've been selling so many houses that *I* worry when I see how hard you're working. How in the world do you do it?"

I sighed again. *"I'm working non-stop so I don't have time to think. I did that when my mother died, too. She died at 9 a.m, and I came into the office to work at 9:30 a.m. because I couldn't think of anything else to do. Remember how shocked Luis was when he asked me how my mom was, and I told him she had just died an hour ago?*

"*But now, every night, I look forward to being so exhausted that I can fall into bed and go to sleep immediately. Otherwise, I start thinking about Jamison and then cry myself to sleep. I decided I'd rather be exhausted by working than by crying. I'm tired of puffy, bloodshot eyes that eye drops don't seem to help any more. I worried that my clients might think I'm drinking too much. I also wonder if I could get addicted to artificial tears. It's crossed my mind every time I buy another bottle.*

"*If you ever need a recommendation for eye drops, please ask. I've tried them all, I think.*"

They both chuckled. A wan smile turned up one corner of my mouth when I realized I had actually made a small joke.

The three of us were quiet for a few minutes, lost in our own thoughts. We were all used to being in each other's lives and sharing all our most intimate confidences. I suddenly realized how much I had missed my Fab Five sisters. I also realized how good it was to be able to say Jamison's name and to talk about him with Krista and Lolly. The three of us intuited that, from now on, none of us would have to tiptoe and be careful not to say his name around me.

Krista said, "We're all here for you; you can talk about him anytime with us. We'll understand."

Feeling their love around me, I softly confessed, "*For several months after he died, I would call his work phone late at night just to hear his voice on his voicemail. But after about four months, it wasn't there anymore. The phone would ring and ring, but no voicemail came on. I felt like I'd lost him all over again. That was a horrible day.*"

Both Krista and Lolly leaned in to put their arms around me and give me a group hug. I felt like I had just woken up from a long sleep—it was really, really good to be back.

Our collective headaches were pounding as the dawn broke. Finally, the missing four agents came out and found us waiting patiently (sort of) on that disgusting curb (or, as they told the story at the office—in the disgusting *gutter*) outside the Donkey Bar. Luis and Bobby hired two taxis and we all went to retrieve our liquor. After fifteen hours in Tijuana, we were in a hurry to get back across the border to find some Excedrin, take a shower, and grab some much-needed sleep.

No matter the headaches, it was all worth it. The Christmas Party was a huge success, and we were heroes to our fellow agents.

That dark, sad place inside me had started to dissipate with the Mexican night. I had looked around me in the filtered light with the understanding that I wasn't alone. I had a family that cared about me, that shared my dreams, supported my accomplishments, enjoyed my happiness, and helped carry the weight of my sadness, too.

By sharing my story with Krista and Lolly, the heavy burden of Jamison's death that I had been carrying by myself was lighter. For the first time in sixteen months, I wasn't thinking of Jamison with such profound sadness and remorse anymore. I was comforted by my memories of our times together, and I realized that I was starting to understand, that in spite of his absence, Jamison had shown me the way to happiness.

Happiness was a choice. Happiness was being loved by the people you loved in return! I had found my happiness in my relationships, not in the money I earned.

I will always feel loved by Jamison and loved by my Fab Five sisters.

Life is good!
Nico

Back L to R: Can't remember, Lolly, Miriam
Front: Bobby, Ginger, Krista, Carmen, Jon, Nico, Luis

EPILOGUE

One Tuesday morning at the office meeting in 1993, Granny grandiosely announced that he was so proud of us and our sales in this difficult real estate market over the past three years, he was going to do something nice for us all. (Over the past eighteen months, he had closed his other sixteen offices, as the bad market got progressively worse.)

On Saturday night, he said, after the close of business at 6 p.m., he was hosting a great party, and he invited everyone to attend. No cheap food or drinks contributed by a title or mortgage company, he assured us: just something nice that he was paying for. He expected everyone to attend, as he had something huge to tell us before he announced it to the newspapers. It was something that would affect us all, he added. Absolutely everyone did attend.

Except Miriam and me.

Miriam was moving her mother into a retirement home back in Michigan. I had seen a psychic for a reading two weeks prior, and he told me he saw the office doors where I worked chained together very soon. He advised me to be making plans right away on where to go, before this happened, and before the other eighty agents in my office were all scrambling for a new place to work.

That whole next week, I quietly came back late every evening to go through hundreds of my closed files. I went through my crammed twin personal four-drawer metal filing cabinets next to my desk and removed the files I wanted to keep.

It went slow, because I removed and shredded any pages with my client's sensitive personal information from those files I left behind. I had cleared out all my personal items to the point where Lolly and Krista had commented that they could actually see my desk, without all the mounds of paperwork normally covering it.

I hadn't told them about the psychic's prediction, for some reason. Maybe I didn't want to be embarrassed if he was wrong. I had also interviewed with a broker down the street, who was thrilled at the prospect of hiring one of Fakke & Co's top agents. I had told him to reserve a desk for me, but I wouldn't be coming until I closed my last two current escrows to make sure I got properly paid.

(Brokers legally own every listing and sale an agent makes, and I'd heard of too many brokers who keep the escrows and, more importantly, the commissions, when a sale closes after an agent has moved to a competitor's office. The agent gets paid, of course, but sometimes it's just a 20% referral, or $2400, instead of the full $12,000 that they expected.)

About 7 p.m. on that highly anticipated Saturday night party, my phone started to ring off the hook. Granny's big announcement was that he had been behind on his rent for over a year. He had declared bankruptcy, and the court had ordered the closing of his last office, our San Marea one. Everyone had to remove anything they wanted to keep from the office within twenty-four hours.

Ginger was the first to call. She hesitated when she didn't hear me panicking on the phone. She said, 'You sh-t, you knew; that's why you weren't here tonight, and why your desk is so clean.

"You sh-t," she repeated, "why didn't you tell me?" (But we are still friends, and we still work together, many years later.)

On Monday morning, the front doors to our office were indeed chained together by the sheriff and posted with 'No Trespassing' yellow tape. When Miriam got back from helping her mother three days later, she had to hire an attorney to get the bankruptcy court to instruct the sheriff to reopen the building for ten minutes so she could retrieve her mail, her Day Timer, her two current escrow files, and her personal items.

Even though her stapler, ruler, closed files, and her desk plants were part of her personal property, because they were under a '*miscellaneous office supplies*' seizure description, she had to leave without them.

Granny had still retained the majority of the $10,000 commission check he held for Miriam during her divorce and bankruptcy, but she was never able to recover that from the court.

WHAT MADE A GROWN MAN CRY

(This is the recounting of the grisly event regarding the Heaven's Gate cult. It happened several years after Fakke & Co. closed, but the story was so compelling, I wanted to include it. Lolly had married her businessman boyfriend, Wade, and they owned a wonderful boutique brokerage in San Marea. Thirty-five of us Fakke & Co. agents now worked for them, along with another fifty high end, high producing agents Lolly and Wade had attracted to their brokerage.)

I loved being around Wally, as did everyone else in our new brokers' office. He had boundless energy and a way of telling stories that made you feel like you were there with him. Wally was a loud, funny Italian through and through, with dark eyes, olive skin, black curly hair, and a charming way of talking and laughing at the same time. At 6'2" and 320-plus pounds, he was a huggable, affable man who could have been a linebacker, but had instead parlayed his size and demeaner to be a bouncer and then co-owner of one of the top nightclubs in the county.

When his partner was caught doing something illegal and the club was closed down, Wally decided to sell real estate. This was still in the 1980s, when agents worked and played non-stop. Other agents who partied with him were treated to line passes at all the most popular clubs, as fellow bouncers treated Wally and his friends like royalty. I had never gone with them. I worked too many hours to enjoy an after-hours life.

So, when Wally wobbled into the office on a Saturday afternoon with a pale white face streaked with tears, looking like he'd seen a ghost, those of us in the office were shocked into silence, to say the least. No one even ventured to ask what was wrong, but we suspected it might be related to his bizarre showing of a home in The Ranch—the one that had been in the news headlines the past couple of days.

Last Thursday evening, Wally had come into the office after a late showing. He entertained us agents working overtime, too, with yet another of his real estate agent tales that was told in such vivid detail, we all enjoyed it vicariously.

Wally had been showing million-dollar homes in The Ranch for many months to one of his wealthy nightclub affiliate/clients from L.A. Rich people usually make for far better clients (and stories) than sweet, first-time buyer couples. Although most of us agents enjoy working with both ends of the real estate spectrum, the rich buyers made for better commissions, and Wally was all in with that.

Like a lot of Buyers, wealthy or first time, his Buyers insisted on 'stealing' something, so when this 10,000 square foot Spanish-styled home in The Ranch dropped its price by $300,000 after being vacant for almost four years, Wally smelled a 'steal.' He had never shown this house to his clients because it was so far above their price range. He excitedly called his Buyers to come quick; but given the horrendous traffic around downtown L.A. in advance of the Academy Awards on Sunday, they were late for their showing appointment.

Adding to that stress, the home had been rented out a month ago, and the listing agent cautioned Wally to be on time. He had said the new tenants were an odd, church-based group, and it might become an issue if he was late to his showing appointment.

When Wally came back into the office about 7 p,m., to the ten of us still there, he seemed both puzzled and excited while he gushed non-stop over his showing and possible sale. We had all seen the vacant Spanish-style home several times. Over the years, as the seller moved from agent to agent, the newest listing agent always hosted lavishly catered Broker Caravan Open Houses. We agents showed up again and again for the excellent food, so the few of us working late had a good visual of the house while he told his story.

The house itself sat so far back from the road that it was hidden from view; thus it was marketed as being 'private and secluded'. It was accessed by a long, dog-legged driveway that curved to the right up the hill and landed out of sight onto an enormous brick-paved courtyard. There was probably enough room in the courtyard to park twenty cars, in addition to those inside the attached six-car garage.

The two-story house was comprised of ten bedrooms and eight bathrooms, per the listing, so it was meant for a very large, possibly extended family; or one owner with a very large, extended ego.

Wally was excited because his Buyers finally wanted to make an offer. The home had started out three-plus years prior at $2.8 million, but the price had dropped occasionally and the house had gotten more tired-looking while sitting vacant for all that time.

Today, the price had dropped from $2.1 million to $1.8 million, as the seller wanted to just get rid of both it and his new tenants, according to the fourth listing agent. However, after showing it, Wally sensed a 'red flag' with the tenant situation. But his Buyers were willing to offer $1.5 million cash as long as the tenants were gone at close of escrow.

Here was the puzzling part: according to Wally, when he and his Buyers finally got there, there was a typed paper sign on the front door inside the ornate front entry gate that said, "COME IN."

Wally had been told the tenants would be home, but no one seemed to be around. The house itself was so sparsely furnished that it felt unwelcoming and empty. The two large leather couches and a couple of dining room chairs that faced each other in the immense 3,000 square foot great room looked tiny, in proportion.

The dining room itself had a gigantic rectangular table surrounded by lots of similar chairs—maybe even twenty, he said. It was eerily quiet. The only thing the three of them heard in the cavernous house, besides the echoes of their own footsteps on the marble floors, were faint clicking sounds.

As they progressed through the house, every bedroom had two or three twin mattresses on the floor and the same amount of small computer tables. People were typing away on every computer, seemingly oblivious to the showing. Initially, because of every occupant's cropped hair and identical black clothing, he thought they were all men, but then realized there were both men and women. He further described them all as wearing identical, brand new-looking Nike sneakers. They sat quietly typing away on keyboards, hence the origin of the clicking sounds.

Wally said it was hard to know how many people there actually were—he guessed maybe even thirty or more—because they were all dressed alike. The desks and computers were all identical too, so room after room blurred together. Not one of them said a word to Wally or his Buyers as they previewed room after room, so he had quit saying "Hi" or trying to apologize to any of them after the first few people hadn't responded to his friendly salutation.

Wally figured they were all mad that he was late. He needn't have worried.

This was on a Thursday evening.

What a difference a week makes! On the following Tuesday afternoon, the sheriff's department responded to a neighbor's complaint that the Spanish-style home in The Ranch had a horrible stench emanating from it. They arrived to find a rear door left open and groups of conspicuously dead occupants in virtually every room.

It turned out to be a mass suicide of the Heaven's Gate Cult membership. According to a suicide letter found at the scene, the group was timing their exit to coincide with the return of the Hale-Bopp comet. They believed an alien spacecraft was following the comet, so they planned to join the spacecraft as it traversed The Universe in the comet's shadow on the day it passed closest to the Earth.

Evidently, Wally was the last person to be inside the house, the previous Thursday. The listing broker declined to be interviewed by the Sheriff until he got clearance from his corporate office. After being pressured to be interviewed about his listing, he offered up

Wally's name to the Sheriff since Wally had been inside the house most recently anyway. The sheriff's office then called Wally, wanting to get details of what he had observed during his showing.

Wally had the presence of mind to grill the Sergeant to make sure all the people were dead. News stories of Mexican drug cartel wars talked about how gangs retaliated against each other by killing rival dealers, and also their entire families so survivors couldn't come back for revenge. He wanted to know about survivors before he could potentially put his family into a dangerous situation by discussing what he saw.

The sheriff's officer told Wally they had found thirty-nine men and women. He assured Wally that everyone in the house was accounted for, and they were all dead. Even though the Sheriff wanted to come out to Wally's house immediately, Wally said 'no'. He was a single parent, and his two kids were getting ready to go to bed. Wally would only agree to meet the Sheriff in the morning after dropping his kids off at school first thing Friday morning.

The sheriff wanted to hear Wally's story first thing Friday morning, but so did the hordes of national and international paparazzi still on vacation in L.A. following the Academy Awards this past Sunday.

Wally came out of his house early Friday morning to take his two pre-teen kids to school and was greeted by fifty or so journalists, broadcasters, and TV crews from all over the world. They had decamped en masse from L.A. when the news of the mass suicide first broke.

The same clueless listing agent had given someone Wally's name again, to deflect all the calls for details. As Wally and his kids stepped out their front door, the tide of journalists rushed them with microphones and cameras while shouting questions.

That was Wally's first taste of being in the spotlight. Not only was it unexpected, unnerving, and unwelcomed, but it scared both him and his kids out of their wits at 7:30 a.m. in the morning. He herded the kids into his Mercedes and drove away without answering a single question.

After Wally gave the sheriff his statement, he found that the journalistic horde had come to our office and our broker Wade had already agreed, with several of the nationally famous TV broadcasters, to go back to the Spanish-style house with Wally to be interviewed live on major TV news programs like CBS *This Morning, Today,* and *Good Morning America.*

Katie Couric, Tom Brokaw, Matt Lauer, and Bryant Gumbel were already in the air on their way to San Marea. Wade knew the story from being briefed by Wally last night on the phone, and he recognized a good potential photo-op for the company when he saw one. On Saturday morning, the San Diego County Coroner was scheduled to start removing the bodies in refrigerated trucks, and the TV journalists all wanted Wally and Wade to give a commentary as the morgue trucks came down the long, graceful, curving driveway.

After Wally ran out of tears and was able to control himself somewhat, that Saturday afternoon, he recounted the morning's events to all of us hanging open-mouthed on his every word while the office phone rang unanswered and incessantly in the background.

The entire group of journalists and broadcasters worldwide had organized themselves while waiting for Wally's interview with the sheriff to end. It appeared that every major (and minor) network in the world was represented, even from as far away as Japan.

An interview scheduler had been selected to sequence the journalistic horde so that everyone got an interview. Priority depended on whether it was for TV or magazine or newspaper. The first interviews were for East Coast television networks, since they were in the earliest time zone. The journalist's position along the driveway was based on what time their Special Report Live news coverage was airing.

Every journalist was given three minutes to ask Wally and Wade their questions while they all waited for the evacuation of the bodies. This was so that three minutes could air on the different networks while the cavalcade of trucks rolled by live behind them.

The list of interviewers ran like a Who's Who of TV royalty. Wade had seen the house and had been briefed in detail by Wally, so the interviewers got one or the other, depending on their employers' star-power. Newspaper and magazine interviews would come later and would be lengthier for more detail.

The sheriff had cordoned off the driveway before it got to the brick courtyard, so the scheduler had Wally and Wade start towards the top of the driveway, dropping down a few feet every few minutes to the next interviewer in quick succession as the refrigerated trucks started to descend in measured increments.

Here's where Wally started sobbing again in earnest, reliving the nightmare in the retelling to us.

Evidently the refrigerated trucks could not hold all the bodies. Plus, the Santa Anna hot winds blowing in off the desert for the past few days had caused the bodies to decompose rapidly. The resulting stench, in turn, had triggered the neighbor's initial call to the sheriff days earlier.

While Wally kept talking and sobbing, I envisioned him with all the press corps standing shoulder to shoulder along that driveway. It was like being in a sports event when the fans in the packed stadium started The Stadium Wave—a phenomenon where they stood up in succession and in sync while raising their arms and yelling, making it look like an ocean wave rolling through each section in coordinated rhythm.

Except, in Wally's recount, no one was yelling. Every single person lined along the driveway was groaning loudly while turning away from the driveway in total sync to vomit after the unrefrigerated trucks slowly crept by them down the hill and the indescribable stench of human decomposition wafted over the crowd. Wally and Wade had not been spared from that involuntary response, either.

At this point in the recall, Wally started gagging again, but because he had already vomited everything out of his stomach earlier, thankfully, it was dry retching.

Wally spent the next two days in full-length interviews with worldwide network journalists, and then he and his kids started counseling. He never spoke publicly again about Heaven's Gate, even after the house was torn down and the five acres it sat on was sold several years later for a tiny fraction of its original value.

(A few years ago, on the thirtieth anniversary of the mass suicide, Wally was repeatedly contacted to be interviewed for several Heaven's Gate Anniversary Special documentaries. He declined.)

SO, YOU WANT TO BE AN AGENT (REALITY CHECK QUIZ)

Real estate selling is still the lowest-cost, easiest to enter, licensed profession in all fifty states. Even people who paint nails have stricter standards for licensing. Most agents sell zero, one, or two properties a year, according to the National Association of Realtors; and live below the income poverty line.

But, John Q. Public gets their license because they imagine that an agent gets paid that 6% commission for nothing except showing a house, ordering a home inspection, and collecting Big Bucks. It looks ridiculously easy; anyone can do it. Right?

You can pass the real estate test if you take it enough times, but the art of selling, working with demanding people, and closing a sale are mysteries that must be solved, alone and quickly, if you are to earn any money and enjoy longevity in real estate as a career. The statistics are brutal—60% of all new agents are gone by six months, and another 25% are gone within a year.

Comparably, of all the men training to become a Navy Seal, only 5% succeed; and the same is true of real estate. After three years, only 5% of new licensees are still using their business card. The biggest differences are: Navy Seals are diligently trained how to do their job to kill the bad guys before going into the field, and they have a consistent paycheck from Day One.

In real estate, we agents work for free while we learn our jobs, and only kill people in our minds.

Do You Have What It Takes to Be Successful?

Start with this self-administered quiz by scoring:

1—Not Ever **2**—Sort of **3**—Probably **4**—Absolutely; this is me

_____ 1. I am a patient person.

_____ 2. I have enough savings to pay my bills for six months.

_____ 3. I am a good listener.

_____ 4. I am not easily discouraged.

_____ 5. I am an excellent problem solver.

_____ 6. I am able to motivate myself even when I don't want to work.

_____ 7. I plan to work more than forty-hour weeks, including evenings, weekends, and holidays.

_____ 8. I will thrive with unexpected changes to my work schedule almost daily.

_____ 9. I understand priorities, am persistent and am focused to attain my goals.

_____10. I know I can learn/improve my computer, social media, and smartphone skills.

_____11. I'm an optimist; my glass is always at least "half full."

_____12. I will cancel a sale if it's in my clients' best interest, even if I need the money.

_____13. I will make selling real estate my only job, even in the beginning.

_____14. I am comfortable saying, "I don't know that answer, let me find out for you."

_____15. I am able to ask people how much money they earn and have in the bank.

_____16. TOTAL SCORE** Part 1

There are no right or wrong answers, this is just for fun.

**There are no right or wrong scores, either—this is to judge your chances of success. The higher the number, the better your chances of still being an agent after two years.*

$_____ Monthly amount I need to earn to pay my bills
x six = $ _____

(Include all household income needed for rent/mortgage, food, car and student loans, credit card bills, entertainment etc. Then multiple by six to see how much you will need to earn or have in the bank, to last without any income until your first commission comes in.)

_____ 16. TOTAL SCORE** Part 1 x $1000 = 16a

16a. $_____ (So, a score of 50 is 50,000) **

17. (16a) _____ x .80 = 17a. $_____

18. (17a)_____ x .005 = 18a. $_____

Congratulations: You've calculated a client's monthly principle and interest payment for an 80% loan with 20% down. (Just kidding? I told you, this is for fun just to see your math skills. You're going to need them to sell real estate.)

_____ * TOTAL SCORE amount from 16a..

19. (16a)*_____ (gross commission)

20. (16a) _____ x .65 = 17a. $_____ (your share after split w/ broker)

21. (17a) _____ x .78 = 18a $ _____ (actual year-end take-home after normal business expenses of 22% are deducted)

Congratulations: You've just calculated your earnings for your first year in real estate. If it's been enough to pay your bills, then calculate your second and third years on line 21 using x2 and x4.

If, after three years, you're still able to pay your bills, you're the only agent out of **twenty** that remains from all newly licensed agents, so forge ahead in your successful real estate career!

*If you work in larger cities on the West or East Coast, then double line 16a. The rest is the same.

GLOSSARY OF REAL ESTATE VOCABULARY

Agent or Broker—Agents and Brokers have different categories of licenses. Agents can only work for a Broker; anyone with a Broker's license can work independently or under another Broker. A Broker is responsible for all transactions that come through the office he owns or manages. Brokers legally supervise and sign off on any transaction—whether it closes or cancels. Listings belong to the Broker, so if an agent leaves an office, his or her listings may not automatically go with them to the new company.

Artificial Surf—this is freeway noise loud enough to resemble the crash of ocean waves.

Back on the Market or BOM – aka Sale/Fail—A category in the MLS before it goes back to Active. This is when something goes wrong in an escrow and the buyer cancels, bringing the house back up for sale to a new buyer.

Broker Caravan or Caravan or **Broker Open Houses**—held on a weekday for agents to preview other agents' listings. Can be new to the market, or new to listing agent, or had price change (re-Caravan). **Progressive Caravans** of no more than eight houses are seen in pre-determined order with all the agents driving together parade-style. Each property is open ten to fifteen minutes as the agents move from one to the next in group formation. Larger geographical areas are open three hours, and individual agents pick randomly from a list of sometimes as many as seventy houses available to view. Usually, time limits the number an agent is able to see to about fifteen or twenty, if they are located close enough together. Food can be offered as an inducement to attract more agents to YOUR house. The more expensive the house price, the more lavish the food offering.

Bungalow—think Hansel and Gretel. Small, one-story with porch and white picket fence.

BTVAPTCOE—shorthand for **B**uyer **T**o **V**erify **A**ll **P**rior **T**o **C**lose **of E**scrow. Some agents think this relieves them of any disclosures, as the Buyer has been warned. This does not work, lazy agents; sorry. You must DISCLOSE, DISCLOSE, DISCLOSE. If you *wonder* if you should disclose, then YES, disclose that too.

Buyers Are Liars—This is what an agent says when he/she has been showing a client the type of property they *say* they want, then finds out they bought something entirely different from another agent, usually after walking into an Open House unaccompanied. These buyers will say they want single story, then buy a two-story. Or they must have a minimum four-bedroom house, then they buy a two-bedroom condo.

Client—can be either a Buyer or Seller or even a Renter who works with an agent (hopefully exclusively, because agents don't get paid until after a sale closes).Customers are found in stores; clients are found in situations where they need knowledgeable, professional advice.

Commission-ectomy—process by which an agent has some of his earnings surgically removed in order to make a sale happen after Buyers and Sellers can't agree on the sales price.

Cottage—small, two-story bungalow, usually one- or two-bedroom, max.

Cream Puff—darling, clean, staged, perfect condition, move-in ready. Agents sometimes exaggerate, but then again, beauty is in the eye of the beholder!

Coastal Contemporary house—two- or three-stories, modern, slatted windows

Cozy—probably less than 950 square feet. Means only one person in the shower at a time, max.

Deeds—the forms that are recorded at the end of a sales transaction. *Grant Deeds or Warranty Deeds* transfer ownership from Seller to Buyer. *Deeds of Trust* or Mortgage Deeds show that Buyer has taken out a loan to purchase a specific property.

Disclosures—means by which a seller and agents let a buyer know of any issues with home that might make them not want to buy. California's sheer amount of disclosures (today, estimated at five hundred pages of inspections, title reports, informational booklets, plus forty, and counting, individual ones) tend to overwhelm most everyone associated with a sale. That's why few, if any, principals in a transaction actually read the disclosures after the first ten pages, although they sign that they have read, understood, and received a copy. In California, it's not necessarily the homes that cost so much money—it's the added cost of all the disclosure paperwork.

Escrow—A neutral (supposedly) third-party, state-licensed service which attends to the many details involved in opening, organizing, and closing a real estate sale transaction. They hold all the deposit, down payment, and mortgage money, paying liens and bills prior to disbursing what's left over to the seller (aka equity). These are the unsung Heroes in a real estate transaction—making sure everyone gets the right amount of dollars. Escrows can be privately owned, owned by a real estate brokerage, or part of a title company. Licensing requirements differ depending on who owns an Escrow.

Feng Shui—the Chinese art of ruining a sale because the front door faces the wrong way. Feng Shui is also known as a "system of laws considered to govern spatial arrangement in relation to the flow of energy, either positively or negatively".

Fixer—desperately needs carpet, paint, and wallpaper removal and new appliances—expected to cost between $10-20,000. Can also be **Major Fixer**—likely more than $50,000 worth of work needed prior to occupancy or **Tear Down** when it's deemed to be beyond fixing. HGTV shows will help familiarize agents to know the difference.

Floor time—A time slot, usually four hours, where an agent is scheduled to be in the office to greet anyone coming through the door with a real estate need. If they don't already have an agent, this is a great source of new clients.

Fog a Mirror Test—A time-honored Urban Legend where brokers will hold a mirror under a prospective agent's nose and if the prospect can fog a mirror by breathing on it, they are alive, and will be hired.

Lockbox—A reinforced, tamper-proof, thick metal rectangular box intended to safely hold a key to the front door of a home. There are many types, from a three-digit, push-button lid, to a four-number dial to line up the numbers (think slot machine) on the lid, a right-left-right dial (as in a safe combination), and, currently, electronic bluetooth ones that are opened by a code entered on a smartphone. Lockboxes all have a shackle with a separate security code allowing them to be opened and securely hung over an exterior doorknob, a hose spigot, gas meter, fencing, or handrail balusters.

McMansion—extremely large house with an imposing façade, extravagantly built on less than an acre. Likely over 8,000 square feet under roof. Occupants can live in 2500 square feet—the rest is occupied by their ego.

Mirror and Broom View– How an agent describes that you can see an ocean view from a home that really doesn't have an ocean view—by fixing a mirror to a broom and raising it up.

Motivated Seller—How a motivated *agent* projects, in the marketing description, that he/she has priced it low enough to get offers. Or the seller has an urgent need to sell quickly, so this description is likely combined with price drop.

Ocean view—Adds dollars to asking price, but actually means that on a clear day, there is some peek, reflection, or distant blue color that is in a westerly direction of the subject property. Depending on the terrain, some ocean views can be seen up to twenty miles inland from the real ocean. There is **Blue Water View,** meaning you can't see the waves themselves, but the horizon is blue when looking the right direction. **White-water view**—this means you can see the white foam on top of the waves. **Laying Down White Water View** is the most expensive type of ocean view.

Preview—agent-only showing to check a property out before showing to a buyer with specific needs. **No Need to Preview**—"spare the poor sellers and show it to your buyers without the extra intrusion of looking first. I promise it shows well." While that may or may not be true, it's best to preview, if you value your Buyer's time and your credibility.

R.D.R—**R**ealtors **D**on't **R**ead. Granny's usual reply to an agent's problems with a contract.

Red Flag—Agents develop a sense of anticipating a problem (a red flag) that will likely come up if their Buyers go into escrow on a particular property.

Reverse floorplan—the bedrooms are on the main level and the living areas and kitchens are upstairs. This is popular in coastal communities, where you might get an ocean glimpse from upper floor.

Smoke and Mirrors—The art of obfuscation, either in a home description or disclosure, usually to make a house appear different/ better than it really is. This is an attorney's favorite real estate vocabulary definition because it is an ongoing source of new lawsuits.

S.O.S.—Shiny Object Syndrome, or the process by which agents are enticed to try one method of attracting a client and then another method, in rapid succession. Very costly to agents trying to take shortcuts to success instead of just investing in hard work.

Snake a Client—The art of the unscrupulous agent to separate a client from his original agent, sometimes right in front of him or her, during a showing.

Title Company—another third-party service that researches and insures clear ownership (title) of property prior to transferring to a buyer. In some states, title and escrow are same company; in others, they're entirely separate.

Trophy Client—an agent's dream Buyer or Seller; or better yet, a client who sells an expensive property to buy another one, concurrently. It's possibly a famous person, an extremely good-looking client (married or single), a cash Buyer, or even a short man standing on a tall wallet. A trophy client can also be someone who sends their agent multiple referrals. Trophy clients expect, and get, extra attention.

Trophy Listing—usually an expensive home that, when you list it, lots of other agents are jealous.

Up Desk or **Up Call**—Agents volunteer to be scheduled in three- or four-hour time slots during business hours for floor time. They sit at a designated desk just inside the front door, usually behind the receptionist, to handle any inquiries or phone calls about real estate. This can be very lucrative in an area where out-of-towners visit, then decide to buy, and don't know any agents.

VAC/LB—no one lives here, so use the lockbox; you don't need an appointment.

WARNING: Use extreme caution when opening a lockbox —

Pandora may be waiting to get out!

Autographed books can be ordered on-line at
PandorasLockboxBook.com

To schedule speaking, or for bulk order pricing
E-mail your requests to:
NicoGriffith11@gmail.com

ABOUT THE AUTHOR

 Nico Lundborg-Griffith is an award-winning, top producing real estate agent listed in the RE/MAX Hall of Fame. Although Nico is not a veteran of a real war, nevertheless as a veteran agent of real estate, she has earned the equivalents of Purple Hearts, Distinguished Service Medals and Red Badges for Courage while selling over 1,000 homes in her illustrious career. Nico sells real estate in Montana where she lives with her husband, Gordon, and her parti-Yorkie, Fannie Mae. To learn more or contact Nico, visit

www.PandorasLockboxBook.com.

"Thank you for reading my book. I hope you enjoyed reading it as much as I enjoyed writing it. I encourage you to share it with your friends, family, and real estate agents. Now it's time to leave a review. Even a few words could help others choose to read *Pandora's Lockbox* also.

It's super simple, copy and paste the URL or scan the QR code to go directly to my Amazon Review Page.

Warm regards, Nico

https://www.amazon.com/
review/create-review/?ie=UTF8&channel=glance-detail&asin=B09QH19W2Z

Made in the USA
Monee, IL
21 April 2023

32212650R00164